What others have to say about
Playing with the Big Boys & Girls in Real Estate

"*Playing with the Big Boys & Girls in Real Estate* provides a fresh twist on discussing what successful Realtors® actually do and how they work with prospective clients to consistently win the listings. Within the interviews of 12 Realtors® are nuggets of great wisdom for new and veteran agents alike. Their advice is worth reading for anyone interested in building a real estate career. Most of them acknowledge great residential education like CRS Courses, as well as mentors in real estate who paved the road to their success. Now it's their turn to become the role models for other Realtors®."

Nina Cottrel
Chief Executive Officer
Council of Residential Specialists

"Some of the best agents in the business are in this book. Every reader owes it to themselves to learn their techniques."

David Knox, CSP
David Knox Productions, Inc.
www.DavidKnox.com

"From Rookie to Superstar the book is loaded with secrets and strategies that guarantee success!"

Terri Murphy
Terri Murphy Communications
www.TerriMurphy.com

Playing With The BIG BOYS & GIRLS In Real Estate

#1 Residential Superstars Reveal All

SUN Publications
Carlsbad, California

Playing with the Big Boys & Girls in Real Estate
#1 Residential Superstars Reveal All

STAR POWER® is a registered trademark of STAR POWER Systems, Inc.

REALTOR® is a registered service mark of the National Association of Realtors.

Publisher's Cataloging-in-Publication
(Provided by Quality Books, Inc.)

Pestrak, Debra.
    Playing with the big boys & girls in real estate : #1 residential superstars reveal all / Debra Pestrak. -- 1st ed.
    p. cm.
    LCCN 2004115319
    ISBN 1-931034-07-9

    1. Real estate agents--Interviews. 2. Real estate business. I. Title.

HD1382.P47 2005   333.33
                 QBI04-200508

Published by SUN Publications

Printed in the United States of America.

FIRST EDITION   First Printing, 2005

DEDICATION

Playing With The Big Boys & Girls In Real Estate

is dedicated to all

the hard working real estate agents

who want to grow their business.

With your busy schedule in mind,

this book was written as

an easy to read, to the point book.

CONTENTS

RESEARCH CONCLUSIONS AND SUMMARY

APPENDICES

ACKNOWLEDGMENTS

Special thanks to the 12 Superstars who gave up their precious time for the interviews in this book. They are all generous and willing to share what they have learned for others to be more successful.

Thanks to Gregg Neuman, Mike McCann, and Mary Ann Bendinelli who went to the extra effort to provide some of their success tools.

An added thanks to Phyllis Wolborsky who, was kind enough to share her key perspectives.

Howard Brinton was very gracious to share some of his success tools.

I would like to thank the people who helped me get in touch with these top performers: Clair Charley of the Sacramento Association of Realtors, Stephanie Pfeffer—GMAC Home Services, Kathy Borruso—NRT, Kimberly Prime and Steve Alessandrini—ERA Franchise Systems, Corey Thomas—Century 21 Real Estate Corporation, Glenn Vatterott—Coldwell Banker, Amy Stoehr—STAR POWER® Systems, Lynda Beighley—Weichert Realtors, Mark Panus from Cendant, Lorin Brown—Lyon Real Estate.

As we all know, without our assistants where would we be. Each of these mega producers' assistants provided follow-up and were tremendously helpful.

In research, there are always people in the background who help validate the data and keep you out of trouble. Thank you Sara Patterson—Council of Residential Specialists and Liz Johnson—National Association of Realtors for your quick response and support.

My extra thanks to Amy Stoehr—STAR POWER for giving me the support to get some of the testimonies for the book.

Thank you Kathi Menard for transcribing the interviews and Paul Wilson for being tenacious in your editing.

Thanks to David Wright, Insight Publishing, a former top-producing real estate broker who gave me helpful advice about real estate and about the needs in the market.

Russ Hollingsworth, Insight Publishing, did an outstanding job on the book jacket design.

The endorsers of this book deserve extra thanks for taking the time out of their busy day to review the book, and provide their opinions.

A very special person in my life is an old high school friend Jim Hitt, who just happens to be a real estate professional. He was my mentor for this project.

And of course, the most important person in my life, my husband. He has been a staunch supporter in my career and in my ongoing projects. Without him, I would not be where I am. His strength and support are invaluable. Thank you honey for sticking with me and giving so much of yourself.

INTRODUCTION

Real estate is a wonderful business that gives you an opportunity to work with people on the most important asset in their lives, their homes, and make as much money as you want. It is truly a business, the American Dream, where the more effort you put in the greater the rewards. You have an opportunity to work with different people every day. It's a business in which you must love people and be flexible. The unexpected is the norm. The people who come in to this business have a vision of what could be possible in their lives.

The biggest thrill is finding that right home to fit your buyer's needs and getting the sellers what they want out of their home, when they want it. This requires the ability to ask great questions; get along well with a lot of different people, in different circumstances; follow through and attend to detail; use market knowledge; and make yourself available when your clients need you.

Allan Domb, number one Realtor in the country, states that 90 percent of all residential sales are made by 10 percent of the Realtors. Gregg Neuman, number one gross commission income producer for Prudential, says that number could be as much as 93 percent being produced by seven percent. If there are no secrets in this business, then how is it possible to have this type of disparity? What do they do that you don't? What do they know that you need to know? That's what you'll learn from this book. That's what motivated me to write it.

You will get mentoring advice from the number-one agents at Century 21, Coldwell Banker, ERA, Fox & Roach, GMAC, Long & Fosters, Prudential, Real Living, RE/MAX, Weichert, and two independents. One of the agents does foreclosures. You are about to learn from the best of the best.

Most agents do not have a college degree. It's a business that doesn't even require a high school diploma. Since 1993 the average age of Realtors has risen. Downsizing, right sizing, and aging baby boomers brought an average of 15,000 new Realtors a month into the business in 2003. Yet, the medium tenure of an agent is eight years and median income is $39,300. The turnover in this business is phenomenal – 180,000 joined the Realtor ranks and 110,000 left in 2003. All of the interviewees come from completely different backgrounds. So background and education have nothing to do with being successful in this business. Anyone who wants to work hard can be successful. This truly is a business that enables you to design whatever future you want.

When Gregg Nueman, #1 gross commission income producer for Prudential, started, he did so because he wanted to be in sales and because, in sales, you can make more money than in most jobs. Why not sell the biggest-ticket item you can, since obviously you can make the most money? This philosophy is also what brings many people to this business. It seems like easy money, but it's not. It's hard work and dedication—commitment. The prices of houses have risen so much, and interest rates have been so low, that it makes it look easy.

These superstars say there are no secrets. Okay, why is there such a large turnover? Let's examine some of the issues people don't address or understand about the business before deciding whether this is for them, and some of the factors that will determine your ongoing success.

Since all Realtors are independent agents, you're running a business. You may be contracted with a major real estate firm, which may provide training, joint advertising, office space, and basic office needs, but it is still *your* business. That means, as a small business owner, you have to play all the roles of a business. Someone has to do the sales, expenses, paperwork, accounting, marketing, graphic design, mailings, lead generation, CPA/taxes, presentations, printing, technical support, Web site design and updates, tracking, and getting educated. The Small Business Administration states that 34 percent of all small businesses go out of business within the first two years, 50 percent within four years and 60 percent within six years. Real estate is not any different. This is a business and has to be run as a business if you want to succeed.

Establishing priorities in your life enables you to have some semblance of balance. Single parents have the biggest challenges. There is no doubt that you have to have your family's support, and it should be before you start in the business. Sit down and have a conversation about what you want to do and what it will mean to your family. They have to be willing to take up the slack and help with the home responsibilities. They have to agree and understand the kind of schedule you will have if you want to be successful and not make too big a sacrifice. If you can't be available when your clients want you, you shouldn't be in this business. Some people want to believe they can start part-time and be successful—that would be the exception to the rule.

For many years, these top producers worked seven days a week, 80 hours or more a week. Now they average 50-70 hours a week. They are available seven days a week. That doesn't mean they work seven days a week. They fit their family commitments in to that timeframe. They go to their children's soccer games and recitals. But they spend 80 percent of their time doing things that produce results—being in front of buyers or sellers, building and maintaining relationships, and getting educated. It's not just time management, but smart time management, doing the right things with the precious hours they have in a day to make them the most productive.

It's not just being a hard worker. Many agents work hard. It's having the right work habits that produce the most results. We establish habits that we don't pay attention to. These superstars share their habits, obviously ones that are enormously successful. At the end of each day, evaluate how productive your day was. Did you spend 80 percent of your time on the 20 percent that produces the most results? If you were to average out your hourly rate, are you making what you're worth?

Anytime we attempt change, we are in a learning process. As we are learning, we typically lack self-confidence until we get comfortable. Confidence comes from doing. Once you learn bad habits, it's a challenge to change. There are many people who have been in real estate a long time and think they know it all. Ah, there's nothing new, and as these top professionals say, there's no secret. However, I think my friend Jim stated it well when he was speaking to another real estate agent who said, "I've been in the business for 26 years," and Jim replied, "Are you sure you haven't been in the business one year, 26 times?" Once we establish habits, it takes a concerted effort to change them. There are a lot of different ways to do real estate. It is working hard, but in the most effective way. If you want to grow, have less stress, and have more time, then it behooves you to be open to new ideas and be searching for ways you can be more productive with your time and efforts.

When we want to be good at something, we have to practice. This requires us to put ourselves in a position of discomfort. The possibility is, we may fail, or we may succeed; but we won't know until we do it. If we fail, that's part of life. We all make mistakes. We learn from our mistakes and move on. These interviewees share how they deal with their mistakes and disappointments.

Some people don't want to work 40-60 hours a week. Then they've decided they want to work only part-time. There is nothing wrong with this, per se, except if they're representing themselves as being highly knowledgeable agents when they're not. All of the interviewees stated that, if you're going to list property, you have to be very, very knowledgeable about the market, and working full-time. Otherwise, you can't represent the seller well, and you will do a disservice to them, yourself, and the industry. If you want to work part-time, stick with buyers. Find a great agent who wants and needs to have a buyer's agent. That way you can be in the business, and keep in touch with what's happening in the market, and have the flexible hours you need.

Representing the seller requires a huge amount of market knowledge. If you know the market, you know what the house should be listed at in order to be sold in the least time. Look at your time on market and what percentage you come in with from listing to sales price. These superstars sell at 99-100.6 percent of what they listed the property for. What is your list time in comparison to the market? These statistics give them a huge advantage in their listing presentation.

Commitment is a big piece of real estate—to your family, your clients, and yourself. Two of the biggest issues in this business are follow-up and follow-through. Performing these tasks requires focus, accountability, caring, dedication, and commitment. Clients want to be kept informed. It's too easy not to return people's calls, and not to examine the contract to make sure it's filled in correctly. It comes down to the details. You make the transaction so much smoother for everyone involved when you are committed to making the deal happen, and in a timely fashion.

These top performers do what's right for the client. They don't compete with their fellow agents or let their egos get in the way of the deal. They know that typically buyers think they paid too much, and that sellers get less than they expected. When you have someone with genuine interest, it's priced right and you know your market, make it happen.

One of the biggest challenges for new people is finding clients, while learning real estate and running a business. Some can't seem to get it going and lose heart and give up. The interviewees said to give it at least a year. It takes that long to get a footing.

Some come in to the business and get going right away. They've figured out what they need to do to be successful. However, others, once they get that taste of success, slack off in that success, and they find themselves with no clients and get discouraged. They had the formula but didn't take consistent action.

Others begin, start getting business, make the money, and get comfortable with what they're doing. It's okay to get comfortable. The question is, do you want more? If so, it's there to be had if you will listen to what these superstars do.

Some people decide they want to work on referral only. These interviewees said, "If you're happy with that slice of the business, good for you." They aren't. Are you happy with it or just comfortable with it?

Very few people like to make cold calls, or like being rejected. However, there are people who don't need your services, so, therefore, you're going to get noes. If you accept that, and know that it's a numbers game, you let it go and move on to the next one. After all, they're not rejecting you; they're rejecting your product/service.

How do the best do it? They advertise. Week in and week out, regardless of the market, they are spending big bucks to get and keep their name in front of potential clients. They want their phone to be ringing. When they have enough business, they will refer people to others, or, by the questions they ask, just not take that person as a client. When they want more business, it is readily available. That way, they are not affected by the market. These superstars grew their business year over year, rarely being affected by the market. Isn't that a better way to handle your business?

Most agents don't want to spend the money for advertising. Sure, they'll send out the Just Solds and Just Listeds, but mailings are not advertising. They are part of your overall marketing plan. With the scarcity market we have been in, advertising hasn't seemed necessary. When you can sell a house in three days or three hours, why bother? That is not how the best of the best think. They know the market changes, and by advertising and marketing consistently, these experts keep their sales funnel full.

These people believe you *List to Live.* Half of them do listings only. They will work with a buyer if it's a referral. However, Karen Hoberg believes you should continue to work with buyers because then you truly know what the buyers are looking for. She doesn't think you can stay on top of what the latest needs/wants are unless you're out there with the buyer. The buyer's agents may not tell you what's not right about a home you have listed, but if you were to take a buyer there yourself, you'd know and be able to better advise the seller.

When starting, one of the key ingredients is finding the market that works best for you. Is it a geographical area, new home sales, condos, For Sale By Owners, expired listing, repossessions, lots, or first-time homebuyers? Become the expert in your area.

The biggest challenge for all of us is staying focused. So many things in a day can draw you away from what you should be doing. It's easy to let someone else's emergency become yours. There is no doubt that you may have the best-laid plans in the world, and by 9:00 A.M. they've been rearranged. It's easy for your day to slip away when you have no one looking over your shoulder, no one whom you're accountable to other than yourself.

All of these powerhouses hired people to handle the things they weren't great at. Usually that's the paperwork. All of them decided, and at different times, when they needed that help. One got an assistant one month in to the business, while for others it was six years. Family members are usually the first employees. Obviously, spouses make good business partners. Many agents will work one deal through and then look for another client. This will always leave you fearful of when and what your next deal will be. You will have ups and downs. You'll find out how these top performers make the best use of their time each day.

Sometimes agents get up in the morning and are unsure what to do with their day. What kind of commitment did you make for that day? What did you want to accomplish? If you don't have anything scheduled, what can you do to get in front of either potential buyers or sellers? If you have no goals or plans, you can't accomplish anything. You will end up spending your day doing things that will not take you toward your dream. Have a plan of action!

Delegation is the key to better time management. We have to realize we are not indispensable, and with the right systems and people in place we can design the life of our dreams.

People have a challenge in finding time for themselves and family. No doubt, with high performers, if something has to go in a day, it's time for themselves. Most of them actually schedule their personal and family time just like it was client time. When you treat it like that, it is more like a commitment. It's one thing to give up your personal time, but it's another thing to make a commitment to friends or family and cancel. In the long run, they won't understand, and your relationships will be affected. When it comes down to family or business, family always should come first.

These superstars say that all good real estate agents have three things in common: integrity, honesty, and outstanding customer service. I think we take these words for granted. Everyone says it, but what do they mean? These role models candidly share their interpretation. They all speak strongly about these keywords that separate top performers from everyone else.

The market is evolving and opening even more opportunities for good agents. Moving out of the scarcity market will force agents to become more knowledgeable about the market, advertise, and strengthen their negotiating skills, if they want to succeed. Real estate agents will have to start investing in themselves and their business. These super achievers all believe that great efforts, in the right areas, produce great results.

Join me, and discover what the best in the industry do to be so successful. The following 12 chapters are these superstars' interviews. Their statistics are for the year 2003.

Here's your chance to get the mentoring advice that can change your business and your life. If you're going to work 40-60 hours a week, why not make 10 times what you're making now? Listen to their words of advice. They all have found a formula that works. Don't be afraid to try something new. If you don't take risks, expect none of life's goodies. Hone your formula for success.

After the interviews, you will find the key points on negotiating, counseling your clients, marketing tips that work, action steps they take, what they've learned along their paths, and the biggest mistakes of agents, and then a summary of what we've learned from these superstars. The Appendix includes some key tools and systems these superstars use and have been kind enough to share, and that you are welcome to use.

If you want to be great at anything, the best way to do it is to listen and watch the best and do what they do. Here is your opportunity to take your business to the next level. Take notes. Decide which things you've learned from these experts that you're going to implement. Then take action. Most importantly—take consistent action every day.

MARY ANN BENDINELLI

WEICHERT REALTORS®
Manassas, Virginia

#1 Transactions National Capital Region
#1 Units Sold: Weichert Family of Companies

- Sales Volume: $33 M
- # of Units Sold: 201
- Gross Commission Income: $1.1 M
- # of Employees: 3
- www.BendinelliTeam.com
- Years in the business: 18

What made you decide on real estate as a career?

I was working as an assistant in an optometrist's office for 16 years. Two real estate agents came in. I, very patiently, assisted them in their selection of glasses and frames. One of them said, "You really would be good in real estate." Within two weeks, I went down to the Northern Virginia Community College and enrolled in the principles of real estate class. Within six months, I was a full-time real estate agent.

What did they say to you that prompted you to take action?

They were discussing how I was able to talk them through finding a frame. They were impressed and thought I'd be great. We talked about what they did. I must have been ready. In real estate I believe you're paid what your worth. You are able to promote yourself and do all the things that make sure your strengths and abilities are appreciated. And you're your own boss. You truly are the business. You're an independent contractor, and I like that part of it; being responsible for my success.

They're working underneath a structure that provides support for them.

The structure and support can really help make a good real estate agent. You have to have it in you, be motivated, and have your own desire.

On support, you have to go out and find where you're going to build it. When I got in to the business, probably the most difficult part was trying to decide where I was going to hang my license.

I thought I knew where I was going, because the instructor of my class was a broker at one of the local real estate companies in town. After I finished my classes and passed the test and did all the things I was supposed to, I went over there to sign up.

When I went in to the first office, there were agents' children playing near the front desk. It was too loud. The office didn't feel right. I felt that it was very important, for image, so I wanted to be affiliated with a company with an image. I had to regroup. Then I interviewed every office in my area. I selected Merrill Lynch Realty. I felt it was more professional. Merrill Lynch was bought by Prudential Preferred

Properties in '89, and then consequently bought by Weichert Realtors in '95. I've never changed companies; I just changed colors three times!

You asked about what motivated me and what got me going? Early encouragement and praise is probably what made an incredible difference for me. Motivation can come from many sources, and it's different for each individual. A good broker recognizes what each individual needs to perform at his or her best. My first broker, Peter Kane, was proud of his agents. He let them know it.

What did you ask about when you interviewed those offices?

The first thing a new real estate agent needs to understand is that they want you as much as you want them. They have very little to lose if you come on board and don't shine. Obviously, they will devote a lot of time and energy in training, and that is expensive, there's no question. But they have a lot more to gain by having you and then retaining you. As a person coming onboard, it is important that you also ask the questions and that you feel comfortable with what they have to offer.

Your first impression of an office is important for your business.

Well, it's based upon people you meet at that office on a day-to-day basis. You want to make sure that, when you make an appointment with a client you've never met, who doesn't know you from Adam, and doesn't know if you're good, bad, or indifferent, he or she gets a good feeling when coming in to the office. The way the agents are dressed has an effect. Everything enters in to it, even the look of the office.

Did location of offices have anything to do with your decision?

Location did. I looked at where each of the offices was situated. But, in our business, a great deal of walk-in is not what we depend on. We depend on our contacts. Whether or not the real estate office was on the main drag, which this one happened to be, or whether or not it was a little bit off the beaten path, wasn't a huge determination for me.

Did you have a mentor?

Mentors were not in vogue then. Mentors were not around. There was education, and I attended the hands-on type things they had to offer. New agents today are very fortunate, especially if they recognize the importance of and can affiliate with a company that's known for educational excellence.

There was a very special lady who has had a wonderful influence on my career. Her name is Valerie Huffman. She's gone through the same path I have, as far as Merrill Lynch, Prudential, and Weichert. She has been promoted to VP of Weichert, which she deserves to no end.

I've take advantage of the educational offerings in the company. My fellow agents were great. I learned a lot just from listening to them discuss situations, or even listening in on their side of the conversations when they were on "the desk," during what we called opportunity time.

That first office was a bullpen setting, rather than private offices. I felt that that was a plus. You got to hear more dialogues, and you got to know a little more about what was going on with inventory.

Those first six months seem so critical to your whole attitude and mindset.

They certainly are. Most of it had to do with education, of learning the nitty-gritty; learning how to write a contract, obtain buyers and sellers, and the processing end of it. I had very strong education in those areas.

I remember the second person I met in my real estate profession. I was showing them properties in these fairly rural areas. We were talking 45 minutes before we got to the first property. I learned two really important things from this particular transaction. The first one was you never, ever, judge a book by its cover. I went out with a couple that didn't talk! Thank goodness they had a six-year-old daughter who was a chatterbox. I was nervous. I was new.

This little girl and I had the most wonderful conversation. We get to the first house, and I'm trying to learn how to get feedback from the client. We go in to the house, and I show them the property. What did you think of the house? Nothing. It was okay. We go to the next house. I'm kind of learning my way through this. Did you like anything more about this one than the other one? I'm really floundering here. We see three houses that day. We go back to the office conference room, not knowing what to do, look them straight in the eye and say, "Which one do you want to buy, number one, two, or three?" The husband says, "Number three." I am in shock. Now I have to write a contract.

I was ecstatic, but I didn't know what to say, so I asked the question. You know, it's "asking for the order." You have to do it. That was in the first two weeks.

I get a call from the lender about three weeks later. We're not going to be able to do this loan because this gentleman won't give us information. He won't talk to us. He won't tell us where his funds are. I call him up. This is "don't judge a book by its cover." I say, "You know, we're really having an issue. This loan company is not going to be able to give you the funds to go to closing because it needs to know where the money is and to get copies of statements. It needs your help on that." His comment was, "Mary Ann, if I pay cash, do I have to talk to these people anymore?" I went to closing three days later. My first transaction was a cash transaction. You live. You learn, and you must learn from what you do. I learned a lot from that. It was just a wonderful, wonderful way to get started in the business.

I had the neatest thing happen. It's probably been about two years ago. The six-year-old daughter [from the above story] bought a house from me when she grew up. She said, "You helped my parents." I looked at her, and my eyes got huge. I said, "You're the six-year-old chatterbox. I've been telling stories about you for years."

Have you been discouraged?

I have always looked on problem solving as one of my top strengths—being able to look at something that comes at you, and try to figure out a way to make everybody happy. That's my goal in life. I think that that got me through any issues. You have to put all of the things that you do in perspective and not take what you do personally. In other words, trying to distance yourself enough so that you can be objective is one of the things that you have to do in this business.

Often, when somebody comes up with an objection or a concern or something that's not right, he or she is looking for more information and needs to be educated.

If you're not getting an objection, the clients aren't talking to you. Then you have to figure it out by asking the right questions. If they're giving you an objection, they're telling you exactly what they need information about.

Exactly right. It's nice to talk to someone who understands. It's not the norm for someone who wants others to come up with a reason why they don't want to do something.

What did you learn along your path?

Mostly, it was how to put all of what I do in some semblance of order; having systems in place is super-important. You learn your strengths. You learn by making sure you get the proper education, and then process those things. You learn by having the same sort of situation, with every one being different. That's how I look at real estate. *Every* transaction I have is different. That's why it's kept me interested in the profession. Each day is a different day from the day before. All the best-laid plans for the day usually get messed up by 9:00.

How do you deal with that?

You have to be ready for anything. You have to have those systems in place. For instance, have your portfolio prepared so that, if you get a listing call at 11:30 A.M., you don't have to put together all the forms you need to go to that appointment. You have your listing folder, your listing presentation, and all of your marketing things you're going to show them. If you get a call from someone and you're in your car heading to Giant Food to pick up dinner for the evening, because you didn't think you were going to have dinner at all, and you get the call that someone wants to write a contract on the house that you showed them that morning, you have a contract folder with you. When you go to a presentation, you have everything prepared so that you can be out the door in less than an hour and be anywhere.

I'm not a firm believer in having this hour set aside for this and that hour set aside for that. I don't want to be that regimented. But I do make sure that I leave specific time for returning phone calls. I want to make myself available at all times to clients.

In talking about systems and making sure they're in place, I didn't realize the importance of having many systems in place until I had a family death. I was needed elsewhere for over three weeks. My clients hardly felt my absence. All went on as if I were there.

How did that happen?

The systems. Everything I do has a way of being done. Whether it's the ad generation, when I list a property, or what happens next, there are systems in place, like I was still there. That makes me feel really good.

That would give you a whole different mindset, wouldn't it, about how prepared you are and how you approach things?

It sure would.

Were you affected by the downturn in the market from '87 through '91?

No. Since I've become a Realtor, my income and the number of transactions have increased every year, regardless of the market. People always need to buy and they always need to sell, regardless of the market. It's a matter of making sure that you put yourself in front of the people who need to make decisions.

At what point did you bring on staff?

I have an unlicensed assistant, Nancy, who's been with me for 11 years. And I have a licensed partner, Shawn Krebs, who's been with me over four years. Nancy came on board during my sixth year in real estate, in 1993; at that point, I was probably making a little more than $90,000 in income. Nancy does administrative tasks:

- processing the contracts and the listings
- making brochures
- preparing and mailing Just Listeds, Just Solds, and Open Houses

- adding names to my database
- helping with the calendar mail outs
- meeting ad deadlines
- doing neighborhood market reports
- ordering signs up and down
- answering my phone, when she's here
- sending me email messages so that I'm constantly aware of who needs to reach me and how urgent it is

The last one is a big benefit. I don't need to call in for messages. I get them on an alphanumeric pager.

I took on and trained a licensed assistant in my seventh year, not necessarily to increase my production, but to have a backup, and to make sure things didn't slip through the cracks as I was getting busier. His tasks included attending home inspections, meeting the appraisers, dealing with termite inspectors, removing lock boxes, and delivering brochures. Since he was a licensed agent, he, of course, could go in to the property. He was taking exterior photos, holding open houses, and showing property. This individual was with me for almost seven years. When he started, I was kind of mentoring him, teaching him the way. We did very well together for those seven years.

Shawn Krebs, my business partner, came to me in 2000 from a mortgage background, and it very became clear quickly that the match was good. He did all the tasks mentioned before, plus he took on other responsibilities:

- interior home features,
- interior digital photography
- virtual tours
- daily updating of my Web page
- writing and negotiating contracts
- negotiation of home inspection items

It was everything I do, which enables me to take some time off comfortably.

How much time do you take off?

I probably take about 2½ weeks a year.

I also take off each of my grandkids' birthdays. I make the birthday cakes. I can easily get away for three to four days. I do that over a weekend. I do that more regularly.

My daughter resides in Spokane, Washington. When she lived here in Virginia, and was 18-20 years old, I tried so hard to get her into real estate. I felt she would be wonderful, that we could be a team. She gave me maybe a ten-second thought on it, and said "Mom, I've seen how hard you work, and I really don't want any part of it." Guess what she's doing now? Real estate.

What do you think caused her to change her mind?

She's very good at it. She has the same caring that I do. I think maturity and a better feeling of self-confidence. As you get older, the self-confidence comes naturally. It does take a special person to want to give up part of his or her personal life to be good.

When should you get an assistant?

I do a lot of things with my company, including teaching new agents and teaching people who have been in the business a while. The time to consider getting an assistant is when you realize you're spending way too much time doing things other than listing and selling. I was putting in about 110 hours a week. My next hire will be someone whose only job will be that of additional marketing. I've been very fortunate. I know agents who have gone through dozens of assistants. That's the hard part. It is so important that you click with a person you're going to be handing things to; he or she is going to be handing them back to you, done.

110 hours is a lot.

I have never begrudged that. It's not something that I feel is bad. My kids were teens when I got in to this.

An agent started about the same time I did. She has four children.

She came to me almost in tears because she was getting so frustrated. She wasn't seeing her business blossom like mine. I sat her down and said, "Carol, you can't compare yourself to somebody who doesn't have to be home at 5:00 at night to fix dinner for four children. You have to do what you need to and keep your priorities straight. Right now, your priorities are your kids." She has to be competitive with herself, which is how I look at myself. I'm not competitive with Joe Blow. I'm not competitive with others. I'm competitive with me. I want to be the best—for me.

You have to understand your priorities in life, at this time.

The guilt you feel is big. A lot has to do with balancing the personal and professional aspect. In the beginning, I did struggle somewhat: time management; feeling I was being pulled too many ways; and feeling guilty that I couldn't be all things to all people in my personal life, because I was absolutely going to be all things to every client.

I take what I do very seriously. I always have. When you're being pulled or you're getting this guilt feeling, you have to step back and regroup and figure out what you can do to make sure that your loved ones feel they're important. This is a team effort with family. I could never be as good, and do as well as I have, without the support of my husband Clay. There's no way.

The resolution we came up with is that I go to the movies every Friday night with Clay. Every Friday night we have hot dogs, popcorn, Dr. Pepper, and M&Ms. We love it. It's the absolute best thing in the world for us. We both know that, come Friday at 7:00—and my clients know—I'm not theirs. I tell my clients that I'm theirs seven days a week, 24 hours a day, except Friday night.

You mentioned giving up things to be good in this business. Give me an example.

In other words, at 6:00 there is no off. Contracts are legally important, but they're also important in that your people are depending on you. There's so much responsibility on the shoulders of a real estate agent. It's not just you who has to handle your own personal affairs. You're handling theirs, too. You have to give up being able to simply turn it off, especially when you don't have someone else who can back you up.

The first 14 years in my career, I felt I needed to be there 100 percent, all the time. I needed to be there for every person I was having any sort of transaction with. The last several years with Shawn and my comfort level with him have enabled me to give up some of that. But I think its individual.

As far as personal, it helped me to realize I have to do something for me. I am making those birthday cakes. I'm up to 31 cakes now, and I'm not that good. They tell me a month in advance that they want SpongeBob SquarePants, Spiderman, a snake, a dinosaur, or a bunny rabbit. I shape the cake. It's a blast. It's so important to them. I have pictures of every cake I've made for every grandkid, with them right in the background, holding up the number of fingers they are. That's what it's about. As an agent, as someone getting in to the business, as someone trying to stay in the business, you have to have those special times.

After the movie, I do have to admit, I call in for my messages, to make sure that something hasn't come up that I really need to handle after the movies. Probably seven to eight years ago, on the way home I listened to my message, and it was a gentleman whose house I had listed two weeks before. He said, "Hi, Mary Ann, this is Jim," and I heard, "Oh my God, it's Friday," and he hung up. I said to my husband, "Honey, listen to this! I have arrived!" I listened to it 10 times. This guy made my month. He thought I was going to rip the sign out of his yard if he bothered me on a Friday night!

What do you do to set expectations with your clients?

It depends, of course, on whether I'm listing a property or I'm taking them out to look at properties to purchase. The education part is really, really critical, and it's key to both buyers and sellers, because when they sit down with me, they're depending on me to help them know what to expect. It's important that a buyer knows which direction the market's going, whether he or she should pay full price or above for a property, expects that my job would be to help with the negotiations, gets and pays as little for a property as possible, and knows what to focus on when looking at property.

It's really, really important to have respect for the company you work with. One of the reasons I'm with Weichert is Jim Weichert, and I feel that he's one of the most impressive visionaries I've ever known.

Handling the changes in the market is easy, because, we, as agents, know what to expect. Then we can pass that on to our clients. I'll never forget listening to Jim at one of our regional sales meetings. He said, "Let them pay!" All of us kind of raised our eyebrows. What are you telling us?

He was referring to changing markets. His concern was our helping the buyers lose one, two, three, or even more properties by advising conservative offers in a quickly appreciating market, and then the clients having to pay even more in the end for a comparable property. If they had been more aggressive in their offering price earlier in the process, they would have settled sooner for less. Let's say the property's on the market for $300,000; we know there are 16 other contracts coming in on that property. If we go in conservatively, and the buyer says, "I'm going to offer $300,000," they're not going to get it. Our job is to educate the clients and help them with those expectations. Our role, as a Realtor, is important. What we do as a real estate agent doesn't dwindle or rise or fall with market changes. It simply changes how we look at and advise clients based on market. It really is how we earn our keep. Our value to our clients is based on market: whether or not we need to be stronger negotiators, knowledge of the reputation of the lending institution, and complicated paperwork. All of those things are part of what we do.

This is where education comes in to play. When I take out buyers and show them properties, and they start to hone in on a specific neighborhood, before we make that offer, before we sit down and write that contract, we take a look at what properties have been selling for in that community, what the trend is. Is the trend going up or down in value? This is before we make decisions on what to offer, so they understand what they're going to have to do to win, and they may lose once or twice until they get to that point. That's okay. They realize the need to be aggressive, and if we're going to get in to this market and if we're going to buy, we'll have to be aggressive in what we're offering for the property.

On the selling side, the street smarts...I guess this is a good word...of the Realtor, in other words knowing which contracts to give more credence to in the case of multiple offers, is an enormous difference in the bottom line for the sellers. They're hiring us to do a job, to help them with advice based on our knowledge. We're not the ones to make the final decision. They have to come up with yes, they're going to accept this, or no, they're not. But I'm a firm believer that sellers won't sell for less than they're willing to take, and buyers won't pay more than they're willing to pay. Our job is to present all the facts.

Don't use our attempt to protect their interests and win by losing. Make sure that you let the client do what the client wants to do, which is to get the property. Don't use our own limitations.

How do you influence your clients?

Education. I don't just put people in my car and take them to look at houses. I have an interview with them prior to that, covering a multitude of things: financing and their options. I may spend 2-2½ hours with them before we even look at the first property.

They have to know how I work, and I have to know what their needs are. Making sure that they know I have knowledge gets them comfortable.

We discuss what they're looking for in a property. They walk in my office, and there are a couple of awards on the walls, which helps. I guess their thoughts are that others have used this person before, so he or she has some creditability. Use your awards. You get diplomas when you complete certain aspects of training. Tote them. Put them up in your cubicle. Have the purchaser or seller you're working with be aware that you've done something. Don't be a secret agent.

You want to make sure that people know your abilities. I don't say first thing that I'm the number-one Weichert agent in the national capital region. I let an award say it, or I let an advertisement that I'm showing them say it. I try to make sure they know they are working with someone who has ability. But it doesn't matter if you're in the business for a day or 17½ years. Your company has ability. If you don't have specific awards yourself, promote your company's award. Promote what your company has done. Getting to the comfort level of the purchaser or seller, they have to buy in to the fact that you are out there to assist them, you're on their side, and you want what's best for them. One of my strong points is that I really do care, and I think my people know it.

I mentioned that I do some teaching, seminars, and that sort of thing for agents. I start many of them out talking about attitude. I promote an upbeat, make-it-happen attitude, knowing what your worth is and not being afraid to justify it. You have these things to convey, and caring, but you also have to be sure enough of yourself and what you're offering them.

Those are the things that make them feel you're worth sitting in front of them. They have a choice when they go looking for property. In our area alone, they have a choice of over 2000 agents. To every person you meet, you have to convey what you're doing and that you're confident, not only in words but also in what you're showing them.

How have you branded yourself in the market?

Probably consistency in your presentation is most important. It's a type of name recognition, the recognition of your advertisement. I use two specific photographs. One is of me holding a camera. I've had people say, "You're the one with the camera." The second photo is on every Just Listed, Just Sold, and Open House flyer. It's of me pointing down toward the photo of the home. I've continued using the same ads for 15 years, just updating the pictures. When you're advertising, you want to make sure that you use the same photographs, but different from someone else's.

How do you negotiate the best deal for your client?

It depends on the market, as far as what that really means. Does it mean making sure that, when you're writing a contract, you've eliminated every possibility for that seller to have any grief with your contract, putting that person in their best light so that they want to pick you and your clients?

How much advice or counseling do you give your clients?

I do a lot of advising, but I don't come up with the bottom line for them. I give them options. I will tell them what they can expect, what some offer may be coming in for, based on what other comparables have been and the market trends. Depending on market, and I've been through them all, what I suggest really differs. At one time, it was discussions of how much less they can pay for a property and how much more closing costs the seller may be willing to contribute. Of course, in more recent years, it's been how to win with the next property coming on the market for sometimes $10,000 more than what the last one sold for.

With the advice, make sure that the buyer knows what the seller may be expecting to see. I talk a lot about the contingencies, what contingencies do to the strength of the contract, and how finance can affect which offer the seller accepts.

How does your finance knowledge influence your effectiveness with your clients?

When I got in to the business, we didn't have Gold Services Managers[1], with the ability to approve funding in our office, as we do now. We can get an approval in 20 minutes without our clients having to go 20 miles away or fax documents to an outside lender. My clients love it because they're able to have everything done in my office. I discuss their pre-qualifications first and how a lender will look at them. I want them to get comfortable with me, before I sit them in front of the lender to get their qualification letter. I want them to have that tie with me because I'm the one they're going to be depending on to pull everything together.

I feel very, very strongly that newer agents need to know how to ballpark qualify a buyer. If they don't have that ability, they need to learn how.

Many times, the contract that's accepted has a lot to do with the reputation of the agent and the lender who's coming with that contract. Lender letters are not all the same. You could have a lender letter and not fund. And that's where the expertise of the agent and where the expertise of knowing which lenders are good for that piece of paper both come in.

What effect do the agents have in the negotiations?

I think they have a strong effect. What we do as agents can help our person win. I do a lot of things to put them in their best light. I love to be able to present in person. If there is any way, shape, or form that I can be

---

[1] Weichert Gold Services is a unique new customer-service program that promotes high-quality customer service being provided by its agents.

in front of the seller and his agent and present for my client, I'll do it in a heartbeat.

I got in to this business before fax machines. Now, of course, it's so simple to fax a contract over. You lose so much when you have just a piece of paper with words on it.

Not all agents "allow" that to happen. It's a shame. I think it should always be the decision of the sellers as to whether they have an agent present to them or have only their agent present during the contract presentation. I try very, very hard to make it easy for the other agent to allow me to be there. This is what I feel has helped get my contracts through when maybe they weren't even the best dollar bottom line:

- One of them is the presentation in person. That's probably the best way, because, as an agent, I look at my mouth as my best asset. I make sure my purchaser knows that I'm going to do everything I can to get an audience. You want to do that because sometimes you can get a feeling for the specific needs of that seller to make it all come together, and I can make my purchaser more human. It also benefits the seller. For instance, the contract date for settlement we've put on the contract is three days different from what the seller really needs. The seller, if I'm not there, can't ask the question then and there of how flexible they are on their closing time. If an agent wants to present in person to me, I welcome it. I don't look at that agent as my enemy. We're not. We're all in this together. They're not my competition. We're all in here to make sure that the buyer and the seller do as well as they both can. We're doing a job. We enable buyers and sellers to have a meeting of the minds.

- Sometimes it means me taking an extra three hours to present in person, rather than just slipping it in the fax. It's not the time that we're trying to lessen. We're trying to make it so that, by the end of that evening, by the time I leave there, my goal would be to have a fully ratified contract. You're going to have a happier client. It is a good relationship builder all the way around.

- The other thing I do if I present in person is to have my client fewer than three blocks away. My purchaser is going to be very close by. If there is just a miniscule change in the contract, it's a dead contract until everybody agrees to that change.

I have my client sitting eating an ice cream cone at McDonald's or a taco at Taco Bell, and they are, literally, waiting for my call. I tell them it may be two hours before I call them, but I need them to be close. Then, if it does turn out that something small needs to be changed, we don't have a ratified contract until the initials are on it by the buyer, which means any other contract can come in during that time. My goal is to get it to them, get it initialed, get it back, and deliver it.

About two weeks ago, there were several contracts on a $400,000 property. I had my people a block-and-a-half away at their parents. I had them programmed in my phone so all I had to do was punch a button. We had one question in the contract. I was the only one who asked to be there and the only one who showed up. There were three contracts. The question was about a stain underneath their couch. They wanted to make sure it was disclosed to my buyer and that they were aware of it before they told the other people the house was sold. I called my client. I said that I could have them there in three minutes. We were able to wrap it up, have them sign off, and have the buyers and sellers hug each other by the end of that night.

I would have never known that if I would have simply faxed a copy and received a counter back to say, "Purchaser is aware of a four-inch stain." Then it would have had to go back again.

Short of being able to present in person, I do a cover letter. I try to humanize my buyer. The cover letter will talk about the things they liked about the house and the flexibility of closing date, because the purchaser is living with family. It will talk about the four-year-old who saw something she loved in the home. I try to have it read during the contract presentation and put a little more personal feeling in my contract.

I'll also do a summary page [included in the Appendix], which makes it easier for the agent to know what's in my contract: price, terms, settlement date, contingencies, all of those things. He or she can have a page to make comparisons between my contract and another.

I love it when someone does it for me, because I have to do that when I receive a contract. If I'm trying to compare more than one offer, I can get the highlights, the points of each contract. It's professional.

You have to keep in mind that you are trying your best to represent the interests of your purchaser. Markets change: we're talking about today's market, when things are quick, when it's very important to get in front of that seller sooner than later. We make everything in that contract as clean as possible. Regardless of market, neither the philosophies nor the way the contract is written would change. When you don't have a scarcity market, contingencies would come back into play.

I have to laugh, because I've been in all markets, and you have a property listed, you're promoting their property, and they're, like, "Mary Ann, it's been a week. What's wrong?" I've been in the market when I have brought cupcakes to celebrate a one-year anniversary for a listing. I'm just as proud of that listing as I am the ones I sell in a day. Celebrating that after a year means the seller knows I'm doing everything I can, and that it's the market rather than me.

How much advertising/marketing do you do?

I believe that, when people list their property with an agent, they're spending an incredible amount of money for that agent to handle the transaction. They deserve to have some of that money spent on them. I do blitz marketing. What I mean by that is, when I take a listing, I automatically know, and so do my sellers, where it is going to be advertised. I don't put one ad together and put it in the *Real Estate Book* and wait for something to happen. I'm going to be in the *Real Estate Book*, the *Harmon Homes*, the *Homes and Land*, and the Internet in eight places. All the things I do marketing-wise are done immediately.

Do you do that with a home that doesn't sell for a year?

Yes, many times I spend close to or more than I make. But you know what, it all evens out.

I do full pages. I have eight to 10 on a page. But by the time the publication comes out in this market, they're gone. But that's absolutely okay. That's something that listing agents have to get across to themselves. You're not marketing or trying to sell that house. You're marketing the lady with the camera and a phone number. As long as you understand that, you don't mind spending the money.

That's a very different mindset.

You have to understand that, or you're not going to spend the money. You're not going to have the other people wanting to list with you. It's a mindset; that's probably a great word for it.

There seems to be a real reluctance, on a lot of agents' parts, to spend money.

They feel they don't have to right now.

My advertising budget has not decreased, even though things are staying on the market less. I'm still advertising in the same number of publications. When someone calls "that lady with the camera," I'll say, "Hi, thanks for calling on that property. I'm sure you're probably finding, that with every call you're making in this *Real Estate Book*, that the house is sold. The reason for that is because the market right now is very, very quick. Has anyone offered to talk with you about your home purchase? Do you have a real estate agent who's pulling up listings for you every day?" That's why I feel strongly that you have to continue to advertise.

How often do they take you up on your offer?

Of the calls I receive, more than 50 percent do not have an agent who they are actively working with.

Then my job is to convince those people that I'm the best thing since sliced bread, and have them want to come in and meet me. My closing on that is pretty significant. It's called call-conversion.

If they say they do have an agent, I say, "If that agent is doing a good job for you, please stay with them. Give them a call. Let them know you saw this ad, because they may want to get in touch. I can keep them posted if anything happens with the transaction."

Oftentimes, agents may not be as handholding as others. If the purchasers start thinking there's something else on the market they haven't seen, they may start to make those calls themselves if they're not getting the service they need. It all has to do with education. Remember the first meeting that buyer had sitting in front of the agent, talking about expectations—what you can expect from me and what I expect from you—that's when you come up with what you're supposed to do as a buyer. Many of these buyers don't know what they're supposed to do. So it's definitely shame on agents who don't prepare their purchaser to be a purchaser.

What other types of marketing do you do?

There are many layers of direct marketing. You have to be careful to spend your money wisely. There are different reasons to do different types of marketing. Mailings alone, done once or twice, are not going to get results. The agents who begin and quit after four or five months should save their money. Name recognition takes a whole lot longer; that's what you're trying to do with direct marketing.

Every time I list a property, I send out an 8½ × 11 flyer that I call a Just Listed. It's not a postcard. It's in a window envelope, and it goes to the closest 250 to 500 names, and sometimes more, depending on the subdivision size. It has a tear-off coupon at the bottom for the neighbors to mail back in their own envelope where they have to write my name on the return envelope. I offer them a neighborhood market report for their subdivision. It doesn't get as specific as a CMA (Competitive Market Analysis). It might include subdivision ramblers, colonials, split foyers, all the different price ranges, different everything. It's talking about neighborhood.

When I sell that property, I send a Just Sold to the same neighbors. I'm doing a double whammy. I use the same envelope and flyer with the tear-off, but the wording's different. It's offering a neighborhood marketing report. The Just Sold is showing that I'm successful. It's more for me. It's not more marketing for the seller. A lot of agents do Just Listeds. The postcard is advertising the agent and the company. What I send is trying to sell the house. It's one more piece of marketing, like an advertisement. It has a picture of the house, and it has information and pricing of the house. It's really important to have that sort of continued exposure in a community in which you want to do business.

Is the flyer in color or black & white?

Absolutely color. I bought a color copier/printer in 1990. I don't know how many years ago I switched to leasing equipment versus buying because of repair costs. I have a very expensive color copier/printer.

You have to be listing and selling in the neighborhood for that to work.

For instance, I do this: Let's say a month and a half or two months have gone by, and I have not listed a property in that particular subdivision. I will send out a postcard with quarterly sales for their community. It keeps your name going there. It's so important.

Where I farm today happened by accident. I got one listing in a Battery Heights condominium. I did a Just Listed flyer, sent a direct mail with an open house invitation, and held an open house. When it sold, I sent out the Just Sold. I received three requests for appointments and listed two of them. Now I'm known as The Queen of the Community. I love it. You must capitalize on your successes, letting the world know of them.

I got a call from this person in Battery Heights, and I pulled him up in the public records. He was the owner of the property. I put together my marketing, my listing presentation. Shortly after I arrived at his house, he said, "Excuse me one second." He walked out of the room and then came back in with a notebook. He tossed it on to the table as he asked, "Do you want to know why I called you?" He opened up this book, and he had every Just Listed, Just Sold, and Open House I had sent for four years. He picked me because I was the "Queen" of the subdivision. Again, that name recognition and making sure you capitalize on what you do well are really important.

How do you hold a great open house?

I have two prepared satchels. I have one satchel that has information if you wanted to list your home. This station gives them information about how I market a property. I have another satchel/station if you're thinking of buying; what is important to know for buying. Looking at your first purchase? There's information they can go to in a corner of the house, which I'm holding open, that they can sit and peruse. I may have something on it that says, "Sample. Please ask." I can get their information, follow up, take them the book, or take them that information. At least I have a way of following up, instead of them just taking and walking out the door.

How quickly do you follow up?

The next day. When planning an open house, I put a front-page ad in the *Washington Post*. Weichert has the front page 42 times a year. I then send out a Just Listed Open, and that goes to the neighbor with a little different scenario. I do a banner across it that says, "Open Sunday, August 29th, 1 to 5, neighbors welcome." I want people who want to sell their houses to come to my open as well. A lot of agents don't realize that people who are thinking about selling their home go around, and this is very smart of them, to see how someone would promote theirs. You're trying to capitalize on that when someone comes to your open.

On Monday of that week, I put a rider on the sign that says Open Sunday. If somebody drives by, they can jot it down.

I put together a booklet called *Active Listings*. It's not just something that I lay out, but it's something that I have at the open, in case someone comes in to the open and says, "This house is nice, but I don't like the backyard," or, "This house is nice, but I didn't realize the price range is where it is. I'm really in this price range." I will have all of the listings, of all of the agents, in the surrounding area in a price range of $100,000 spread of what I'm holding open. It gives me the ability to have additional conversation with that person rather than the person saying, "This house doesn't meet my needs. Thank you so much. Goodbye."

I have a four-page sign-in sheet that is carbon. Underneath where they sign in, I write in any conversations I had with them, and whether I should send them the neighborhood report for their house they may be selling in a year. If I have 20 people coming through an open, when I leave I won't remember whom I talked to about what.

When they come in, I say, "Hi, I'm Mary Ann Bendinelli. I'm representing the seller today. If I could have you, please, sign in." I have a clipboard, and often I sign in for them because I can read my writing; sometimes I can't read theirs. I want to be able to have them be open and honest with what information they're giving me.

I say, "If you don't mind signing in, that way the seller knows who's been through their home today." It's a way of putting it back in their perspective. If I had a bunch of people in my house, I'd want to know who went through. Then I will hand them a brochure and ask, "Did you come from the signs or did you see the advertisement in the *Post*?" I'm trying to determine whether they know what price range it is. If they came from the signs, they may not have a clue. I'll go into the price range right upfront with them. If they came from the *Post* ad, I may say something like, "It's so wonderful to see that my advertising dollars are at work," just something, information, trying to start a conversation.

I escort them through the house. I don't do open houses with just me there. There's a safety issue today that there didn't used to be. That's one of the reasons why I escort them through, for my own safety and keeping track of the house.

If I have a three-level house, I'll have three people there. I'll have one on each level. I'll use the newer agents who really, really love to be able to do an open house with me so they can see how it's done. They are so appreciative of an agent who will share.

What other things do you do about the security issue?

When I list their property, when I'm talking about my worth, and justifying my worth, one of the things I bring up is safety. I used to meet people at vacant houses and show them the property. I don't do it anymore. I have them come to my office. We talk about what their needs are, and then we talk about income and debts and assets. Then we go out and look at properties.

I bring up objections before they do. In my presentations, I bring up things so that we can address them before they bring them up themselves. What I would say is, "One of the things that concerns me is that you're at work (I'm pointing to the husband), and Sandy, here, is home with the kids, and somebody knocks on your door and wants to see your home. You wouldn't let a stranger in your home when it wasn't on the market. Why would you start now?" I bring the safety issue in along with reasons why.

How have you invested in yourself to become this knowledgeable?

I've taken GI courses, broker classes, and appraisal. I believe education is very important. I'm afraid that, when they first get in to the business, and this is the toughie, agents are absolutely inundated with education. Unfortunately, at that point, they don't know enough to absorb it. They haven't written a contract. They haven't gone out on a listing appointment. They haven't put a keypad in a lock box. All the things that you learn by doing, you're being told how to do.

Going back after you've had training, after being in the business six months to a year, and taking some basic classes, you're going to get so much more out of it. It's enabling you to absorb and understand. Oh, that's what they were talking about.

You're getting the knowledge, but not thinking that you can get it all done in the first three months. In 2003, I had 97 hours of receiving and about 40 hours of giving real estate education.

How do you stay motivated?

I want to be good. I want to be the best, and I think that, in itself, motivates me. I've not once woken up in the morning and said, "Oh, I have to go to work today." I don't necessarily look at what I do as a job. My mom, before she passed away, used to give me grief about the numbers of hours I worked. I got her to understand when I told her, "I work eight hours a day just like everybody else. The other eight hours a day I work is my hobby. "

Two compliments that probably mean more to me than anything: One was from someone I sold a house to. Whether they're buying a $100,000 condo or a million-dollar property, I look at them the same. They both need the same amount of attention, handholding, whatever. This particular one was a $100,000 condo. I remember her saying to me, "Mary Ann, I don't know how you do it, but I always feel like I'm your only client." That was big. That's what it's all about.

The other compliment I got was from a fellow agent. It was one that they didn't know I heard, which are sometimes the best ones. It was at an awards ceremony where I was number one maybe for the fourth or fifth year. The agent said, talking to a group of about seven other real estate agents who were at her table, "You know, she does so much business, and she's even nice." Those are the things that are really important.

What is a typical day for you?

I usually get up around 7:30; if I have an 8:00 appointment, I get up at

6:30. If I have a 9:00 appointment, I get up at 7:30. I don't have an alarm clock that goes off at the same time every day. I do preparation for the next day in the evening. I'm a late-night person. I get up at 7:30, take my shower, and get ready. I'm out of the house by 8:20.

I got rid of an office in my house seven years ago. My husband and I share office space. I work out of the Weichert office when I'm meeting clients, but most of what I do is at the other office. I have some very sophisticated equipment there. That's where Nancy works. My database, my files, those sorts of things, are in this office, and clients don't come to this office.

I have about an hour a day during which I consciously make phone calls either to past clients or for lead generation. It's when I am touching base with people. I try to do that four times a week. I'm not always perfect about it, but I try really hard.

Most of my days have one or two listing appointments, and I'm back to back throughout the day. I'm either showing property or writing a contract. I usually finish my day with clients about 9:00 at night. I come back to this office and do a debriefing, where I go through and update the information in my database to make sure I'm ready for the next day. I pull files for the following day. I make sure that I put together the neighborhood market report, the CMAs, and the trend market analysis, so I have everything I need with me. If I'm going to a closing, I make sure I have their file and everything I need for each of my appointments.

You do that and not your assistant?

I do that. Nancy puts together the neighborhood market report for me. I give her parameters of what I need pulled, and she puts those together for me. But as far as pulling the files, I do that myself.

At what time do you stop your day?

Between 11:00 and 12:00 at night. Often, I have a laptop, so unfortunately sometimes that makes it home. When I go home and it's already 11:00, I can't talk to anybody anyway.

My husband and I eat a lot of our meals together. He owns a power and surge protection company and is on the road a lot, and he works crazy hours, like I do. Often, we meet somewhere for dinner. I don't do a lot of home cooking, but I love to do it. I exercise three times a week, and I'm pretty religious about it. I did join a gym.

Where do you fit that in?

It depends. It's usually best in the morning because it's before my day falls apart. It's usually at 7:30. When I get up, I go directly there. I have a locker, and I change and make myself pretty and then go directly to an appointment. I much prefer an evening to a morning, but that doesn't happen very often. I've been doing that the last two years. As you get older, you start putting things in place that you should have had in place a lot earlier.

Before you got Nancy, how did you prioritize your day?

I always tried to make sure that I got through the A-B-C stuff. A is imminent; it has to be done for a transaction, listing, sale, or settlement, that sort of thing. The B things are things that have to be done that day. But they don't have to be done at a specific time. And then the C things. I try very hard to make sure everything gets done that has to be done by the end of the day. That's why, sometimes, that 10:00 or 11:00 at night was 11:00 or 12:00, or later. That's when you start realizing you need some help.

Your ego in this business can be an incredible help, and it can be an incredible hindrance. Feeling that you're the only person in the world who could do it right is tough when you realize you need to start delegating. I think that's probably what took me so long to get to the point where I could hire a Nancy. Letting go. I really don't need to do a lot of things, but realizing that took me six years.

Is there anything else you'd like to share?

Make sure your client becomes a partner in the process. When you're having discussions with your client, make sure you present suggestions, not ultimatums. When I list a property, I'll go through it with them, and I'll make suggestions of things I found through the years have helped someone sell a property, either more quickly or for more money.

I might give you 10 suggestions. If you do one of them or 10 of them, I won't love you any less. I make them part of what's going on and make sure they know what you're doing. Probably the biggest complaint that sellers and buyers have about their agent is, "I don't know what they're doing. Did they advertise this week? Did they do this? What are they doing for me today?" Make sure you convey what you're doing, as you're doing it. They can't read your mind.

You send copies of the ad to the seller?

Absolutely, Nancy does that. They also know if something's coming up. I try on a weekly basis to talk with people whose houses I have listed. That is the other thing that agents tend to fall short of; if they don't have anything to say to them, they don't call them. It's so important that you call them to say, "I don't have anything to say to you."

Those are the things I find help a lot in the relationship. Everything we do is very strong in relationship: whether it's listing a property, taking buyers out, or talking with your fellow agents.

Probably one of the most important things is how I look at what I do. Make sure you treat every individual with caring and respect, and I'm talking everyone: your termite inspector, your lender, a renter, the workman, settlement offices, and more importantly, your fellow Realtors. You are across the table from them all the time. And you're reputation is the only thing you have in this business. That's it. It's not hard to have that reputation be tainted. It's so important to always, always remember that.

What type of systems do you have in place?

The importance of "being prepared" for the day to day tasks and having a system where someone else could take up the slack in an emergency is paramount to your own sanity AND to the well being of your clients.

- I have an advertising form that is kept current that shows all active properties vertically, then across the top are the mediums that we consistently advertise in. When we place an ad, the date is filled in, so that we make sure our advertising dollars are distributed properly and I can keep the client informed as to where their property has been promoted.

- I have a generic listing folder presentation, as well as multiple folders with all the forms needed for listing a property or writing up a sale. These are available in a file drawer, "pre-packaged" so that I can grab them at a moment's notice.

- My "open house bag" is a tote bag with 3 separate tote bags inside - broken down into 3 "stations" that will be placed in 3 different locations in the home...designed for a seller, a buyer and one station describing all the Gold Services offered (mortgage, title, ins, etc). This dramatically reduces the preparation time for an open house.

- I have templates designed specifically for when I "JUST LIST" a home that immediately goes to the neighbors ...and a template called "JUST SOLD" that goes out once a contract is ratified.

"Systems" are ways that have helped to increase my productivity...and remain sane.

<u>JOHN BEUTLER</u>

CENTURY 21 – Beutler & Associates
Coeurd'Alene, Idaho

#1 Gross Commission Income – Century 21 Worldwide

- Sales Volume: $77.4 M
- # of Units Sold: 281
- Gross Commission Income: $2 M
- # of Employees: 1
- www.C21Beutler.com
- Certified Residential Specialist (CRS)
- Years in the business: 27

How did you get started in real estate?

I went to school on a golf scholarship. I got my degree in marketing. I was in the golf business right out of college for three years. A gentleman named Derrel Cedarblom, who was in real estate, came up to me and talked real estate, and I ended up buying a little cabin from him for $10,000. About a year later, he came up to me and asked if I wanted to sell it. I said sure, and I sold it for $17,000. That was twice what I was making in the golf business, and I knew that golf wasn't a hobby anymore. I love to play golf, but it wasn't my passion like it was when I was in college.

The golf pro Jim Griffitts, whom I was working for, had his real estate license, and he was taking some real estate courses in the evening. I went over with him on a couple of occasions. That's how I got interested. $10,000 to $17,000 in one year seemed like a lot of money to me.

Did you go to work for that Realtor who sold you the cabin?

Yes, I did. I interviewed with three different brokers, and the other two didn't really give me an opportunity, or didn't seem interested. Derrell always did, but I thought I should check around. He was the vice president with Fuller Brush, and he retired from it about 20 years earlier.

How do you find the right broker to work for?

That's a good question. I tell people they should look around. People have gut feelings about who they feel good about. You don't know that until you get out and interview two or three brokers. They have different philosophies and different personalities. You need to interview two or three different people and ask tough questions.

Such as?

What's their business philosophy? Our philosophy is to do the right thing. We started our office in 1990, with the idea of quality marketing, taking care of our clients, standing behind what we said, doing what we said we were going to do, and taking responsibility and blame when things didn't go right.

How did it go for you at the beginning?

Derrell's philosophy was knocking on doors. I knocked on a lot of doors. Nowadays, there are more efficient ways to farm properties. It didn't go well, but I made $22,000 my first year in real estate. That was in 1978, my first full year. In 1978, the local real estate association named me Rookie of the Year.

That was a lot of money to me because I'd worked a full year in the golf business, and I'd made about $6,000. It wasn't even about money. I enjoyed real estate, the people, and the freedom. It blossomed from there. That was in '78. During '79-'82, our market was in the tank. Our market area had 750 Realtors, and the interest rates went sky high, to 16 percent, double digits. We went from 750 Realtors in our area to 110.

How did you survive?

I wasn't married at the time. I went from $22,000 to $13,000 in income in 1982. But I was hanging on. I decided I needed to get some education. I started taking my CCIM course. Anytime I could go to a course or class, I did. I had to borrow money from my parents. I hated to do that, but I had to borrow. One time I had to borrow $500, which seemed like a lot of money.

Was that to survive, or to get your CCIM?

A little bit of both. I'm taking the CCIM course in Oakland. I'm gone for two weeks having made $13,000 the year before. I could hardly afford to do that, but the market wasn't very good. I needed to take some time to get educated. If you want the same results, do the same thing you're doing. If you want different results, you need to make some changes.

After three or four years, the market picked up a little bit. Rates went down. I think I made $33,000 in 1984. That was a lot of money. I remember those years were really hard. I always went up from there. I felt like I was in the top tier of our area. I liked what I was doing. I like people. I kept at it.

What enabled you to learn the business and become successful?

I found that, by going to these classes, you learn a lot. It gives you a little more confidence. Then I started taking the CRS classes, two at the same time. I learned. You think about two or three things you can incorporate into what you're doing on a daily basis. There are things you might not learn from anybody in your own marketplace. You always pick up some things, and I try to be consistent and incorporate those things in what I'm doing. Maybe there are some different farming ideas, such as different mail ops, or whatever it is. I incorporated that in to what I was doing. Try to be consistent with it. I also visited with other Realtors who were not afraid to share their ideas with someone outside their areas.

Did you have a mentor or coach along the way?

Derrell, who got me into real estate, was probably my main mentor. He'd go around with me and knock on doors and things like that. He was pretty good. Over at Century 21, we have an incredible learning system for people who get started. Back then, it was, "Here's your desk. Here's your phone. Good luck." You're on your own. That's how it was. If I had what we have nowadays, I'd have gotten off to a lot better start. You learn through trial and error, and hard knocks.

What transpired in your business during that 20-year timeframe?

The interest rates went down. Our economy in Coeurd'Alene was strictly lumber, mining, and agricultural, and some tourism. When the rates went up, you had this Spotted Owl, and things like that, in the timber industry and the mining industry, and things went in to the tank.

A group of people in town formed Jobs Plus, an economic development group that was successful in recruiting companies to move in to the area. Now our area's very diverse. We have a beautiful area and a tremendous quality of life. The community leaders took an aggressive path on recruiting more diversity into the area, as far as jobs, and that helped. Our county population in 1980 was 59,000; in 1990, it went up to only

69,000. Today, we have 115,000 in the county, and 900 Realtors. Our market area is a fifteen-mile radius.

How do you differentiate yourself in the market?

You have to spend some money to make some money. I was always very consistent in my marketing. Show people you're willing to spend money and they notice it. You don't take one page in your local magazine for one month and then quit. You have to be consistent and people see that. Nowadays, you should promote yourself as much as your listings.

My reputation means a lot to me. I have a very good reputation. People are always calling, asking for me, because of the way I've treated people over the years. They keep calling and referring my name. A lot of that is treating people right. It doesn't happen overnight. But if you are consistent, it really pays off. People know if you care about them.

How long did it take to establish that kind of reputation?

You have to figure, '78-'83 was kind of a no-man's land. It was so bad. I don't think anybody noticed anybody, unless they didn't take care of business. But, I'd say I was very consistent when dealing with marketing stuff from '83 on. Probably three to five years of that and being consistent in what I was doing. I have gotten more business every year.

Doing all that cold calling and getting your face in front of people paid off.

I would sit at my home on Thursday night, waiting for the paper, and I would call all the For Sale By Owners on Thursdays and Fridays. They're the hardest to work with. They had an interest in selling. I was very consistent with that for six months. Today people still remember me knocking on their door. I worked that really hard. It was a lot of work. There are smarter ways to do things like that now.

If you were going to do it again, how would you farm your market?

I would pick an area I wanted to farm and put together a marketing plan based on a mail-out program. Everybody works a little bit different. You need to find something that you can do consistently. Keep people abreast of what's going on in your marketplace and prices in the neighborhood. Whatever area you pick, you must let people know that you have to be one of their choices. You do that by being consistent in their marketplace.

What did you say to them so they would decide to use you?

I don't know if I was that successful with them. For Sale By Owners always have an idea that they can sell it themselves, so they don't really want somebody else's help. It created a work ethic that I was consistent with. I had a lot of rejection, but I kept after it. I didn't bug people. I wasn't overly aggressive. I got a few of them.

The main thing is, when you're recruiting or trying to convert a For Sale By Owner, you need to explain to them that you have 900 Realtors in your marketplace working for you, and they're not going to have every buyer. If they can sell it themselves, great. They save the commission. But most times, people are their worst negotiators. They offer you a price, and somehow you always come down. I'm my worst salesperson for myself. I tell For Sale By Owners that Realtors can help them keep their price. I will qualify the buyers and do all the paperwork.

How do you keep that price up?

You don't get the seller and the buyer together. If the buyer and seller negotiate, the strong person will win. Most sellers will compromise their position to get a sale, as opposed to being away from the sale, having the Realtors working on behalf of their clients.

How do you work with the other agent on behalf of the client?

Every transaction's different. First, you have an idea what the property's worth. Maybe the seller doesn't quite understand that. You also have an idea what the competition is. Usually the seller doesn't know that. Based on what you think the market value and the competition are, you can keep the price at a level you think is fair. Or, you can recommend to the seller that this is where he or she should be. Your recommendation and his or her acceptance of that, when you're communicating back to the other agent, is pretty powerful.

Do you ever meet with the buyer and the agent?

Mostly, the agent. Very rarely with the buyer, unless I'm working with him or her, and that's a whole different ballgame.

What do you say to the other agent that enables you to maintain integrity with your client?

It depends on the transaction and the seller's motivation. If an offer comes in that's close to the selling price, some sellers will say, "I'm not going to wait around for the extra one or two thousand, or whatever it is. I'll take it." You have it priced right and go back to that agent, saying, "Listen, we priced it at what we think is a really fair level in this marketplace. Here are the CMA and the comparables if you want to look at them."

As an agent, you really have to know what your competition is. When properties sell, they're gone, so they're really not competition anymore. I might have a house listed for sale at $100,000 and need to know what people are looking at that's going to compare to that home. If the competition is $100,000 or higher, I know I have a really good value if my listing is at $100. You have to know your market and the competition. If you really believe that you have it priced right, then you convince your seller. "This is where it needs to be." Ultimately, the seller will make a decision. Some people are better gamblers. Some sellers want to make their first offer work. Others want to hold out for the highest nickel, and, ultimately, they can lose. That's where you have to know your marketplace, and you really have to know the transaction so you don't lose a good sale, thinking it's a good price. Maybe it isn't. You don't want to get yourself in a situation in which you recommend to your seller, "No, let's hold on for this price," and then you're sitting on it for six to nine months if the deal doesn't go together.

How much counseling do you give your clients?

A lot. Much of the counseling happens at the point of the offer. When a buyer makes a low offer to the seller, one of three things happens if the seller counters back. The buyer will:

- reject it and walk away
- accept it
- re-counter

Normally, if a buyer likes a property enough and committed to make an offer, he or she will probably accept our counter back. You have to decide whether or not you want to counter with this seller and where you think the buyer will accept. That takes experience and really knowing your marketplace. That's where Realtors have a lot of value that you don't even know about; your value is that you know the marketplace. Most buyers and sellers go to their jobs every day. They don't know the market like you do. That's what they're paying you for.

That's where you have value. You can't be shy about it. You should be proud that you know what's going on in your marketplace, the values, the pricing, and other stuff. That and your MLS are valuable. That's what people are paying you for. That's what gets the seller and you the higher value.

How many of your units sold are based on a seller versus a buyer?

I have both transactions about 28 percent of the time. Normally 52 percent are my listings, and 20 percent are my buyers'.

How do you get the listings?

At one of my classes, a guy told me that you could work with as many sellers as you want. But you can work with only so many buyers. You have to have inventory to stay in the business. This was probably back in '83-'84. I decided I needed a mindset to get a lot of listings. I needed to build up a listings base, because then I can have other Realtors working on those sales for me. That's no secret. It's not easy in a competitive marketplace. Right now, we have 1,200 listings in our marketplace. There are 900 Realtors. Twenty percent of the Realtors are doing most of the business, so you can figure that out. But I usually carry at least 20-30 listings and sometimes more.

What are you doing now?

I still farm areas. I still mail out. Today, 90 percent of my business is past business. It's past clients referring me. They've told a friend. It gets a little bit...I won't say easier, because sellers and buyers still have the same demands. But it's easier for me to get inventory now. I give away a lot. I refer many to people in my office.

How do you keep in contact with your clients?

At Christmas, I have my past-client list, and I write them all a Christmas card. Century 21 has a program in which you can keep in contact through different mailings that you sign up for, on every closing for five years. They're getting something from me three or four times a year. You pay for that, but at least they know you're thinking of them.

I've gotten involved with community things. It's important to do that. You have to give back to your community, especially in a market like we have, to be out there and visible. You have to do it because you like to. You have to feel good about giving back to your community.

How did you decide to open you own office?

It evolved over maybe two or three years.

Were you working for Derrel Cedarblom, or was that a transition?

It was at a place called Forest Brown Realtors.

Why the change from Forest Brown to Coldwell?

In fact, I went from Forest Brown to Acuff Realty. Forest Brown closed down, and the brokers in that office all went in different directions.

I went to Acuff Realty and worked for Pat Acuff, for whom I have a lot of respect. He's very honest and very ethical. I was there for three years. Leaving Pat Acuff was the hardest decision I had to make, because the market was not doing very well, and it was a struggle whether or not they were going to keep their doors open. Coldwell Banker was a bigger office, and a little stronger, and I went there for five years. It had probably 70 agents at that time, which is a lot, and I was its top agent every year.

What made you different from everybody else in the office?

That's a good question. My assistant, Anne Sumner, who has been with me since 1990, says that I treat everybody the same. I never thought about that. I could be working with this $50,000 buyer or a million-dollar buyer, and she says, "You treat everybody the same."

Consistency in your behaviors and in the way you deal with people, with integrity and honesty.

It means a lot to me. I may make a mistake. I look for opportunities to say, "I'm sorry. I made a mistake." I take the blame for it; I have to. Nobody likes someone who points fingers. They want someone to be accountable, and I try to be accountable. Usually it involves money. If you make a mistake and there's money involved, take care of it. I've never made a mistake intentionally that would cost somebody money. I sell a lot of houses and waterfront property, and a lot of times I bought dishwashers and garbage disposals and who knows what else. It wasn't my fault. But the seller left town and the buyer's upset. He or she looks to you. It's really goodwill.

That's what you get remembered for. You're not perfect, and you make mistakes. You can't meet everybody's 100-percent expectations. Though you try to be perfect, you don't know what's in their mind. You better be able to read people pretty well, if somebody's upset about something. If they are, take care of it. I don't mind what it costs, at any cost, because if you're in real estate, and you're in it for the long haul, you better think about it that way. There are too many people who have a shortsighted approach to value.

How did you learn to read people?

If you have empathy and you care about people, you can see what they're thinking. It isn't always trying to put that deal together. Maybe there's something better for them. Be honest with them. Just because you like something doesn't mean they're going to like it. Be honest with them about it. Don't try to put a deal together because you want to get it done. Do the right thing. It's easy to say, but for a lot of people it's hard to do.

You wondered one day, "Why don't I own my own office?"

Yes, there were some things I realized weren't going to be perfect about working for someone else. You have to trust what's going on, and you have to have people who trust what you're doing, too. I felt that I needed to make a change. I realized I was going to be in it for the long haul, and I thought I could do some things better.

I opened my own office, and we were John Beutler & Associates in 1990. I bought this building downtown. It was my wife Ann, who has an accounting background, and I, and three other agents. Two were from Coldwell Banker, and one was an independent. He was tired of running his own office. My wife was office support and management. I would not be where I am without her.

Opening the office was one of the hardest decisions I made. I called my mom. Whenever I had to make a tough decision, I always called my mom. Mom would listen, and she would say, "John, you've always made good decisions, and you'll make the right one now." I can almost cry when I think about that, about her and when she says that.

My wife came over almost immediately with a list of things to do and bookkeeping stuff. I'm thinking, "Gosh, I never thought about that part of the business."

Today we have 90 agents and a staff of 16. Our office was the third largest in the nation last year. I have one assistant, Anne Sumner. She's incredible. She knows me like the back of her hand. She has sort of the same philosophies I do. She's a really good person. Together, I would not be where I am without Ann and Anne. This past year I hired an assistant for my assistant Anne.

We've been John Beutler & Associates for six years. In 1977 or 1978, when I got in to the business, there were 78 real estate companies in town. Today, through consolidations, Internet Web sites, and all the technology, five offices in our town control 95 percent of the business.

In 1996, I had an opportunity to purchase a Century 21 office in town. I used to drive by Coldwell Bank and Century 21 every day, and I thought I would love to have one of those franchises.

What would it do for you?

It would give me stability, name recognition from outside the area, a lot of tools I don't have access to, and Web presence. I felt that, if we stayed an independent office, we would be moving backward. It's proven to be one of the best decisions we ever made.

Now it's Century 21 Beutler & Associates. We had a meeting with all our agents, and 85 percent of them voted to keep Beutler with the Century 21 name.

At my office, we hardly ever lose anybody. The hard thing is that, having a high producer as an owner of an office, other offices say they don't want to work for me because I'm a competing broker. On the contrary, I bring in a lot of business I can't handle. And I never compete with anyone in my office. If there's anything that is a competition, conflict, or compromise, I always back away. But I'm unlike any broker in town. I know the market better than anybody. I add a lot of credibility to our office that way. I have my office and my assistant, and I'm not really involved with management in this office. I'm listing and selling every day, which is what I like to do.

Who's doing the management?

My wife and Todd Sankovich, a manager we've recruited through the Century 21 system. Stacy, our bookkeeper, has been with us since almost the beginning. Our office support staff is incredible.

It's my assistant Anne Sumner and I. That's what people don't understand, that's pretty incredible. I have one assistant and she's licensed, but she doesn't go out and sell or list property. She handles my clients and all the paperwork and will occasionally show property if I get in a bind. She does all the coordinating for inspections, lenders, title companies, and appraisers.

What would be a typical day for you?

Usually I'm in the office by 7:30-8:00, somewhere around there, until 6:00 or 7:00 at night. I'm not an early riser. I'm usually in my office at home from 8:30 or 9:00 at night until 11:30 or 12. Monday, Tuesday, Wednesday, Thursday, and Sunday nights, I'm in that office doing a lot of paperwork, things that can't get done in a normal day. I spend my days in the field and about 20 percent of my time in the office. The evening is when I do my strategic thinking and planning. I've been doing that for years. It's my hobby. I like people, and I feel I have a responsibility to the people I'm working for. I have to get things done.

Wouldn't it be better to have another staff person to do the paperwork instead of you?

Yes. I could do a lot more business if I wanted to, but then I would really be competing with everybody in my office. If there's something I can't handle, I refer it to somebody in my office. If I own the office, and I have six staff working for me, it truly would not look right. Let's say, if I feel it's an area where I should be working, and maybe there's an agent in my office who works there a little better or more consistently than me, I'll look to give it away.

How do you have any kind of a balance with three teenagers?

I hardly ever miss an event. I have coached their basketball teams. When they were born, a guy told me to spend as much time with my kids as I could, because they grow up really fast. I've always remembered that. Even when I came home and I was dead-dog tired, if my daughter or son asked me to do stuff, I would do it. It's always energizes me.

You always make them number one?

Right, probably to a fault. I love being around my kids. I try to be there for them. Clients understand when you have something that's family-related. They really do.

Did you prioritize your time differently before you got Anne?

I never really prioritized my time. If somebody called me and it was real estate related, if I had the time I'd always do it. They could call me at 2:00 in the morning, and if I wasn't doing anything, I'd probably go show a home. That's kind of how I've been. I've always tried to be available. I would just do it.

You talked about getting your CCIM and CRS. Do you continue to invest in your education?

Not as much, because I find that I don't have as much time as I did. When you get started in the business, that's a great time to take classes. I probably tried to do something every year. At 51 years old and 27 years in the business, I can always learn, but I think I have gotten to a point where I need to be.

There's not much more I'm going to do differently. I'm producing as much as I want to. I haven't gotten lazy about how I treat people, but I'm very comfortable in what I'm doing. However, when I do attend seminars, I always pick up something new.

What caused you to reach that comfort zone?

What really drives me in real estate is that in the early '80s you were always fearful that you'd never have another deal. This can be my last deal. I never take anything for granted.

What keeps you motivated?

Sometimes people get burned out. Maybe it's because they're not happy with what they're doing or they're not doing it well. I like what I'm doing.

I like the people. I don't know what drives me, but it's not the money, I guess. There's a certain amount of ego, being number one in the world. It took me a long time, in my mind, to get where I am. I feel very, very fortunate to be that. You do what you did yesterday, because of where you are today. I've been very consistent. It's kind of ingrained in me. It's a habit. That's how I work.

I don't set any goals. I'm a driven person, I guess. I'm very competitive. I hate to lose. But I won't lose at any cost. When I play golf, I'm like that. As a little kid, I loved basketball. I'd be out shooting basketball in the snow sometimes. My mom said I've always been a hard worker.

I read a lot of articles on real estate. I love reading really good books. When I read books, it's usually not real estate. I don't have a lot of time to read books, as I wish I did.

Golf keeps me motivated. That's a passion. I love playing in golf tournaments. That really keeps me going.

Having my wife in the office keeps me motivated.

And my mom. I'm proud of my past, where I came from, and I think about that sometimes. I'm always thinking about my father, and what he would do.

Some real estate people have poor business habits about time, how they work, taking action, and follow-through.

I believe that about 87 percent of Realtors do not make a follow-up call. That means that they may get a call, or have an interaction with a client, but they never get back. They never follow up after that initial contact. Somebody may call in on an ad, and he or she gives them all the information, the name and number, but they never call back. I think 20 percent of the Realtors will follow up 80 percent of the time. I think 20 percent of the Realtors make the money.

The 20 percent who follow up will do well. Think about this. They call you. They don't even know you. You think you're the best salesperson in the world. But they don't know that yet. They don't know who you are. You have to earn their trust, and you don't earn it by not calling back. You have to call back and give them some reason to trust you, to know that you want to work for them. You need to follow up. Follow-up is a huge thing in any sales business.

I get a kick out of people who say they never get any leads. They do, but they don't do anything with them. For instance, a guy calls on a $150,000 house. You give him all the information on that house, and you sit around waiting for him to call you back. "Well, if you want to see it, give me a call. I'll be happy to show it to you." It's never going to happen because they're calling other Realtors, too. You need to get back to them maybe within a half-day, or a day, and say, "Listen, if you didn't like that house, there are some other options for you."

They're looking. You need to give them some other options. Right away, they know you're willing to work for them. If you could meet them, and meet their expectations and start a relationship, you gain trust. Once you have trust with a party, it's hard to lose it. Once you lose the trust with somebody, you'll never get it back.

How do you build that trust?

By doing the right thing. Do what you say you're going to do. I think about that constantly. My parents were awesome that way. My dad was in the car business, a hard business to be in. After he died, people would come back for years asking for my dad because of what he did for his clients.

What is the best use of an agent's time and money to really learn the business and be successful?

When you get in to real estate, you have to give it a year. It's almost like an apprentice program. You have to develop a plan, and your broker can help you, or your sales manager can help you, if you have a good learning system for your office. But develop and work a plan.

A plan would include what?

Cold calling, contacting friends, working the neighborhood, being available, doing open houses, and anything that will help you in the direction you want to go. You'll give up a lot of things. Open houses are a great way for people to meet buyers. I think agents should do that. Be in the office on the weekend. You'll be surprised how many calls you'll get. You have eight hours in a day. Now you're your own boss. You have to give yourself some duties.

You said you don't set goal, yet having an action plan is a goal.

It is a goal. People starting out need that action plan or road map to get them somewhere. You can't come to the office and sit around. You have eight hours or more in a day, but they go by so fast. I don't feel like I'm clocking in or out. It noon and then it's five, and I love that. You have to keep busy, and you have to give yourself a plan. If you're in it for 20 years, your plan becomes ingrained, and then you do what you need to.

You have it in your brain, instead of putting it down on paper?

Right. And you know how to do things better. You could do a whole lot of things in a day. If you followed me around in a day, you'd probably be amazed. A lot of Realtors ask how I do that. I have a couple of guys in the office who say that my time-managing skills must be incredible. I do prioritize things, but I get a lot of things done because I just do them.

Every day, I register every call on this 8 × 14 yellow pad with a note. When that pad gets filled, I'll put anything remaining on a new yellow pad. I'm always referring back to it. Every night I go through that, making sure I haven't missed anybody and that I called everybody, made the right contacts, and did everything I could. It's a great follow-up tool for me. It's hard for me to put that on a PalmPilot[®]. It's too much. I have a PalmPilot for names and phone numbers.

I have a Day-Timer[®]. I write down my schedule there. I tried a computer schedule, but this works for me.

[®] PalmPilot is a registered trademark of 3Com Corporation.
[®] Day-Timer is a registered trademark of Day-Timers, Inc.

I tried a recorder in my car for jotting down notes, but then it had to be transcribed. It was easier to write it down. Then I could go back and review it.

Exactly. That's what I do.

What type of lessons did you learn along your path?

Do what you say you're going to do, but don't over-promise. Don't say things you can't do. I've learned that you need to be prepared. You don't go in to a situation, a listing presentation, unprepared. Even when I had to give talks, I realized that the more prepared I was the better things went.

Don't take anything for granted. Don't go in to a listing appointment thinking you have it. I always like it when somebody else's competing for it.

How do you compete for a listing?

I make sure I'm prepared and that I have all the information I need: sales, listing information, and marketing. I tell the sellers that every agent coming in here will give them, hopefully, pretty much the same ballpark figure. It isn't so much the price. It is, how can I market? What am I going to do to sell your property? That's where I think I have the best marketing plan of anybody.

What is your marketing plan?

It's really simple, but I put it in writing. Everyone's a little different. If I say I'm going to do a virtual tour, I get it done right away. If I say I'm going to color-advertise in all the magazines, I do that. I'm really consistent. I bring books along that show where I've been advertising. Also, you can compare that to what the competition is doing, seeing that what I do is better and more consistent. I tell them what I'm prepared to do, and I'll do it until I get the property sold.

Give me some examples of what you do.

There is no real secret. If I list a home, I will have great pictures inside and out, especially for the Internet. We have two local real estate publications where I advertise in full color. I've had my pages for fifteen years, and have them reserved for as long as I want in the *Real Estate Book* and *Homes and Land*. I periodically advertise in the newspaper. They won't get in every week, because you have to rotate, but at least one a month. Networking among the Realtors. A lot of little steps, but those are the major things. If you have it priced right, and you're doing these things consistently, spending money marketing, it's all you can do.

Are there secrets to holding a great open house?

Sometimes sellers want them. Sometimes you don't get anybody. They're really to get buyer leads. The secret is advertising. Make sure their ad is in the press, and you have good directions. I think it's important to invite all the neighbors. They're going to come anyway, so you might as well invite them. Try to find a house that's a nice home. Normally, open houses work well in new subdivisions because they also have model homes that are being promoted by the developers/Realtors/builders. You have a lot of activity. It's important to have an open house in an area with a lot of activity, or a lot of traffic, and usually you'll find that in a new subdivision.

Any last words of advice?

Anything worthwhile takes time. You have to give it time. I don't think there's any get-rich-quick formula. Be consistent. Give it time, and you will be successful, especially if you like people and want to help them, and you're willing to work hard. It will happen.

Get the education. But real estate's a situation in which there's no limit, so-to-speak, to what you'll make. It's up to you. Develop a plan and give it time. It's like planting seeds. Some are going to grow and some aren't. If you're willing to work hard, you care about people, and you have a plan, you should be successful.

If you lose a client, or whatever, you need to ask yourself if you did everything you could to help him or her. Then you have to forget about it and move on because you can't satisfy everyone. If the answer is no, hopefully, you'll learn from it and remember it the next time.

Keep in mind, when you have those sales, those are clients. You can imagine the energy they'll create if you treat them right. You can't stay in touch with everybody personally; there's no way. But if you do a good-enough job, they're going to remember you. Treat people right, and do the right thing.

<u>CHERYL DAVIS</u>

PLATINUM PROPERTIES
GMAC REAL ESTATE
Las Vegas/Henderson Nevada

#1 Gross Commission Income: GMAC

- **Sales Volume: $36.5 M**
- **# of Units Sold: 55**
- **Gross Commission Income: $1.15 M**
- **# of Employees: 2**
- **www.Cheryl-Davis.com**
- **Years in the business: 22**

What made you decide to get in to real estate?

When I was growing up, I didn't wake up one day and say, "I've decided to be a real estate agent."

I had taken my real estate license in San Antonio, Texas, passed the test, but never got in to real estate. I decided to move to California to pursue my unique modeling career as well as being a professional ballroom dancer and trainer. I did a magazine shoot that did uniforms for real estate companies. When my options in dancing went sideways, because I had some knee problems and surgery, I wondered what career would enable me to stay with, meet, and be exposed to people, and still feel like I'd done something for them, and real estate was the first one that popped in to my mind.

I was very fortunate that my first job was at a Beverly Hills boutique. I had a mentor who was one of the best in the business. I was grateful that I got to train with the best and move up from there.

How did you end up in Henderson?

After the boutique, I went to one of the majors. Next, my husband at the time decided we were going to move to Las Vegas, and he was going to start a new business out here. Of course, I followed.

Did you stay with the major firm when you moved?

When I first moved, it was a major firm, *Better Homes and Gardens*, but I didn't practice real estate. I got pregnant, had another child (I have two), and didn't practice real estate for about a year. The plan was to go back and do it part-time, because financially, I didn't need to be in the business. I just wanted back in the business. Shortly thereafter, we got divorced, and I needed to be in the business. So I moved from a whole different city with absolutely no realm of influence here and no contacts.

When you came back, did you return to a major company?

I went back to a major. My theory in this business is that, if you have a sphere of influence, you can pretty much be anywhere because you already have your sphere there. Most of my business is referrals. At this point in my life, I could probably be Cheryl Davis & Associates and do the same production in business that I do now, or certainly close to it. But, if you're not completely established with a long-time clientele, the majors just have so much to offer, because name recognition alone will get you in a front door.

Since you moved to Nevada and you didn't really know anybody, how did you get your business going?

Hard work! I had my first elegant *Homes* open house and decided that that was the market I was going to work in.

How many hours a week did you work?

I don't think I've ever worked less than 60 hours a week, and certainly I have doubled that more than once. I don't care what anyone says, they're magicians if they can do it for less.

You work hard, you play hard, and you have to take time off to be with your family and your vacations and to get rejuvenated. Again, you're doing a lot of production and have people's lives in your hands. Because, let's face it, when you're selling two-, three-, four-million dollar houses, customers expect you to show up and to represent them, and you have to be there to do it. It's not a nine-to-five job, and I'd be surprised if anyone who treats it as such is very successful.

How do you balance time with your children?

In this business if someone tells you they're in town for six hours and they're going to buy a house, you have to make your time available during those six hours. My kids have suffered through the years on this. It's made them a lot more independent and self-sufficient, but I still struggle with balance. I wouldn't say I have that one down.

My kids are the most important things in my life. Hopefully I work for their benefit as well, but I think they've missed a lot of time over the years. I don't think it's hurt them as far as their character, their skills and whatnot. But there's probably a little resentment here and there for that.

What made you realize you really could be outstanding in this business?

I was very fortunate; my mentor, the boutique owner, took me under her wing. I had no other patterns to choose. My pattern was cut out with one of the best in the industry. She's now the president of a board in Palm Springs and the manager of a large company out there. From day one, she taught me that, after a certain amount of time in the business, everyone has the same knowledge as to what the comps are in an area, what the value is of a property, or where something is. Once we know our contracts, the locations, the areas, and what a professional should know in any industry, what puts us aside from everyone else is how people feel about us and the service we provide them.

Really, being above everyone else is your customer service and having a personal relationship with them. If you're interviewing three agents, the person you could talk with the best and who understood your feelings more than anyone else—not just being out there saying that I'm the top producer in the city—that's the person you're going to go with.

How do you establish that kind of relationship with your clients?

That's truly something that you can work on and perfect. But, you really have to like people in order to be successful in any "people" business. The first thing I do is to try to find out who people are personally; finding how much their house is worth is easy. Put 100 of us in a room, and probably 90 of us will come up within five percent of the same pricing. But, coming up with what someone's needs—I need to do this because this crisis is happening in my life or I just inherited a million dollars and I'm moving up or whatever—is much harder.

Most people don't share their personal stories with you unless they feel comfortable with you. I think the comfort zone in any relationship is letting someone else speak. I'm no different from anyone else. If you listen to me intently, I'm going to like you, because you're listening to me, and the whole universe is revolving around me at that time. I have the best communication when I ask some very key questions, and shut up and let them start talking about themselves or their situation or life, and they're comfortable with me. You've made a friend. It's a comfort zone where someone feels warm and fuzzy, instead of that someone trying to take money out of their pocket.

It's truly all about relationships.

Completely. But I think life is all about relationships. I don't think the real estate industry is any different than going on a blind date. You're looking at a relationship with two people who have never met each other, trying to find a common ground.

How do you differentiate yourself with customer service?

I have a team of professionals who I hand picked to work with me. We have outstanding customer service because my motto is to treat everyone like we want to be treated. It doesn't work 100 percent of the time because you have life that gets in the way, and you have mistakes that happen, and you have breakdown in communications, whether it's your staff or the customer or clients you're working with. But I always feel that, as long as I treat people and deal with them the same way I want to be treated or dealt with, it keeps a very open communication, and people are comfortable with me.

How big of a staff do you have?

I work with three people. Whenever I don't feel I can give 100 percent of our customer service to you, I refer you to another agent.

Another agent at GMAC or within your group?

Within our group or company. We have approximately 150 agents, and if it's someone whom I don't feel I can give the time to or it's not specifically my arena, like if someone's a first- or second-home buyer, I usually refer him or her to someone who can provide the attention he or she needs. I primarily deal with higher-end custom homes and builders.

I just took my largest listing to date in our area, for $10,700,000, and it's barely out of the ground, and we already have an offer coming in on it. I have the buyer, too. Also, it's the way you advertise and whom you're throwing that property in front of. About 65 percent of my business represents both the buyer and the seller. On the high-end, that turns out to be substantial income.

I just had four offers—that's why I was saying that it's been a crazy day. There's a group coming in that wants to buy several homes for two million dollars; they've made offers on five of mine, and I'm representing both sides of the transaction. We're selling about 60 percent of your own product. The other 40 percent are your buyers of other people's products. It's lucrative. I never work for the paycheck. I always work for the end result. If you really look at this industry, and you really listen to people, you know what they're looking for. You don't waste their time and get them frustrated.

How do you determine the difference between what they say they need and what they really want?

I find that, if you listen very carefully to people, they give you a broad scope as to what they want. A perfect example: I had a client who wanted only a one-story house, 6,000 square feet, on a golf course with a city view. They ended up buying a two-story house that had only partial views, but the master bedroom was downstairs. I find the biggest mistake in real estate is agents trying to show people everything and confusing them. Then they're frustrated because they don't feel you've listened to them, thinking, "Why are you showing me this when I told you I wanted that?" Really listen to what people want, and show them a couple of things. If what they said is not really what it is, and you go to that next level—oh, this is what they want if it were here—then you can really narrow down the time you're spending with them. You shouldn't waste their time and yours. Tune in and hone in to what they can afford and really want and put them in the right place.

A lot of people don't have any foresight. They're saying they want something that's fully done, or fully finished. But if you find them the perfect floor plan and get them with the right designer, because it's still within their budget and realms and you can create the visualization that they need to feel comfortable, then you're going to have a sale there, too.

How do you move from a single-story, golf course, full view to a two-story, partial view?

You're actually giving them 60 percent of what they want. The single-story, 6,000 feet, full view at two million dollars is going to cost them three million. They already know that that's not within their realm or their budget or what they're comfortable spending. But, perhaps you already know what really captures their attention, such as a gourmet kitchen, or if they don't cook, they don't really care much about the kitchen, but they're big entertainers who like the outside verandas and the lagoon pool that has the swim-up bar. There is no such thing as a perfect home, in most cases. I mean, every now and then I hit the jackpot, and it is the perfect home. But in most cases, you really do have to make allowances. You get to that house that's really a two-story, but it has that perfect kitchen, and the master's downstairs. They really don't have to be up and down stairs all day, and they have that fabulous pool. Okay, it has only partial views, but three-quarters of the house they love. Then people start saying, "You know what, I could live with this."

If you really get in to people's emotional psyche—if you're a good listener, you feel when they get excited and know when they're turned off and what's absolutely wrong for them—then you can make those judgments for them and put them where they need to be. Trust me, sometimes it's taken me a year or two to find someone a house. I don't bug them every week to go out and look at everything else in the city. I call them up and say, "I think this house is for you." Because they have enough respect for my knowledge and my communication with them, and they know I know what they're looking for, eight times out of ten they say that I'm right.

How much convincing or advice do you give your clients?

I don't try to convince people to buy homes. If it's an investor, that's probably where I use the most negotiating skills. If I know my market well, which I do, and I know they're looking for a profit down the road, I'll say, "Take this, this is something you really need to get, you're going to be sorry if you don't," or whatever. But, in most cases, I try to massage what people are looking for. If you can bring in to the negotiation where they want to be and how they want it to be, then you've become a facilitator instead of a salesperson trying to convince them that it's a good deal.

How do you negotiate the best deal for your clients?

My favorite saying in real estate is that you can't put a circle in a square, but you can, hopefully, grind that circle down a little bit to where it might not be the perfect fit, but it's a win/win for everyone. You might not get everything you want on either side, but if it's important and comfortable enough, you have to make allowances—you know what, we'll give you $2.1 instead of $2.3 but we'll close quickly. As a facilitator, you almost have to try very, very hard to get along with the other side of the transaction, which is another broker in most cases.

We're dealing with a lot of egos, and some people feel their ego is more important than doing the best representation for their client. When you tell the clients to stay adamant, full price, you're really doing them a disservice if it's the right buyer who can fulfill the client needs to get them out in a timely manner. Or if it's the right seller and the buyer, maybe the seller's not going to get that extra $25,000, but they're going to know for a fact that the buyer is a solid person and that they're going to close escrow. When you're dealing with another agent, whether they're in-house or outside, the communication between the two of you is really what makes or breaks a deal in most cases. I love representing both sides because I know I'm the only one who can break down the communications.

I have a saying: "My greed has never exceeded my need." I mean that so sincerely because that's where the breakdown comes. I negotiate commissions probably as much as I negotiate properties. An inspection report comes back, and they want literally everything fixed and sellers, of course, who are in love with their property, say, "How dare you!" You have to ask them how much money we're talking about—and let's just use a number, two thousand dollars—to do everything. Are you willing to lose the transaction over two thousand dollars? Some of them are adamant that they are. My theory is that, if you've gotten to that point, I'll pay for it, or why don't we split it with the buyer. Let's put a monetary value on this instead of a physical contractor coming in and doing it. You start soothing feelings and ruffled feathers. It's an emotional time for buyers and sellers. Buyers think they pay too much. Sellers think they left money on the table. That's our business. You have to get everyone to a point where they think that at least they did the best thing at the time.

In black and white, everything looks mean. I could say to you on the phone right now that your voice bothers me and explain why, and then we would be comfortable with each other. If I wrote on a piece of paper or emailed you that your voice bothers me, just as an example, all of a sudden you've taken it personally. Once someone starts taking things personally, instead of looking at it as let's get from "A" to "B," I feel like you have a communication skill breakdown. I see the names of certain agents, and I just hope their property works for my buyer because I love working with them due to their sharing my mentality. Let's get the deal done and make sure it's a win/win for everyone, or it's at least the best situation or circumstances. If it doesn't work, we are not attacking each other. It's okay; we tried. You see other names in this industry, and you don't even want to show the property, because you know, coming in the front door, it's just going to be a nightmare!

Some agents act like paper pushers instead of facilitators.

People do not hire us and give us the type of income we make to push a piece of paper. People hire you for the value you can bring to the transaction, which is why the Premier Service[1] mentality is wonderful. An offer comes in that might not be full price, but all the other terms and conditions are exactly what that seller needs to make his or her life move on. Price is only a very small part of the transaction. If you could work around making a buyer happy with the price, it's the rest of the transaction that you're trying to get through. People who just throw it at them and say, here, counter it, are doing them a huge injustice, because they're not looking at the overall picture, and what's going to be the benefit to both sides.

In cases like that, you can lose deals and the clients.

More than once, because you don't have the exposure to the other party, whether it's the buyer or seller. You don't know where their breakdown was. Did I know the seller said, "Absolutely not, I won't accept this," or did they fax over the offer and say, "Tell them what you want"? If you're

---

[1] Premier Service is a new concept that GMAC has launched that follows the philosophy Cheryl is talking about—service is number one.

only going to put it on the MLS, and you're only going to fax over an offer to someone, they really don't need you. All you're doing is looking for a paycheck.

I've had more than one agent, once I started probing them as to what their reasons were, get very frustrated and hang up on me because they felt like I was insulting them, when all I was trying to do was find out where we were and why.

Does the agent's experience, patience, knowledge, and willingness to participate have a significant effect on the salability of the property?

I don't know if experience is all that it's cracked up to be. Somebody who has been in the business six months can have the same experience as the person who's been in the business for six years. I'd much rather have a brand-new agent who's excited, and still has that enthusiasm and passion to get the job done, than somebody who's been in the business but really doesn't care anymore.

How have you dealt with the market changes?

The market conditions have changed, and being in the business as long as I have makes you more experienced as to how to handle the changes. The conditions change. If you're in a buyer's market, your strategy for your sellers is different. If you're in a seller's market, your strategy for your buyers is a little different as to how you're facilitating the transaction. The way we handle the business has never changed. I learn something every day, and my ego is very small when it comes to the business because I'm amazed at how much I can learn from new agents. They always have that one thing that I forgot about.

I think the As, Bs, and Cs of the business are just like the alphabet. You have to learn the alphabet before you learn to read. You have to learn to read while you're learning to write. But you're not going to be a great writer unless you know how to read what you wrote.

Is more of your business on the listing side or the buyer's side?

I'm primarily a listing agent. I probably have over 100 million in inventory right now. But I sell 50-60 percent of my own transactions.

The way I market my properties, the buyers call me directly. They don't have other agents who come in and say that they saw you in the MLS or that they want to see your house. Of course, that always happens, but I'm a firm believer that you really have to expose your properties. I use all the national periodicals, *Dupont Registry*, *Wall Street Journal*. We have seven to twelve Web sites up at all times. We look at each property strategically. In the higher end, if I can get someone to my Web site, whether the property I'm advertising is the right one for them or not, because of the way the site is set up, I'm going to get them to call me.

I had a client who called from the Chicago area. She said, "I don't know you from Adam, but I am so loyal to you because I've been on your Web site for the last six months; I wouldn't even think about calling another broker because I would feel I was cheating on you."

And how did she find your Web site?

Through the *Wall Street Journal*, *Dupont Registry*, or *Distinctive Homes*. If I get a resort-type property in a resort destination, for example, perhaps in Las Vegas, and it's in the middle of winter, I'm probably going to advertise that in Chicago, New York, or Minneapolis because it's cold. If it's one of our properties that's in the golf course communities or one of my new builders, I'll probably go to northern and southern California and run an ad in the *LA Times* or the *Orange County Registry*, in San Francisco, or wherever. As I share with my sellers, as long as I'm in the *Wall Street Journal* in a property that's close to your price range, and my Web site's on it, they're going to pull me up. It doesn't have to be your property. I don't think any of us has enough money to advertise every single property we have in all of these magazines and periodicals and nationals and internationals every month. Let's face it, everyone, in almost any price range, is going to be computer literate now. I'd tell a new agent to get a Web page even if they pay only $150 a month for it. You can always have the little clicker, for a little money, that puts them through the whole MLS, but they're staying on your site.

Do you have a specific budget for advertising?

If I look at the property and the seller says they don't care if I sell their house for six or eight months, let's list it for a half million more than it's worth, then I'm not going to spend my hard-earned dollars putting them in every single place I can put them. At the end of the year, I probably spend, between my assistants and all of my advertising and all of my outside sources, 30 percent of my income.

Think of the business you wouldn't have without it. I also think people waste money, a lot in this business, going out just saying it's all about me. Most sellers are not impressed when they get a flyer in the mail. I'm a stickler on sending out listeds and solds with pretty pictures and offers of this and that, because I'm presenting the property. I never send out something that says use me, with my picture on it. You would toss it in the trash.

That's where people spend a lot of money in this business that they shouldn't. I firmly believe that human nature is it's all about me. And in this business, you're talking about real estate. I also believe if you're not going to do it right, don't do it at all. If someone sends you a beautiful postcard that tells you the details of the house—it's a pretty picture of the house and there's a tiny picture of the agent, but the rest of it is about the property—all of a sudden you're interested because that property has something to do with you in your life. You mean I have an extra $100,000 equity because my house is better than this house, or vice versa. By advertising the properties, instead of themselves, you would get ten times the results.

In most of my neighborhoods that I "farm" religiously, there's always someone else who steps out and gets his or her name out there. There's always going to be the agent who's going to tell the seller that their property is worth 30 percent more than what I would list it for. They do get properties, and they get a lot of them, but they get them for a very short time, because they don't sell. If I say to someone, "Your property, at best, is worth $2.5," but someone else is willing to take it on for $3.5, I'm not going to get that listing, because I'm not going to take it. I'm wasting their time and mine. Believe it or not, they're going to be angry with me.

Some people never end up buying from an agent, or they'll be working with an agent and they go someplace else. Is it about relationships, about asking the right questions?

People skills, above all else, are important. There's always going to be that person whom you've worked with for six months who walks, and breaks your heart. I've been very, very fortunate and feel blessed in this business, but nine out of ten people I work with are very loyal to me. You're always going to have that percentage for which, no matter what you do or how you do it, it's not going to work out. If it happens to someone over and over, they absolutely do not have the people skills or they don't know how to communicate, and, for lack of a better word, to find out what people are looking for. Because, if someone's a ready, willing, and able buyer and you know your market, they have no reason to go to anybody else. If you've worked with someone for five months and haven't found them a house and then they find one with someone else, you didn't listen to them. You didn't know what they were looking for. There was a communication breakdown there.

It's the same with someone who has ten properties listed for six months and not one of them sells. You did not share with them what the market was. You didn't tell them the truth. That's why they went down the street, and the other agent got it, for 10 percent less than what you had it listed at, and they sold it in three days.

What do you think differentiates the average real estate person from the top performers?

Tunnel vision. In all fairness, everyone I know who has been at the top of the industry has been very focused as to what his or her job is. They have a job description, and they go to work every day. They're independent contractors. Sometimes, people don't treat this as a business. I feel good today, so I'll think I'll do this or I'm going to blow this off. Or, they don't show up in a timely way or whatever, and I truly believe that everyone I've ever met in this business has three characteristics that always seem to come up. The ones who have been successful year after year are the people who:

- Treat this as a passionate business. They own this business. If they don't show up, then they're going to close their business down. Once you get one property in escrow, if you don't have another one in the pipeline, you're out of business.

- Have integrity. I think you can lie and cheat your way through a few things for a little while, but the real estate industry is, like anything else, a very small world, and bad publicity gets around

100 times quicker than good publicity does. If you do the wrong thing over and over, you're out of business. And integrity speaks miles and volumes over someone who's a hustler.

- More than anything, have confidence in themselves, knowing that, when the going is bad, if they show up and do the right thing every day, they, too, will get past this. I've had times when I thought I'd have to take a second trust deed out on the house, because of whatever the market condition was, to stay in business. Tenacity has everything to do with someone who's a top producer over and over, because they all have good years and bad years.

Some people don't understand the sales funnel: How many do I have to have in escrow, when am I going to get my money, what kind of lifestyle do I want, and how many houses do I have to sell to design that lifestyle?

My theory in life is that, if you don't have a map, you're probably not going to get there. If I wanted to go to Laguna Beach from Las Vegas, and I'd never gone to Laguna, if I didn't have a map showing how I was going to get there, I'd be hitting and missing all over the board.

Everyone, from the McDonald's gal who gives me a Coke to what I do in my business, has to have a business plan. If you don't have a business plan, you're not going to get anywhere. My theory is that I get two referrals out of every person I'm doing business with. Everyone's excited when I am first listing their house or taking them out to show property. If I don't get the referrals, I have done something wrong. Once you get the escrow and things are starting to go sour, and the lender's not doing his job and the escrow officer forgot your file, they're frustrated. Are they going to refer you right now? You have them on that emotional roller coaster and they're upset. It doesn't matter how good you are, by the time it closes, they're not upset anymore. This is when you ask for more business, but I find that the best referrals are when you first meet someone, because that's when they like you the most. That's probably my trick in the business.

Some think you come in to this business and it's sky-rocket straight up and never run in to challenges.

It's hard work. We all get lucky on occasion. I call that kissed by the angel. I've had my kisses by the angel, where if I show up at the right time at the right place and something good happens. But, if you don't show up, nothing's ever going to happen.

Where did you have challenges?

We were at a stagnant market at one point, three or four years ago, but I don't like to dwell on bad experiences. The houses I had listed were sitting there. Mind you, these were upper homes and estate properties. The buyer funnel was very small. My advertising costs were about 100 percent more than what I was making, because you still have to maintain the advertising, even though something is not selling. If you don't, you're going to lose the business, and you're not going to have any future business anyway. It was a buyer's market. Our market had changed so drastically and it continues to change, as far as being more stable and getting the rises of 10-12 percent, or 30 percent a year, as far as your equity positions are concerned. But if you bought a new home, you better want to keep it for two or three years, or you're going to have to sell it at a loss because you're competing against the builders or brand-new construction on a custom home.

It was very challenging back then. There was more than one time I thought I was in the wrong business. Oh, I should just give this up. Again, if you stick to your guns and believe in yourself and your product, you get through it. It's a life challenge. It's like one of my kids going to school and flunking their math test. You don't quit school over a math test. You study harder, and you go back and take the test.

What are a couple of key lessons you've learned along your path?

My biggest lesson—and I don't know if I've learned it yet, but I don't cry as much as I used to—is not to take things personally.

I'm exposed to people every day, I find I can either feel responsible for everything bad that someone tells me or says about me, is unhappy with me about, or thinks I didn't know enough about; or I can think this wasn't against me, this is something that happened to them, and I can react one way or another. That's probably been the most valuable lesson. I don't think I've mastered it because I still spend some time crying when I've had my feelings hurt, something hasn't gone the way I thought it would, or I lost to someone whom I felt was a lesser broker.

You have to love people, because you deal with so many types of people, in different circumstances, like death in the family, divorce, and people who don't want to sell but have to sell. You have to deal with all those emotions.

My biggest lesson is to stay passionate. Anything you have passion for exudes out of your personality. People love to be around people who have passion. Sometimes you have to go home and lick your wounds and say that it wasn't you and shame on them. My theory is, if you don't love what you're doing in the business, get out of it.

How do you keep yourself motivated?

I think that's a personal issue with everyone. For me, it's when you get up and you know the next day's going to be another challenge and you're going to be able to, in one small or slight way, change someone's life. I truly love what I do. I know how many people I've made happy in this world, and how many lives I've changed. If I can do one valuable thing daily, whether it's for another agent to make them feel good; to a client who's been dejected, rejected, or whatever, or gotten the deal of the century, or unloaded the property that they really couldn't bear anymore; I've done something good. I stay motivated. Again, I'm not monetarily driven, because I know I'm always going to get paid, and I set my standards. I'm not going to do less than so much. Except for that one point, my income has always increased 10-20 percent per year. That's because I've gotten wiser to what's effective and what's not.

What types of things are most effective?

I'm probably being repetitive, but the most effective thing that anyone can do in this industry is listen. I love to talk, because I am an A-type personality, but every time I'm excited, every time I listen and shut up, things just get better.

Also, I listen to many different types of tapes. I read a lot. I read a lot of motivational material and a lot of self-esteem and meditation material. I don't read as much as I want to.

So few people think it's necessary to invest in reinforcement tools. How can you get better?

I completely agree with you. Even if you have it, how much do you retain? Whatever materials I've used, I can go back and pull a book out that I read a few years ago, and I haven't retained 20 percent of the material. All of a sudden, the light bulb switches on. Oh, yeah!

Does the 80/20 rule apply in real estate?

Yes. How many people just want to slide through and want to be a victim, and how many people want to step up and change people's lives? Gee, I'm a victim because this person just took my buyer away from me. Or, gee, I'm a victim because these people just told me how bad I am, and it's really not my fault. I think I get more frustrated with people who blame their environment, their situation. Attitude, to me, is 90 percent, and 10 percent is the physical abilities that we have out there. I've seen a lot of people who I would have never thought could make it in this industry, based on their background, lifestyle, people skills, and verbal communication skills, and you know those are the people who have that attitude of "I'm going to make it," and that's all. I've just learned so many lessons that way.

Can you think back to a deal in which you had some challenges?

Throw some pennies up in the air. The hardest transaction, and it's always the same thing, is when people lose confidence and faith in you because of what's happened outside your ability to control it. I have a recent one. There was a property I had listed, and the first offer came in, but the earnest money never came in. Of course, the seller was very upset with me, but it wasn't my buyer. So, it was an outside circumstance. Then we sold it again, and on the contract the earnest money was going to be in escrow within 24 hours. Two days later, it wasn't there. The seller wanted to fire me. That's when you start to take things personally, and you have no control over those types of issues.

But I think the hardest thing is being an A-type personality and wanting to control my environment. Sometimes you can't control it. It's very difficult to get through anything that you have absolutely no control over. One of mine was with a lender; we're talking about a $2½ million deal they had $300,000 earnest money on. The lender did not fund on time, and my buyer was losing $300,000, because the seller was not going to give him an extension. That's a pretty substantial amount of money. It was like *me* losing that $300,000. Of course, the buyers want to know why I can't do anything about it, but it's not my seller. Circumstances you have absolutely no control over are the ones that really make you want to lose it in this business.

My buyer did lose the earnest money deposit, and they ended up getting another house from me. But, you're lost, and you can't pull anything out of a hat, because there's nothing to pull. I don't blame anyone else, but as I told them, the way we put this contingency is that, if you didn't have your loan in place, we could pull out at this time. The client knew it was their fault, because they believed an outside source who promised them the world and couldn't come up with the product. All you can do is say that you've done everything possible. But I went through probably three weeks of total depression because of $300,000, or $25,000, or $10,000, depending on whose income it was and who they were. That's a substantial amount of money.

My biggest fears in this whole industry are lenders and appraisers. With an appraiser, you don't have any control whatsoever. If they don't appraise it out, you're in trouble. If a lender says he or she is going to commit and doesn't do it, you can't pull that money out of your pocket. In fact, I was just talking to one of my clients this morning, and we were laughing, and she said, "Cheryl, this industry is either a drama, *Law and Order*, or it's a sitcom." It literally is. One day it's drama and the next day it's funny.

If you look at transactions gone bad, in most cases, it's outside influences that you can't control, and I don't know how to tell that you can control it, because I haven't learned that lesson yet. The only thing you can do is to be the professional you are, and try to protect your client the best you can. You have people whom you're relying on to do their piece. Sometimes people don't do their piece. But there are going to be times when there's just absolutely nothing you can do about it. You have to forgive yourself. I really do love my clients, what I do, and being around people, but there are some times when I'm going to get depressed, no matter what, because there's nothing I can do about the situation or the environment. That's the day you crawl in bed and read a book or pop in a tape and tomorrow morning's a new day.

What types of things do you do to revitalize yourself?

Not as much as I should. I'd spend a lot more time on vacation. I'd eat better. I'd drink less.

My newest thing is doing a little bit more exercise and spending a little more quality time with the kids. They're all growing up. But in a perfect world, I'd be doing a lot more of all of it, but again, there you go back to time management, and I haven't perfected that skill yet.

Do you actually write down your goals?

Oh, absolutely. In fact, there are some days when I have to write them down two or three times, because I have to feel they're really embedded. And, if I don't write it down, I forget it. If you don't look at it after you write it down, then you might as well throw the paper away. Actually study it. Okay, my goal is to make $100,000 this year, and I've never made more than $30,000. Well, what am I going to do after I say $100,000? Am I going to go sit at two open houses a week? Am I going to go out and distribute flyers? You have to have a physical action, after you've had the goal or the desire, and that's why I have a tendency to write a lot, because I write lots of goals down, but I have to continue doing it, so I'll get to it.

There's never enough time. Priorities are where a lot of people get bogged down in this business. They spend their time on lukewarm leads. I find a lot of people have their priorities confused.

A lot of people are very comfortable failing because then they don't have to step up to the plate once they've been successful. It's that mentality—"Well, let's kick it up a notch. No, not comfortable here, let's go back down."

I try really hard not to set up to fail. I've always felt that, if I have it in front of me, come hell or high water, I'm going to get it. I don't try to do things that are beyond my realm right now. It's like a rubber band that you keep stretching. Little by little, you stretch. From my humble background, nobody would have ever thought I would be in the position I am right now.

I'm still uncomfortable when I go on a listing appointment and I don't know someone. I'm still a little nervous because I don't know them yet. The uncomfortable part, of a possible rejection, holds so many people back from just really pushing out there. Rejection is painful, and if you take it personally, it's more painful, and it's very uncomfortable to meet anyone. Everyone's your best friend. You're uncomfortable, but so are they, so you make them comfortable first.

About how much time do you spend with a client?

On my listing presentations, I spend about 20 or 30 minutes going over my presentation, and probably an hour to get to know them. I would say, at a minimum, an hour and a half. I don't think you can know what people want, need, or think in 30 minutes.

Do you have a specific routine?

No, I don't, because I don't ask the same people the same questions, and I'm a true believer in mirroring people. If someone's very quiet, I try to lower my voice. If someone's very obnoxious and loud, I fit right in.

I have to slow down a lot with speech patterns because I speak very quickly, and already have my next thought in front of me. Obviously, there are always the same questions. I have them show me their property or try to find a picture or something that's personal for them that I can relate to: the dog, the cat, the grandkids, the boat, the water skis, or whatever can create some sort of communication line to where we have something in common. I think my questions change depending on whom I'm with, because if someone doesn't have kids, I'm not going to sit there and have a conversation about my kids. If someone's an avid reader, then we'll probably spend 20 minutes because we found something we have in common. What books did we both read, what movies, or you're from this part of the world and I was there. I could sit in a cowboy bar and drink beer and throw peanuts or I could be at the best black-tie affair in town. It's just wherever you're comfortable and can mold yourself into the environment. In this business, you have to be a chameleon if you're going to make everyone around you comfortable. You don't have to change your personality. You have to adjust to make someone else feel more comfortable around you. I'm not going to lie to someone or cheat them, and I'm not going to have any integrity issues. I'm just going to slow down, or dress up, or I'm going to soften my speech, or I'm going to yell a little louder.

When I used to negotiate multi-million dollar contracts, I would always walk in the door knowing the least I would take, but here's what I'm going to go after, knowing very well I was probably going to have to back down, negotiate part of it, but also be very clear when I would walk away. Do you go through that process?

Oh, absolutely. I do not negotiate my commissions up-front. I have a favorite saying for that. I tell every seller on a listing appointment that— and I'm a six-percent agent, because I do the higher-end—if we can establish a price that you're comfortable in selling your home, and I get you that price, and I've done everything I'm telling you I'm going to do, I want six percent. However, if we get to a point where you don't get what you want, and I'm in this position, I say that my greed never exceeds my need. We'll work on the commission. If we're $5,000 apart, there's nothing to worry about. If we're $100,000 apart, we never had a deal in the first place. I've never had a seller who hasn't been comfortable paying a full commission, as long as they get what they want. There's give and take in everything, but not on the front end. If I negotiate my commission on the front end, I guarantee you they're going to take some more away from me on the back end.

I would never disclose or expose my seller's minimum amount they would take, because, obviously, I want them to walk away from the table with as much in their pocket as I possibly can give them. However, if someone said to me, "I won't take a dime under $2.5 million for my property, but let's put it at $2.75-2.8 million," and someone came back and said, "We'll give you $2.45," then we're going to try to come back at $2.65, and then hopefully get them to their comfort zone. But that is life; you are negotiating what everyone's bottom line is.

Since you don't typically meet the other side of the party, it's pretty difficult to really understand what's motivating them.

That's out of your control environment. Did the broker fax it over to them? Or, is the seller just adamant about this price? If they don't have good communication skills, or they're intimidated, or they really don't know their profession, I mean you're in a very tough position.

What I usually do on those is ask them if I can present my offer—especially if they come back with a stupid counter-offer. "Would it be okay with you if I sat down and presented our counter-offer back to the seller?" A lot of them would say no, because they're intimidated by you at this point. And they're exposed.

I then ask, "Would you have your seller put in writing that they do not want me to present this counter-offer?" Most sellers don't know that you're even having these conversations with someone else. And most people don't think to ask.

You can absolutely tell another agent you want their seller to sign in writing that they don't want you to personally present it, because your buyer has requested that you are physically there to present the offer. They've told me no I can't, but then have your seller sign off on it.

In most cases, they don't say they won't have the seller sign off. I guess there's nothing you can say except, "May I write your seller a letter?" By that time, they know you've tagged them. They will either give some excuse to the seller as to why I want to do it, or, in most cases, they'll let me talk to him.

A lot of agents are scared to death to put a buyer and a seller together. I'm scared to death to put a buyer and seller together without having an agent in the picture, because you never know what's going to happen, and it's really out of your control. But if it's a monitored meeting, nine times out of ten, they find something they like about each other, and then they don't feel bad about buying or selling from each other.

I don't usually like the buyer to sit with the seller on the first go-around, but if I feel we're only having communication problems, I will just ask, "Can my buyer meet over there and talk to your seller about the pool equipment, or this or that?" Then, when you have the contact between two people, you become human, and they're not looking at an offer that upset them. They're looking at a communication with a human, they really do like my property, and maybe there are some allowances here.

You also have the other broker's ego out of the way. I've had the worst experience with what was probably a newer agent, the best buyers in the whole world, and the most wonderful seller. The agent says the seller won't agree to this, won't agree to that. My client and I happened to be there one day when the seller was there. The seller told him to shut up, leave me alone, let me just deal with these people.

Now you might not ever get to the right price, because maybe you are too far off. In most cases, you can mold it, meld it, and play with it a little bit to make it happen.

The seller wants someone to live here who loves their home. I just had an offer today for $2.7 million, an investment group, which was full price on a property. We're negotiating $2.55 million on the backside. The people for $2.55 call it their dream house; they're in love with it. He said, "I don't know these investors. I'd rather take $150,000 less, knowing that these people love my home."

That's because they met each other, they bonded. "Wow, we love your house. This is our dream house," as opposed to an investor who says, "Here's full price. I don't know what I'm going to do with it."

Any other advice on how to be successful?

If I were going to look for anything in the industry to tell me what to do, it would be an ABC Guide as to what I need to do every day, ABC, in order to get to the next level. They've already gone through their training. They need to know what they have to do every day. Mark your 90-day goal. Whether you've been in the business a million years or you haven't, if you don't have a lot of inventory, you better figure out what you're doing for the next 90 days.

They always tell you that it takes 30 days to make or break a habit. But when you start looking at goals, career, and movement, you have to give yourself 90 days just to put yourself on the map. If you are new, or if you aren't doing well in the business, you have to log down what you need to have happen to you in 90 days. After you know that, you can decide whether you have to have two open houses, knock on some doors, make some phone calls, or get involved in a civic organization where you're in front of someone. Again, when you meet someone, it's the happiest time of their life, and once you meet them, they're going to refer you to two other people, which in turn is going to get your wheel spinning and the pipeline going, and then they're going to refer you to two more people.

No one likes to cold call. I've never been a cold caller myself, but I have been able to reply, if someone says thank you to me, "You know, the best compliment you could give me right now is to provide me a referral to someone who's either going to buy or sell some real estate." That was my favorite line for at least the first five years in the business.

In Las Vegas, there's a party every day. But I go to parties and people ask for a card and I don't have one. I just don't use that part of my life for networking. I think if you network that way in a social situation, and you get aggressive, it turns people off.

I was at a barbecue at a dear friend's house the other day, and I happened to have sold their house. They had their brand-new house, and they were all happy with it. One of their son's friends had just gotten his mortgage broker's license. I said, "Yeah, give me a call sometime." I mean, not giving him a card, nothing. The guy haunted me for two weeks. Finally, I said, "I think it's great to be so tenacious but now you're stalking me. Leave me alone." And I think that's how people feel at parties. You're trying to have a good time, or socializing. During the conversation people will find out you're in the real estate industry, and then they bring the conversation up. "Oh, I have a house I just bought," or just sold. If you need to get exposure out there, the best way to get it is to wear a name badge all the time. If you're in a grocery line and someone wants to buy real estate, they're going to start up a conversation with you. If I'm in the grocery line, I don't want to talk about real estate. I want to get my groceries. Wherever you are, whether it's church, you're in a grocery line, or you're at the drycleaners, you will always come across someone at some point who's going to need some real estate.

I approach life on a lighter sense; I'm not that serious. I love it when I can have a captive audience. Even when we go out, I lock the car door and say, "You're my captive audience. You're not going anywhere until you do something with me." This breaks the ice, because they're already thinking, "My God, this girl's going to try to sell me something." Let's break the ice right now.

How did you get your clients?

I've been very fortunate because I'm very good about asking for referrals, but there were a couple "For Sale By Owner" builders when I first moved here.

In fact, my one client brags to everyone that he was my first listing. He was a "For Sale By Owner" builder, would co-op but wouldn't list, and had never used a broker before. I had my song and dance straight from Beverly Hills; I can sell your $700,000 house, which was a lot of money 14 years ago. I said, "I'll tell you what. If you can sell your house to someone who's just a regular principal while I have it listed, then you don't have to pay me a commission." So it was really a win/win for him. I was listing it, and I got a high-end listing in a guard-gated community, and I just took it from there. I started advertising it, sending everybody the comps, and doing the beautiful pictures. All of a sudden, I am the queen of The Fountains, which was the name of the neighborhood. He did sell it to his own buyer, and did not have to pay me a commission because of the way I set it up up-front. He's still my client, and I've probably done $20 million worth of real estate over the last 15 years.

I could have spent the same $15,000 I lost on that commission, marketing myself, saying all about Cheryl, with no product to market. I would have rather done that freebee and gotten myself to where I'm in an established neighborhood, on the higher-end, where everyone's going to start seeing my name. And then I got the next phone call. That's where the ball rolls. Of course, he referred me to everyone in his whole sphere, because he felt so guilty that he didn't have to pay me a commission.

Sometimes, you get referrals over guilt. There are some clients whom I have taken around for two to three years and have never sold them one piece of property. But I guarantee I've made one to five transactions on those people, because they refer me to everyone. Make some lemonade out of the lemons. Okay, these people aren't going to buy. Well, the highest compliment they can give me is to refer me to someone.

ALLAN DOMB
Independent

ALLAN DOMB REAL ESTATE
Philadelphia, Pennsylvania

#1 Realtor in Sales Volume and Number of Units: United States

- Sales Volume: $235 M
- # of Units Sold: 834
- # of Employees: 12
- www.AllanDomb.com
- Certified Residential Specialist (CRS)
- Years in the business: 25

How did you get interested in real estate?

In November, 1978, I worked for Phelps Time Lock Service making $15,000 year. I was listening to a radio show called "All About Real Estate" on WPEN, a Sunday morning talk show in Philadelphia from 9:00 to 12:00 at the time. I heard the radio talk show person, Jay Lamont, talking about Temple University's Real Estate Institute, and he was a director, and you could get your real estate license. The show interested me. I have been listening to it since then. I started my real estate courses at Temple, went for my license in 1979, and started in January 1980.

Interesting time to be going in to the marketplace.

It was a very interesting time, because in '81-'82 interest rates went over 20 percent. In fact, I was able to obtain city mortgage money for someone in 1982 who gave me a bottle of champagne because the city mortgage money was 15 percent.

There's a fascinating statistic that we should realize today. With interest rates hovering around 5½ to 6 percent, the home that I sold in '81 or '82, at a mortgage rate of 19 percent, for $300,000, had a higher payment than the home I sell today at the 5½ percent mortgage rate, for a million dollars. So you bought $300,000 in '81, '82; today you buy for a million. Today, your payment's lower—more than three times the home size, but lower payments.

What was it like starting in the market during that time frame?

I was working part-time for 1980, '81, '82 because I didn't want to give up my full-time job of receiving $300 a week gross. I worked in the morning, from around 6:30-7:00 until 8:30 at the real estate office. Then I went to my main office, where I was the general manager of the Time Lock company. For lunch, from 12:00 to 1:00, I went to the real estate office. And then from 6:00 until 10:00 at night, I worked in the real estate office, and I worked Saturday and Sundays. So, really, I had two full-time jobs. I made more the first year in real estate than I made at my Time Lock business. I made $35,000 or $40,000 in 1980, part-time, and that was pretty good, part-time. Then I went to like $75,000 or $80,000 the second year and then just kept growing from there.

In 1982, part-time, it was a tough market. I won the award in Philadelphia for top salesperson, selling $6.3 million worth of real estate. I was the top Realtor. I was part-time.

I decided, after I got that award, that maybe this is a good thing for me to do full-time. I left the Time Lock business. They had given me a raise at that point to $16,000.

By the way, I took their business in 1977, which had a gross of $230,000, and within four or five years, took them over $600,000 in gross. They had been in business since 1904.

What enabled you to be so successful, working part-time when you started out?

The work ethic instilled in me by my parents. That was a very important factor. They were great role models. I remember my parents going to work when I was young, leaving early in the morning, coming home late at night. My father would work six days a week. They were workers. I just thought that was what you were supposed to do.

You have goals, not just financial goals. You have where you want to get to in your career. That's one of my mottos: I always try to go above and beyond what people expect; I always try to do the best in whatever I attempt to do, to be the best in it. I guess that's somewhat of a competitive drive in me.

You had specific goals?

Always. I never compete with other people. My competition had to be me. It had to be what I wanted to get to, not to do better than the next person and then stop because I did. I know agents who say I just need to do $500,000 more than my person next door to me or something. That's not really the goal. The goal is what you want for yourself. It's like golf; you want to get the best score possible.

In real estate, my whole goal was to create a method of becoming independent, having cash flow and assets, which didn't require you to work. And to a degree, the real estate business was the method of being able to buy real estate and keep it and rent it to accomplish that goal. That's the big goal. I started buying real estate in 1978. Actually, I bought my first piece of real estate in 1971. My father had to co-sign. It was a piece of land in Florida. I had a development called Palm Coast.

Even back then, you were being that entrepreneur, get-out-there, do-it type of a person.

In fact, when I was 12 years old, my mother had to go to the public school because I had two paper routes, one at 6:00 A.M. and one at 3:30 P.M., and the teacher kept saying I was falling asleep during class. She didn't make me give up the paper routes. She just went to school and spoke to the teacher. I tried to stay a little more awake during class.

Do you write down your goals?

I think that's important. I do write down my goals, goals that I see on a regular basis.

How did you learn the real estate business doing it part-time?

I learned a lot from the radio show. I took courses at Temple University. I learned a lot personally from Jay Lamont, who was the head of the Real Estate Institute. He taught me an enormous amount. Then, over the years, I've learned a lot from fellow Realtors and people like Howard Brinton, who has taught me a tremendous amount.

How did you decide which real estate office to work for?

In 1980, when I started, I really wanted to work for a company called, at the time, Poquessing, now a Coldwell office. The broker/owner of the office was Joseph Fluehr, who sponsored me for my real estate exam. But then when I interviewed, to see if I could work part-time, they did not feel that I had the material to succeed. Unfortunately, they did not hire me, or fortunately, they didn't hire me. I went to work for a broker, Jane McDonnough. I worked there for two years. Then I went to work for someone else for a year. Then I opened my own office after three years, which is a requirement in Pennsylvania.

Later in my real estate career, I became friendly with Joe Fluehr, and he got me involved with the board of Realtors. In 1988, he was president.

In 1990, I was president. It turned out to be a very good friendship where I've even spoken at his company's sales meetings. I've needled him by saying they all had an opportunity that I never had, and that was to work there.

Why would they sponsor you and then change their mind?

I think they just didn't have the openings at the time. He probably saw this guy—what's this Lock salesman? He's not going to succeed in real estate. Look at this schleppy-looking guy.

What made you decide to stop working for Jane McDonnough?

Something had occurred in her office that I didn't think was proper, and I wanted to own my own business.

What was it like to open up your own office?

Actually, it was very easy, because I made friends with an attorney, Nelson Wooman, who was also helpful in my real estate career. Even though I was working part-time, he enabled me to rent space within his law office and pay an overage fee of a secretary for 15 hours a week. I was not going to do this on my own. That saved my life.

I set up my office more like a lawyer's office than a real estate office. I immediately got a Dictaphone. I approached the real estate business like a true professional with the law practice, and realized that time is money. The highest and best use of my time is doing one of four things: prospecting, listing, negotiating, or selling. Someone else should do everything else. He gave me a support system and really helped me tremendously. I'll never forget that. He really helped me get set up. He was very instrumental.

Agents seem to be reluctant to be independent.

I'm in a sea of Goliaths here. I paved my own path.

Being an independent means taking on all the areas of the business and being able to do that successfully. How did you do that?

We have our own mortgage, title, and property management companies. We manage over 500 properties. We have our own rental department, where we rent over 300 or 400 apartments a year. On top of that, I do a lot of development in addition to the brokerage.

I completed a building called the Saunders Building, where I sold seven single-floor homes that were 3,000 square feet each. Each sells for raw space $700-800,00, and $1.3 finished.

I bought Barkley Square, fifty-two percent of a hotel, which was 240 hotel rooms, 156,000 square feet, that I converted to 55 to 60 new luxury condominiums. Now I'm doing a building called the Lanesborough, which is a 19-story building, where I built three town homes, on the top three floors, of a 260-foot high building, where there's one home per floor. Everything in the building is brand new. They sell for $1.6 raw and $2.7 finished. So it's really the luxury-end of the market.

What made you decide to get in to all these different avenues?

The big difference between me and anybody else is that I'm out there every day selling. I can see what the market wants. That's a big advantage.

What made you decide to do development?

I didn't start until '99. I got my feet wet for the first 19 years doing brokerage. I was always tempted to do it. I always said, "I'm not doing it; I'm not doing it." I would help other people. I finally said, "You know what, everybody's picking my brain and doing these things. I can do this. I have the wherewithal to do it." Every year I would try to buy several investment properties, put them on 15-year mortgages, and not sell them, keeping them. I've accumulated quite a few properties that way. I would say that the properties are more valuable than the brokerage.

What motivates you to continue to do so many listings?

I've asked that of myself several times, and the answer, I believe, is that I still enjoy working with the buyer and seller and helping them in the transaction. I still get a kick out of helping a first-time buyer. I also feel that I can maintain what I would call the "eye of the tiger" (that movie *Rocky*)—by being on the front line to the market and seeing every day what people want. That gives me a huge advantage in designing and developing a building. I can see what's not in the market, what's in the market, and what people are looking for in the market. We're pretty much on the cutting edge of what people want because we're in it every day. Then we can sell it. We add our own inventory to the market.

You got this real estate knowledge through Jay Lamont?

I would listen every Sunday to Jay Lamont, and really, it's continuing education. I went to every NAR convention. I also got involved in the Howard Brinton program. I was a consistent listener of the Howard Brinton Star Power tapes. It took me 45 minutes, and if I got one idea, it was worth it. What I found is that you're not going to implement a lot of things, but if you could do one or two things, and really implement them and maintain that implementation—because many people do something and then they forget about it six months later—then each day you are, as Howard would say, tweaking your business.

What do you do to be so great at prospecting?

I once read an article called "Prospecting Is Like Shaving." If you don't do a little each day, you're a bum. The key to sales is prospecting. In prospecting, there's an expression called PLATS: the Prospect becomes a Lead, which turns into an Appointment, which becomes a Transaction, which eventually becomes a Sale. If you are making a lot of sales and you are not prospecting, I guarantee that, within a month, you're going to have a slump. That's the biggest problem with salespeople. They go through this process of highs and lows constantly. To maintain a constant high, you must focus every day on prospecting.

Time management is another goal. I'm very in to time management. Every day, to this day, I try to make at least 100 phone calls, where I've left a detailed message or spoken to somebody on the phone, every day, 100 phone calls. In addition, every day I have a top-ten list—a top-ten list of my most dollar-productive activities. Typically the top-ten things are transactions I'm working on. If I have only 15 minutes in between appointments, the first sheet I pull out is my 10 most productive things, versus calling somebody about wanting to sell me pens. I'm negotiating an $800,000 contract. Which one do you think is more important?

One of the things I try to do is under-promise and over-deliver, which means I'm always trying to do better than what I tell people.

When I sell a property, for example, every two to three weeks, I'll call the buyer and seller and leave them a message just to check in and make sure everything's okay. What I'm doing is servicing them extremely well. That becomes a great forum to get prospects because most of my business is now referrals.

In addition, I maintain lists of people looking for specific types of properties, and I'm constantly calling them. Or, if I see an investment property for people who have bought homes, I'm constantly calling them. Or, if a listing comes up next to somebody who owns the property, I'll call them and tell them, "The property next to you came up for sale. Maybe you want to buy it; you can rent it out; maybe you want to expand. You may want to take some of the space. You live in a house in the suburbs; you can add on to your home. When you live in high-rise condominiums, you don't have the luxury of expanding your house, unless you can buy the space next door. It's not always available." The opportunity to buy it is something they should seriously consider when it becomes available. That probably, by the way, is the key to the business. We are one-street specialists, specializing in luxury high-rise condominiums in Philadelphia.

But the prospecting is every day. Today, for example, I had eight people who closed over the last whatever years. I called them and wished them a happy anniversary. Every day I may have eight or 10 calls like that, of people who have had closings.

How do you track this? What kind of system are you using?

Through On Line Agent. Phenomenal software, like $500 or $600. It's preprogrammed.

If you bought today, I may call you. I don't want to be intrusive. In other words, I value my time, and I believe everybody I deal with values their time. If I have two numbers for you, during the day, I will call you at home and leave a voicemail so I don't bother you at work. I'm just going to call you and say, "Debra, this is Alan Domb. I just want to say happy anniversary. Today, three years ago, you closed on your property. Hope all is well. Just wanted to let you know the market is X, and hope you're doing well. If I can help you in the future, let me know. 545-1500. Take care." Done. You come home from work, you hear that message, and it makes you feel good.

How do you get listings?

Let's say you lived in the Academy House. I'd call and say, "Hi Debra, I just wanted to let you know that, in the Academy House, we handle almost 85 percent of the sales that have occurred over the last four or five years. More than eight out of 10 houses that have sold, we sold." That's a pretty powerful statement.

I don't think anyone has that dominance of the market share. We dominate about 75-85 percent of the luxury condominiums and the buildings that we sell in. That's three out of four. That's a huge domination.

Why would anybody want to use someone else?

Unless you have an aunt, an uncle, a brother, or a cousin in the real estate business.

How have you positioned yourself?

We are a one-street specialist. I've learned everything about that building. Knowledge and availability, those are your two keys to success. Have the knowledge of your market, knowledge of financing, knowledge of math, knowledge of your whole comps, and of your marketplace, all that information. If you live in the Academy House, or the Dorchester, and you call me and say, "Alan, I'm in 609 Dorchester," I'll tell you that that unit has 623 square feet, and the condominium fee is $387. The taxes are $154. And last year's sales of that apartment, without even looking at it, are $260,000 or $275,000. Have you put in a kitchen? Have you changed a bathroom? What equipment do you have? I can do the listing over the phone. That's knowledge. That's more knowledge than the other agent you call at some other company. Somebody says, "Which building is it? The Dorchester. Where is that located? In House Square. Okay. And you have 609? Is that a studio, two-bedroom?" It's a junior one bedroom with what they call a sliding door between the bedroom and the living room, like a Dexter, junior. It has hardwood floors. I can draw the floor plan, without even looking at it.

And availability means if I want to see an $800,000 home, Thursday at 10:00 A.M., can you see me? Yes. You have to be available.

What else have you done?

I studied everything. I specialize in luxury condominiums and about 23 buildings. I know the market cold. So this is just not something you jump in to. This is something you have to become an expert at.

I read a book called *How to Sell a Million Dollars Worth of Real Estate* back in 1978, which was a big deal back then. The author said one thing that stuck to me: become a one-street specialist. Learn that block better than anybody else, so that people will beat a path to your door and seek you, out of the specialists in your marketplace. That's, to a degree, what we've created for condominiums. We have become the best Realtor in Center City, Philadelphia, in luxury condominiums. We're not the best Realtor for an office park, or an office building, or a town house, or a suburban home. We don't even take those listings.

What do you do with them?

We don't take them, and we won't take the buyers. We are one-street specialists. If you want to buy a condominium in Center City, Philadelphia, we can help you. If you want to buy a three million dollar house in the main line, call this person.

I don't think many people have gone to that extreme in specializing. By the way, that's the key to our success.

Being in a major metropolitan city where you have so many condos makes a huge difference, too.

But you know what, you could do the same concept in Punxsutawney,

Pennsylvania, where the groundhog is, okay? You can specialize in an area in Orlando where they have new developments that have 4,000 homes.

There's a guy by the name of David Roberts, I think his name is, Ralph Robert's brother, down in Florida, Royal Palm. He specializes in luxury properties on the waterfront in a golf course community. I think there are 1500 homes, and that's his area. That's his market, and he dominates it. He drives around the area in a golf cart.

Jerome Depentino, in Longport, New Jersey, specializes in Longport, which is a Jersey shore, high-end community, with sale prices from $500,000 to $5 million. He has 1500 homes in that market, and he dominates that market. Same concept. He specializes in one area.

So niche marketing is definitely helpful.

Niche, especially for a smaller firm because you become the boutique specialist. There are really two types of companies left: the Goliaths of the world and the boutiques. There is no room anymore for the middle market, to a large degree. They're getting squeezed both ways.

That's a driving force for me. I love dealing with entrepreneurial businesses; the bank I deal with, and the restaurants I like going to. I have a great affection for that level of energy. To me, a large driving force is being a thorn in the side of the Goliaths of the market. I love that.

What enables you to get the best deals for your clients?

It depends on what I'm representing: if I represent sellers, if I represent buyers, or if it's a dual agent.

It's not so much the best deal as it is being totally truthful and honest, presenting all the facts, and giving them my opinion. They'll make the decisions. I'm dealing in an educated marketplace.. Everybody says to me, "But I'm paying the highest price today." People say that, today, because the market's been pretty good. And I'll say, "You're right, but for the last five years, everyone has, because in a rising market, everyone pays the highest price." Think about it. Tomorrow, it looks like a good deal.

What effect do the other agents' abilities have on your negotiation?

I have come to the realization that 90 percent of the business is completed by 10 percent of the Realtors. Having said that, I have a full-time person who deals with all cooperating brokers. She gets paid to deal with them on a one-on-one basis, which takes it out of my control. This way, I don't have to spend my time dealing with that. No irritation, no issues, nothing, zero.

You're not dealing with the other agent directly?

No, I've delegated it to someone in my office.

That's probably lowers your frustration level.

Lowers it totally. They don't like it. They think that I think I'm above them. But, quite frankly, it's not the highest and best use of my time.

One of the keys to productivity is constantly knowing your hourly rate. How much are you earning an hour? How do you increase that hourly rate? The only way to increase it is to analyze what you do every day, every hour, and say, of all these things I've done, which five have been the most productive and which five have been the least productive? Of the least productive, how do I delegate them to someone else? The five that are the most productive, how do I do ten of those?

Then you opened up this office. How did you grow from there?

Very slowly. We're not a big office. I think I have 12 or 13 people. Now remember, in that framework, I have a mortgage person, a title person, property manager, assistant property manager, receptionist, bookkeeper, secretary, two maintenance people, and two rental people, and then I have one and a half assistants. We're not really big.

In fact, we have fewer people now than we did ten years ago. But we do rely more on the computer now than we did 10 or 15 years ago. I believe your first assistant should have the full knowledge of your computer.

I had to bring in Jim Casey to train my people on a daily basis so they understood how to use On Line Agent, because we had the system for so many years and nobody was really using it to its maximum. People really don't know the full capability of that software.

At what point did you decide to go in to the mortgage and title business, and become almost a full-service office?

In 1982, I started in the mortgage business with a company from First Boston called Shelter Net. I believe, in 1983, I opened my title company. I said, you know what, this is a time management thing. (A) In 1982, not many lenders wanted to lend on condominiums, so I had a mortgage company. And (B) I wanted to have the closings in my office so I didn't have to run all over the place. The title company enabled me to do that.

What are some of the things you've learned along your path?

Stay focused. Specialize. Someone told me early on, " The most money you're going to make in real estate isn't selling it. It's buying it."

It surprises me how few real estate agents actually invest in real estate.

Stupid.

You have access to the best deals out there.

We have a policy in our office. We don't buy anything that's listed with us or is going to be listed with us, even though if you disclose it, it's okay. I feel it's a conflict of interest. We have to buy things that are either listed with someone else, or listed For Sale By Owner.

What kinds of major challenges did you run in to along your path?

A lot of jealously with other agents within my marketplace. It's a very jealous business, and that was a major issue for many people—not for me—but for other people.

A lesson I learned in the early stages was that I probably should not have sold any of the 20 or 30 condominiums I bought over the years.

One example, a two-bedroom, I sold five years ago for $180K, and I just helped the seller resell it for $550K. Multiply that by 20 and it adds up a little.

Fortunately, I still have much more real estate that I own than I ever sold; it's in the hundreds of units.

Why is it that most real estate people are so ineffective?

Real estate is not a career or profession that is sought after when you go either to high school or college. It's a profession that people fall in to when they're looking for something else to do or have failed at something else. It's not like you want to become a lawyer. I think if you took a poll in the high school right now of how many want to become a real estate agent, you'd find very few. I think part of the fault is that a lot of the people coming in to the business aren't the highest caliber people in the workplace. Many times, they look at it as an easy way to make money. They think it's easy, but it's not an easy business. People who think this is easy have no knowledge of the work and effort that goes in to it.

How many hours do you work?

When I started out, I worked 70 to 80, and today, I work 70 to 80. And when I'm not working 70 to 80, I'm probably thinking about it. I'm not a person who says, "I can't stand it, I can't wait to get out of this." A lot of my peers are asking me, "How are you going to exit out of this?" I don't want to exit.

What's a regular day like for you?

I'm exercising at 6:00 A.M. until about 7:15. Usually I have a cup of coffee at 7:15, go home, check my emails, make a few calls to people I can call at 7:30 to 8:00, or 8:15, or leave voicemails for people. Get showered. Go to work, by 8:30. Usually have meetings or appointments in the early morning. I have appointments throughout the day, or stuff in the office, or I'm at development meetings. Every Thursday there is a development meeting on my $30 million Lanesborough project from 8:30 to 10:30.

Today: I was out showing properties; negotiating on an office building that I want to buy that may be possible to convert to condominiums; dealing with an apartment building that I own, 88 units in Center City, Philadelphia; dealing with buyers and sellers; negotiating transactions; and closing two deals today. I don't mind attending the closings, but I'll go in for two or three minutes, congratulate the buyer and seller, wish them well and just, what we say, I guess, press the flesh.

However, we do prepare the client on how we are going to do business. Once we sell a property, they get a letter generated by my secretary that says, "I just wanted to let you know that this will be the procedure during the closing period. Debra Metzman, our contracts manager, will be calling you in the next forty-eight hours to coordinate your transaction. She'll be your contact person. Kim Kruger, our mortgage person, will be contacting you regarding a mortgage. Jean will be calling you about the title. I'm always available to answer any questions, or my assistant, Theresa, is also available. Every two or three weeks, I'll check in with you. I just want to make sure everything's going okay. If you need me for anything, just let me know." Every two weeks, I have a meeting for 30 minutes with all those people to go over every transaction. This process eliminates my sitting in a settlement for an hour and a half when I could be showing/selling two more properties.

How much marketing do you do?

We do a lot of direct mail because, really, we don't have any signs. No one's looking on the 32nd floor of a high rise for a For Sale sign. It's all direct mail and advertising in the local newspapers, whether it's the *Philadelphia Inquirer* or the *Philadelphia Weekly*.

Every month, we send out sold cards to our farm areas. Our farms consist of maybe 7,500 to 8,000 homes. We've sent them something every month, religiously, for the last 18 years. Every month.

We advertise in the local newsletters, and I also do a lot of direct-mail letters when we have a new listing. For example, on the 12th floor of a building, I'll advise everybody on 11, 12, and 13 that a new listing is available, and if they know of anyone who may want it, have them call me. In the early time of my career, I had people say to me, "Allan, you never told me that was for sale. I would have bought it." As a service to them, let me tell them, because I don't want them to be upset with me.

Is there a percentage of your budget that's earmarked for marketing/advertising?

We have it down to a science, but I don't know the exact percentages. We're spending, over the last four-five years, roughly the same amount of money, plus or minus $30,000 or $40,000 on marketing and advertising.

Agents seem to be reluctant to spend the money required.

I spend it. But, when I get a commission check, I pay myself if I'm the listing agent, like any other listing agent, or if I'm the selling agent, like any other selling agent. I don't leave the money in the business. I pay myself. If you work with me and I listed your property and sold your property, I had both ends. I would pay myself half the commission, which is 50 percent, and the other half goes in to the business. There are two pieces going on here. (1) I want to pay the salesperson. And (2) I want to be paid as the business owner. And you have to make sure both work.

Too many salespeople say, "I've sold a hundred million dollars." They have nothing to show for it. Well, that's not good. That's not what this is about. This isn't really about how much commission income you're selling, or how much your sales volume was last year. This is about, really, how are you creating wealth?

What things help you move the client along the decision process faster?

You know what I try to do? God gave us two ears and one mouth, and I try to use them in that proportion; I listen a lot. I learned that, actually, from Bob Wolf. If you listen carefully, they will tell you exactly what their needs and wants are and how to close them.

This is like going to a doctor's office. If you have something medically wrong, the doctor: (1) takes four hours to run tests, tries to figure out what is wrong, and comes out of the office and says, "I'm not sure, but you may have A, B, or C," or (2) has you fill out forms, meets with you for five minutes, and says, "This is what you have, this is why, and I'm positive." What do you think?

I like B.

Most people do. The key to this business is quickly figuring out what people want, understanding what they want, and speaking to them on their level. I deal with a lot of high-end people. They appreciate that I can talk to them on their level. I deal with the people on the lower level, and I'll talk to them on their level. You have to identify with whatever level they're on.

Is that something you learned along your path?

You learn it by making mistakes. Now why did that happen? What did you learn from your mistakes? I make mistakes all the time, and I just say to myself, "What happened there? What did I do wrong?" And I find out. I think it through, and then I say, "What can I do to correct that?" rather than beat myself up over it. It's done. Over. The only thing I want to make sure is that I don't do it again.

What do you do to work *on* your business, instead of in it?

Buying real estate and working on getting my debt down, my asset value higher, and my cash flow increased are all items of building on my wealth, my business. But I think it's bigger than my business. It's a little bit about wealth. You happen to choose real estate as the vehicle to get to the wealth. What is the wealth I have built and the income generated from it?

I don't think anyone's done extremely well without investing. So many people I know have invested in the stock market and are not happy about that return. But, think about this, if you not only bought the home 20 years ago that you should have bought, but you bought 10 of them, look where you'd be.

At what point did you get your CRS?

Very early on, because I read an article that said CRSs make three times the amount of money of non-CRSs.

Do you think that's true?

I really do. I think that they are the ones who are more committed, want to be more knowledgeable, and are the 10 percent of the population doing 90 percent of the business. I do believe that.

What words of advice would you give more seasoned agents to become more successful?

The advice people gave me. You'll make money selling real estate, but you'll make real money buying it. That's a great expression.

How do you deal with the changes in the market?

Markets go up and down. The key is not leveraging yourself really high. I'm not leveraged over 50 percent, for example, which is not a high leverage in this business. You have to be able to weather the storm. There will be a storm. We don't know when it's coming, but there will be a storm. There always is. The storm will come, you batten down the hatches, and it creates an opportunity to buy more

What is your market prediction?

I'm not sure. It depends on the area. In my area, we have a unique phenomenon. Baby boomers are driving our market. They are the biggest driver of any market that we've ever seen, and it's just the beginning. They lived in Center City back in the '70s, and they moved out to the suburbs in the '80s and '90s. In the 2000s, they're coming back in to Center City, selling big homes, and buying a home in Philadelphia and the Jersey shore. I do notice that, when people have big homes and they're selling their homes, they want the nice home in Center City, or on the shore because they want their children and grandchildren to come to that home. They want to keep their family together.

What's happened in Philadelphia at least, 25 or 30 years ago, was that people were lucky to have one home, and today, many have two and three. That is a unique phenomenon that is only going to continue. As people live longer, their homes aren't coming available as quickly as they did. You don't have as much inventory coming up. The population is still growing because of the medicine available to keep people alive. More and more people are saying, "I'm not going to go to assisted living. I want to stay in my home and bring the people in."

What is your philosophy on doing what is right for your client?

In the end, you get paid back tenfold. You want as little brain damage as possible on every transaction. Also, people call and say, "I want to buy." We tell them, "You should rent." Even though we're turning down business, that's the right advice.

How do you use your negotiation skills?

First of all, I don't get involved in the home inspection negotiation. My transaction coordinator does, and she is very good at that. The negotiation could be that you're showing a buyer a property, and the buyer says that the property needs a lot of work. You know what, I can estimate what it's going to be. Let's play a little game. I'll give you the estimate, "To paint this apartment, it will cost $700. To put new carpeting in will cost you $1200. To change this kitchen, of a quality that's nice cabinetry, GE Profile™ appliances, will cost you $14,000. But to back it up, in the next 24 hours, I'll fax you proposals from the three subcontractors we use to document what the numbers will be." We're renovating 30 to 40 kitchens a month. We're doing a lot of volume.

Are the contractors who do that work part of your staff?

I don't want to get involved. I'll tell you why. I have my own contractor, and if my contractor does work for you, and you call me back in six months screaming at me that something's wrong, you're not going to give me your listing back. I don't want to get involved in that business. I'll use other contractors. Let them make their money.

Also, I have a policy that if you were the seller, and the buyer, for whatever reason, the day of, two weeks, or a month before closing backs out of the deal, I will buy the property for the price, if you want me to. Nobody has that policy. When you have a deal that's failed, you have unhappy people on both sides. And two unhappy people tell fifty people. I go through that extreme, and I'd do that for you because you'll tell 50 people what I did. "You're not going to believe this." Then I'd keep it and rent it.

What if it's not a good rental?

We take all the lemons and make lemonade. I bought a penthouse that was a million one and rented it. After five years it's worth a million eight. I bought a property that was $145K four or five years ago. Today it's worth $500K. I'm not unhappy I bought those. You may lose money in the beginning, but in time they'll come around.

I've learned a lesson. So they lose a couple of thousand dollars, or $10,000, $20,000, or $30,000 in the beginning. (A) I'm getting a commission; (B) I'm not involved in a legal entanglement, a lot of upset people, and a lot of time and energy in a negative area; and (C) I've turned that negative, negative situation and immediately made it super positive, and gone above and beyond, which none of my competitors can offer. Nobody will step to the plate like we will.

<u>SUE FRYE</u>

ERA LANDMARK REAL ESTATE
Bozeman, Montana

#1 Gross Commission Income—ERA

- Sales Volume: $62 M
- # of Units Sold: 302
- Gross Commission Income: $1.6 M
- # of Employees: 3
- www.SueFrye.com
- Certified Residential Specialist (CRS)
- Years in the business: 21

How did you get started in real estate?

I was a stay-at-home mom because I had all my children when I was 18, 20, and 23. I worked for a couple of years when they were tiny, very tiny, before I got pregnant with my third child. Then I stayed at home until my kids went to school all day. Later, I was a waitress at the age of 35. I worked at a place called Froggy's. I was older than the manager. I did very well. I won the liquor contest and sold the most specials for the month. I've always been a good salesperson. I sold Avon. I was in the President's Club while I babysat and raised my children.

We moved to Bozeman, Montana when I was 37. My husband was 41. We had visited Bozeman and fallen in love with it and thought this would be a great place to start the second phase of our lives. My husband is a builder and a contractor, but because we were new to this town, he worked at the contractor's office. I worked as a waitress for about ten months. I didn't want to be 40 and be waitressing. I think I've always loved real estate. I wanted to be in real estate when I was in California because my father was a contractor. But I felt that it would be too hard on my children. It's very difficult to be in real estate if you have young children. In order to be good, you need to give it your all.

I got in to real estate May 28 of '83, and I sold my first two houses, one to the cook and one to a waitress.

At the place you worked?

Yes, and I did it the first two days. As soon as my license came, I sold them. The first year, from May to November, I won Rookie of the Year. I sold five million dollars-worth the second full year in real estate.

What enabled you to do that?

I knew only two people here. However, I have a lot of confidence. I'm very comfortable around builders. No one had ever gone after the builders here. They let the builders "For Sale By Owner" or sell on their own. While waiting on one of the top builders, I talked to him about listing, and he'd joke around. Finally I made a deal with him. "Look, why don't you do this? If you give me a thirty-day listing, and I sell one of your condos, you'll give me a listing for longer."

What I did was—and I didn't have a whole lot of money, I can tell you—I got a little invitation card and had that published in the paper. I put in this big half-page ad, where it said you're invited to the brand-new condos. There were 88 units. I talked one of the furniture companies in to coming out and furnishing a model. They'd never done that before. I had 100 people come to my open house. I sold it that day and wrote the offer at the table.

The builder then gave me that listing, and he gave me three other listings for three years. One had 60 units, one had 88, and the other had 30. I was off and running. That's how I was able to sell five million in the second full year. I had been talking to him, and I just kept showing him properties. I'd have him take me around, showing me some of the new construction things that were going on.

I got a reputation, sort of like the condo queen. He did spec houses. I did everybody's open houses and everybody's floor time on the phones. I enjoy what I do. I have a photographic memory, which helps. If I've been in a house, I can recall what it looks like, and I'm very good at prices. I memorize the listings, not only mine, but everybody else's.

What gave you the confidence to go to this builder and say, "I know I can do this in thirty days?"

I believed I could do it. I figured the worst-case scenario. If it took me a little bit longer, at least he'd give me "A" for effort. But I didn't expect that I'd fail.

Did you go into debt to take out that ad?

No, my husband was a roofing contractor and a builder; but starting in a new town, he went out and roofed a house in order for me even to get my license. I still worked as a lunchroom waitress for two months. I don't think you can do any job part-time and do it well.

You have to spend a little money to make it; and you still have to do it when you become successful. I think some agents are so afraid. If you did have to take out a loan, it wouldn't hurt. But, you know what, if you have to work a little harder, if your husband has to—mine had to go out and do an extra roof.

You have to learn to live on commission. But commissions come and many people spend it all at once, or they spend it before they get it. When you have commissions, you have to make sure, until it closes, you don't have it. But, commission is a great way to go because you can make as much as you want. It's how much you work, how hard you work.

What kind of lifestyle do you want?

I find most people's expectations are too low. You need to set them a little higher, even if you only achieve 75 percent of it. But if you set them so low, you make it too easy to achieve, and then you never reach a little bit farther.

I set my goals high. I didn't set them so high that I couldn't reach them. But, I set a goal I could reach, and if I reached that goal, I would reward my family or myself. Maybe I'd take the kids on a cruise, or I'd take my mom. Whether it's a new car, or new curtains, or a new couch, whatever it is, you need to have some kind of goal.

A lot of times in these classes, they'll ask, "What do you expect to make this year?" I watch people put down the minimum. You want to put more than you really need. If you say, "I'm going to sell $10 million," and you sell only $9 million, you've done real well. It's really easy to attain $1 million these days. The million-dollar club, anymore, should be the multimillion-dollar club.

You're self-employed, so by the time you pay self-employment tax, and pay for your gas and all your other expenses, selling a million dollars is nothing. You need to sell more than that to make good money, because you don't have a job where somebody's paying your 401(k), insurance, and paying/matching this and matching that. You're paying. You're an independent contractor.

How did you learn to deal with all the different areas of a business?

A lot of times when people start in sales, they think, "I don't have the money for education; I don't have the money to get my GRI" (Graduate Real Estate Institute). I got mine right away because you learn from people who are successful. You want to surround yourself with people who are successful. That's why I wanted to work with a company that I felt had more to offer. I started out with a small company. By the time I sold my first two houses, within four weeks, the lady had dissolved the company. I thought, "I'll never go with a small company again. I'm going to go with a company that's a nationally recognized name, and that has a broker and other people supporting them, such as secretaries and marketing directors." I don't mind paying a percentage of my commission to a good broker. Some people resent that. What they don't realize is that you need that good support group around you. You need all of them. You need your family and your company. They help make you successful. Sometimes people make a little money, and they want all of it, and they get too greedy.

For me, it was good to have a company and a broker I could count on. My broker was a nice guy. He wasn't the number-one broker by any means, but he had a good product, and he had a great office manager, who is now my broker. You don't have to be good in everything if you surround yourself with people who are good at what they do.

I believe there are key things you learn when you're out there. A lot of agents start out and start doing all the things that made them successful. They go to the multi-listing meetings, they tour the homes, and they preview. They do all of that when they're a rookie, and then they have a little success and think, "Oh, I don't need to do that anymore." You know what? They end up falling by the wayside, because you need those other people. You cannot do everything yourself. You can do a lot, but you need a good support group, and it's good when you're peers and you like each other and work together. You accomplish a lot more when there's a group, when there's a team, than when there's just one person.

Before it was fashionable to have assistants, I first hired a college girl to come in and help me do some of the paperwork. We're pretty hands-on here. It's a small town. We handle ordering our own title insurance and things like that. We still don't have a closing agent. We send it to the title company and get everything set up. We have a lot of hands-on work. We still make appointments for inspections, because we don't have any real countywide permitting. You need other people. I had an agent who came to me. She was an older lady, and she was not good at closing or selling, but she had a master's degree in English, and she was very good at paperwork. I hate paperwork. She came to me and said, "You need an assistant." In real estate, you have to have somebody who's licensed in order to answer questions about real estate, about somebody else's listing. That's a rule. She worked with me, and then finally I hired another gal. That way, it freed me up to do nothing but list and sell. That's why I'm not only a listing agent. I list a lot of property, but I sell a lot of my own property. That's why my volume is high. I sold $62 million last year, and I've already closed about $45 million this year, in a small town.

Then my sister decided to move to Bozeman, and she said she was going to give me a year as my real estate assistant; now, she's been with me nearly 12. Then, I have another assistant, Sheryl. But I think you need the assistants to free you up from the paperwork. Some people have buyer's agents, but I do not. I like to have control of my own sales and my own listings. That way, if I'm going to be responsible, I'm going to take care of my own mistakes and not have to worry about somebody else. That's how I work.

I like what I do. I've never had a slump. Every year I've done better than the year before. Every year, I think, "Gosh, if I could just at least meet or do a little bit better than last year." I always set my expectations up there, and if I sell only $55 million, that's a lot of real estate.

What enabled you to continue to grow?

I follow the trends. It's more important to follow market trends. In other words, you have to be on top of what a buyer wants, and you have to make sure that you're accommodating your seller and what he needs. I still do open houses. I know some people think that's old school. But, this is a small town, and you meet a lot of people. People like to see you face-to-face. Sometimes people let success go to their head. You're the same person, whether you sell a lot or you sell a little. People need to know that you're human. After a while, they get this thing that she's too busy to do this. And I want to let them know that I'm not too busy to do things that made me successful, and I appreciate that they have faith in me.

How do you follow the market trends?

I go to all the national conventions. I read a lot. I'm an avid reader. I'm a CRS, Certified Real Estate Specialist. I got that early on. They are only the top two percent in the United States, and I've been a CRS since my third year in real estate. Some people will never get it, and some people wait until after they've had a lot of years. We have a great board in Bozeman. It brings in some good speakers. We have accountants, attorneys, and 1,031 exchange people. My company has weekly meetings. I don't think you're ever too old, or have been in the business too long, to learn something. I learn something every time I go to a conference. The busiest people always find time. I always hear people say they're too busy. If you go to any of these top conferences, the busy people are always there. The other people say, "Oh, I didn't have enough time to go."

Or, go to an education seminar. We have a lot of those. I love to go to real estate seminars, motivational speakers. I love it. I always learn something. They always get me jacked up. When I leave there I feel good. I got to meet Dr. Phil at our convention this year. I got my picture taken with him. I've always liked people who inspire me. I think there's always somebody better than the next person, and you can learn from him or her.

Have you had mentors or coaches or both?

If I was trying to learn something, I would always go to the agent who had more experience, or I'd go to somebody in commercial and ask him or her questions. People are complimented when someone goes to them and wants their advice. I would go to different people in my office. There was a fellow who sold a lot of land, and he took me on a tour of the valley of different land. I learned land that way. I would visit the guy at the window store, the carpet store. I would go to different places so that I would have some information on a little bit of everything, or, at least, know where to go.

When people buy a house or a piece of land, it's generally the most expensive thing they ever do in their lifetime. It's important for me to give them a feeling of confidence when they buy from me or work with me.

I try to learn as much as I can. I do that about construction as well.

People are more knowledgeable. Buyers are more knowledgeable. They have access to computers and a huge library of information. Often, when they get to you, they have some good knowledge, and they want to make sure that whomever they're working with has knowledge. They don't want somebody who says I don't know, I don't know, I don't know.

Talking to vendors in the industry kept you up on market trends.

It would. I would also go to different seminars in which somebody would be discussing market trends. I also watch programs like the kitchen and bath shows. What sells a house, the kitchen and the master bath or is it being a one level?

In this town, almost everything was a split entry. It's an inexpensive way to build; you get more square footage for less money. But as the population is aging, they want more one-levels. You have to build what the market's buying, and you have to be ahead of the next person.

If the prices go up in houses then with townhouses, you can get a lot more square footage because you're sharing a common ground or a cluster of smaller homes. You have to move with the market trend, and part of that has to do with interest rates and building costs. It's a myriad of things, and you have to be on top of all of them. I often will talk to the lumber company and see what lumber prices are doing. When gasoline prices go up, everything else goes up accordingly.

People should talk to builders, engineers, well drillers, all of them. They know what's going on; they're the ones paying for those things, and you need to find out what it costs. It used to be, you could survey a subdivision and then there's your subdivision. You can't do that anymore. You have to have all these impact and traffic studies. A lot of agents think all they have to do is write an offer; it's not the case.

How much control does the agent have in the negotiation?

You have a lot of control if you are knowledgeable. If you're not knowledgeable, you have no control. If somebody makes an offer on a house and it's less than full price, if you're not knowledgeable about your market, how can you possibly instruct or counsel people on why your market sells within two percent or another market sells within 10 percent? If you don't know what your market trends are, you don't know what the cost of construction is, and you can't be a very good negotiator. If you are knowledgeable, you're going to be good in all fields.

I have a reputation with the agents that, if they give me an offer and it's reasonable, I can make it work, because I have enough information about the market and about the particular property that I have listed. I sell probably 65 percent of my own listings.

I have to make sure that I'm pricing it at fair market value. I have to be able to show that buyer they're paying fair market value. If you are knowledgeable, you can do that. I'm very comfortable. I resell some of my houses three and four times. I have to make sure that I'm competent enough that, if they hold it for two years, they're going to make at least as much as they paid for it, if not more. Almost always, it's more. I don't want to sell them something that, if they try to resell it, will not be worth what they paid for it. I'm in for the long haul, not the short term.

Do you give your clients options and instructions?

I counsel them when I list it. I also counsel buyers. When they give me price points they want to be in, if they're under $250, I never move them out of their comfort zone until they're ready to move out of it. I hear complaints from sellers and buyers all the time. They say, "I told that Realtor that I wanted this or I wanted to do that, and they just showed me things I didn't want." People say, "Buyers are liars." I don't believe that. Sometimes people don't know what they want, but I believe that, if you start out showing them what they think they want, they will find what they're looking for.

If they qualify for $250,000, is that what you show them?

That's what I show them. I might show them something within two percent of that $250. But I never move them out of their comfort zone, until they're ready. In fact, I don't ask them how much they can afford. I ask them how much they're comfortable with. The difference is, it's not what somebody qualifies for. It's what he or she is willing to buy. Somebody might qualify for $500 and want to spend only $300. I want him or her to spend something they're comfortable with.

They say they're comfortable with $250, but then they find a house for $300?

On my way to that $250 house, if they ask me, "Sue, how much is that one?" I can tell them. As I told you, I memorize the other part of the market, so that when I drive by another house that's somebody else's listing, or my listing, I know all about it. If I'm going to a listing for which there are two houses on the street that are $249 and $232, and we pass one that's $269, I make sure I know the price of that house, and also how big it is, some information, square footage, age, stuff like that. If they say, "We might want to look at that," I ask, "You told me you really wanted...?" They go, "I know, but we could go a little bit more?" But I wait until they tell me. I don't say to them, "I picked up four or five houses that were around $250; one's $260, and one's $270." I feel like they have to tell me when they're ready to go there, and sometimes they can't go there. I don't want to make them feel uncomfortable. I certainly don't want to waste their time, and I don't want to waste mine.

How much time do you spend when you meet the seller?

I almost always spend pretty close to an hour and a half to two hours. I'm a one-stop listing person. When they give me their address, most of the time I already know where it is. If I have not seen it or something in the area, I'll drive by it before I go out there. I'll have one of my assistants pull up the information on: square footage, a history of when it was built, how many bedrooms, tax notices, septic reports, or whatever I need. Then, based on my knowledge of the market, I can pretty much pinpoint within five or six percent of where it's going to fall, without having seen it. Then, I already have kind of an idea when I go there that they're going to fall within this $25,000 to $50,000 range. It's like a high/low type of thing. Then if I go out there and find out they have solid granite instead of granite tiles, and they have 12' ceilings, instead of 9', I could adjust for the square footage difference in what it costs to build something like that.

Unless I'm doing a specialty property that's an unusual acreage, or a very customized home where I need to look at it first, I generally price it and list it at the same time. I rarely go a second time. I'm very good at being able to list property within two percent to three percent of what it sells for.

Do you consciously think about how you influence people, or is it being so knowledgeable in the market?

It's probably a combination of both of those. It's very important, if I'm knowledgeable, that I'm very comfortable about influencing them because I truly believe that what I'm telling them is exactly what they need to hear. If I'm not sure about what I'm saying, I won't say it, because I'm very conscious that I'm influencing them. I want to make sure that, were something to happen, if they were ill, if they lost their job, that I could come back and competently sell their house. Sometimes you can do every single thing right and something doesn't sell, because the right person didn't happen to see it. It doesn't mean that there's anything wrong with the market. Usually when markets go bad, they go bad everywhere.

However, in Bozeman, we aren't influenced as much by interest rates. Obviously, it's always better when they're lower. People chose to live here because we have no major industry. It's a college town, and agriculture and tourism are the number-one industries. But we're not a Jackson Hole or Vail. We have ski resorts, blue-ribbon fishing, cross-country skiing, hiking, and all that stuff. But we aren't the more glitzy. It's more family-oriented instead of a corporate retreat or vacation-type thing.

We get business and we get vacation people, but they're not the same. A lot of people who come here live to fly fish. A lot are in my age group who live in Florida, Alabama, Mississippi, and Arizona. It's too hot in the summer. They start out coming here as a vacation home, and then they end up spending as much time here as they do where they come from. We used to sell second homes, but now they're like dual homes. They have one here and one there, and they spend an equal amount of time in both.

There must be a lot of entrepreneurs.

There are. With the Internet, people can work anywhere. They can work out of New York and then work in Montana and then fly there once a week, once a month, or once every two months. There are a lot of people, and they're not all wealthy. Many people think that everybody who buys a second home is wealthy, but they're people who may come from a market that's more expensive than ours. They sell their major home, and they come here and buy a home. They have enough left over to buy a condo or a small home there and have two homes.

There are all sorts of things that can keep the house from closing or issues that come up. How do you deal with those?

We do encourage people to have inspections. Generally, if they're not structural, in other words, major surgery, and they're cosmetic surgery, you can fix cosmetic things. If it's a good buy and the right location, you may have to spend a little money to paint, or do something like that. Obviously, if you have a crooked wall or a crooked floor, you need to look elsewhere unless you have the expertise to fix it. A lot of people like the older homes, and you're going to get sloping floors. Something that was built in 1910 is not going to be perfectly square.

But I make sure they have the expertise to do that, or the money. Sometimes young couples get caught up in the ambiance of an older home and the glamour and the feel, but they don't really have the back-up money. When you remodel and you tear something down, you have to pay to have something torn apart and then put back. You have twice the expense. I try to make sure they understand that, if they think it's going to cost them $10, it's probably going to cost them $20.

You need to make sure they have full knowledge. If they have the money to do it, they should have an inspection. They're not an expert in everything. They spot things. Then if you think there's a problem, you need to contact an expert in that field, whether it's a plumber, a roofer, or an electrician. That inspector is just like me. I can spot some things, but I can't plumb the house or change the electrical. I can look to see if it has old wiring or it has a frayed connection, but that's all I can do.

They should get bids if it turns out that it's going to be a major undertaking. Then they need to take more care and maybe get some bids from contractors so they're comfortable. Often, what you're paying for is the land value of that older house that's gone up so much. You can't reproduce that location. When you buy an older home, even if you have to spend a little more money, you won't lose money, because the land is valuable.

How do you convince people they ought to do these inspections?

I say, "Make sure you don't get yourself in a pickle." In other words, you want to make sure that, whatever it is you're undertaking, you have full knowledge of it. I want them to have full knowledge when they go in.

I had a couple that had $30,000 from their grandma. I said, "The one thing that's nice about me is, my father was a contractor and my husband's a builder, so I do know what I'm talking about. I built several homes. Even when you have full knowledge and you're married to a builder, a lot of times you'll end up spending more money, because you'll think, 'I need to do this and I need to do that. Oh, it would be nice if I had a better light fixture or a thicker pad, or better insulated windows.' Pretty soon, that $20,000 has gone up to $50 or $60."

As long as they go in with full knowledge, I'm comfortable. I had a couple once say to me, "If you don't take this offer, we're going to go to somebody else. This is what we want." I said, "Okay, just make sure that what you want is what you're going to get." That way, they can't blame anybody but themselves.

Do you have to put that in writing to protect yourself?

I never have had to do that. Really, 99 percent of the people you deal with are really upfront and honest. This is a very friendly town, a very friendly community. Montana people are genuinely helpful, and even people who move here from areas where they didn't always trust their neighbor, or became a little cynical, find out that people really are what they seem. I can't say that in 22 years I haven't run into three or four challenges, because you always do. But, the bottom line is, if you know deep down in your heart that you did everything you could, you need to stand by your convictions.

When people make mistakes here, they're honest mistakes for the most part. I don't think they set out to deceive you. I'm a really optimistic person. I believe the best in people, until they give me a really good reason not to. Everybody's entitled to a mistake; you just have to make it right. We're human.

What happens when you run into a challenging personality?

I generally don't do business with them, but sometimes you don't find out that somebody's not truthful until after the fact. This is a cute story. This orthodontist called me from the airport and said, "I saw your listing; I want to know about it." I said, "I can videotape it and send it to you." He made an offer. I never met him. He used to call me very late at night from New Jersey. We got him inspectors, engineers, and all this stuff. It had a forest service access easement on it. The forest service has certain rules. You cannot give anybody a written guarantee on the forest service. This guy kept on and on. Finally, I said to him, "Maybe you shouldn't buy this house." He said, "What are you talking about?" I said, "Look, you've talked to the forest service. You've talked to the engineers. You've talked to the inspectors. You've talked to everybody you can talk to. Sometimes you just have to go on somebody's word. If you're not willing to do that, then you should stay there and not buy this house. We've done everything we can. If you're not comfortable, don't buy it." Well, he closed on it. And the day I met him he came and gave me a big hug. His wife said, "I'm so glad you're patient with us. He didn't take his medication that day." I never had one complaint, never anything. He's still living in the house after six or seven years.

How do you deal with people whose houses need work?

I tell them, but I tell them the things that are important. There's no sense doing things and trading dollars if you're just going to tack it on to the price. What I have them do is things like declutter the closets, shampoo the carpets, or paint the trim. If they don't have a lot of money, you can still get it scrub-cleaned and trim the bushes. If you have to make an allowance for paint, or things that you don't have the money for, like somebody who's lost a job or gone through a divorce and they don't have the money to spend, you can do the things that present it, and then make an allowance for those other things, or you have to adjust it in the price. I always tell people, "The more you can do to make it present itself the better, because you get only one chance to make a first impression."

A lot of times they say, "I don't want to do that: I don't want to spend the money." I reply, "Most people will take off two and three times what it cost to replace that." If you have the money to replace a warped face board, and paint it, or if the window seal is busted, change the glass." Eighty-five percent of the people who buy are visual. If they see something, that's what sticks in their mind. It's just like good news/bad news. You're supposed to buy with your head, but your heart, you know.

It's what you see when you go in to a house. If all the stuff was out of it, it was perfectly big, but if it has three students in it and they have dishes piled up on the sink, and a smelly cat box, and their dirty, smelly clothes, what do you look at? You look at all that stuff. You don't look at the space in the room because there's no depth perception when you have all this stuff in your way.

People have a tendency to blame somebody else. If it's my fault, if I failed to tell them or I don't do something, then I'm responsible. I can't do anything about some things. If you're behind a warehouse, you can't move the warehouse. But you can do some things to help that situation visually. You can plant a tree, put some flower boxes up, or put up a fence. People are going to feel good. It's a feel-good thing. You can make that disappear in somebody's mind. But if you have a burned-up yard and your garbage can is sitting in the alley behind the warehouse and you look right out there, they are going to see the warehouse and all the other crap around it.

It's just like when people listen to noise. When you're in your house, most of the time your TV's on; your coffee pot's going. It's not dead silence. When somebody has a street that's two doors down from traffic, and your standing out in the yard focusing on it, you can hear every car. But when you're in the house, doing things, it doesn't affect it. It's visual. It's perception a lot of times.

How do you differentiate yourself in your market?

Part of it is, in my market, people know I have this phenomenal memory and that I can do 10 things where somebody can only do three. I'm noted for it. People know who I am. I had one agent say to me, "If I didn't like you, I'd hate you." Always, there's some form of jealousy. For the most part, the agents are very ethical and very friendly and nice. It doesn't mean that you don't wish that you had it, or it doesn't mean that you don't go against somebody and try to get the listing, but it's done in an ethical way. The people who aren't ethical usually don't last that long. There might be one or two who fall through the cracks, but you know, when they get a reputation for not being fair and honest, people don't go around them. Maybe in a bigger town, it's harder to see that, but in a small town, it's pretty evident.

Not only that, my record speaks for itself. I was the first agent ever to sell as much as I did, and I continue to do it. People know that, if other agents bring me an offer, and if they ask me questions, I'll do everything I can to help them. I try to be the same person I was when I started. Just because I sell more doesn't make me a better person.

Did your life change when you started making all this money?

I have to say my life didn't change a great deal. I still look for bargains like the next person. I like to work. If I ever won the lottery, I'd still probably do the same things because I like to help people. I contribute a lot to the community, to the university, to the Boys & Girls Club, to Big Brothers and Big Sisters. I was a Lioness for 15 years. I like to do things for children. My husband and I both give away a portion of the money we make because this community's made us a very good life. I have a lovely, wonderful home with a lot of acreage. I don't dress any differently than I did then. I don't do a whole lot differently, other than, it's easier, and I can take all my grandchildren on a cruise instead of not being able to do that. I've been able to make it easier for my grandchildren to go to college, and help my children get established. I like to do those kinds of things.

I like people who are real. People who have money can be just as real as people who don't. In fact, sometimes people who don't have any money are more jealous, when they can get off their butt and go out there and make it, too. I don't feel sorry for them if all they do is whine. I had to go out and make mine. If the real estate market went in the toilet, it wouldn't bother me to go out there and sling a little hash; I might be a little tired.

Attitude is half the battle on anything, even if it is an illness. I've had challenges in my life. A lot of times when you're successful, marriage is very difficult because your husband gets a little jealous of all the time you've given to other people. We've had to work through some challenges. But, you know what, if people would work as hard at their marriages as they do at their job, they would be successful as well. Unless you have somebody who is abusing drugs or abusing you, or something like that, a lot of times, people just give up on things too easily.

What kinds of challenges have you faced in your career, and how have you overcome them?

People say you have to swallow the frogs. Do the biggest one first. Often, the anticipation, whether it be a move or a problem, is far worse than the actual thing. I hate to tell anybody that their deal's falling apart.

If you do have troubles at home, with your children or your spouse, you can't bring those in to work. You have to put it aside while you're at work and not blame other people for it. But you have to deal with it, too.

A lot of it is just really talking about it with your spouse, your children, your clients, or customers. It's the same thing even with your family. You have to talk about things. You need to hit them head-on. You can't be afraid, because they're there still, waiting for you. A lot of times, I'll come out and ask them. They don't go away. Consult with a counselor or whatever it is you need to do. My husband used to feel left out and stuff. He realized, "I have the best of both worlds; I have a wife who makes a lot of money. Who said it was a crime for a woman to make more than her husband?" The deal is, be happy. You reap the benefits. Men have always worked for years. I waited. My husband worked his butt off. I enjoy what I do. Everybody goes through passages in life.

In real estate, a lot of times it's somebody listening. Deaths and divorce are very sad occasions. It's final. You have to deal with it. Sometimes they need counseling. Often their Realtor is their counselor, and all they really need is a sounding block. They need to talk to somebody. You don't have any major advice; it's just to listen.

You can't please everybody, no matter what you do. As long as you've tried just as hard as you can, there are some people you're never going to please. You're going to have to face that fact and move on and not let it bother you.

How many hours do you work?

I put in probably 50 to 60 hours a week. Some weeks, I put 70 or 80 and sometimes I put in 40 or 50. But I'd say it averages 50 or 60, ten- or twelve-hour days, and I do work on Saturday and often on Sunday. I just took a week off and went to Sturgis and took two weeks off in March and went to Europe and saw some friends I sold a house to. I took a week's cruise in January, and went down for my granddaughter's graduation. I work very hard when I'm here, but I also take time off. I take my mom for lunch. I pick her up. My mom's 82 and works at Wal-Mart here. My granddaughter's here, so I meet them for lunch. If I'm busy and have an appointment in the evening, my husband will meet me for dinner, and then I'll go to my appointment. You can make time.

What's nice in this town is that I had a listing appointment on Saturday, and I took my granddaughter with me. It's a more laid-back market. I said to the man, "My granddaughter just got here. Rather than going all the way back home, I hope you don't mind that she's going to sit on the deck and read her book while I do the listing. He said, "No, that's fine." Sometimes, just asking people, they're happy to. My sister works with me. While I'm out of town, she takes over for me, and once in a while she has to take her nine-year-old son with her. People don't care. People take their dogs everywhere. I carry water, and I have a blanket in the back. It's too hot to leave the dogs sitting in the car, so I take them with me. When I show property, they love it. People are back there with their kids.

You asked me to think of a sale that sticks out in my mind. And, it could happen only in Montana. This young fellow was probably in his late 20s, early 30s, and I found him a house that he liked. It was on about four acres, on a side hill, and owned by a chiropractor. The seller had a pet bobcat. He'd had it for a couple of years; it was like a big cat for him. The buyer thought it would just be wonderful if he owned that bobcat. I've never had anybody ask to keep a bobcat, not a real one. We'll give it a shot. I wrote up the offer and said he wanted the bobcat, like you'd ask for the refrigerator, the washer, and the dryer. The seller said, "I don't mind. Now that we're going to move closer in to town, it's probably not a good idea to have the bobcat anyway. We'll let him have it." About a month later, I get this frantic phone call from this young guy, and he goes, "Sue, I don't know what to do. This bobcat hates me. I can't even go in the garage. I just open the door and throw something out at him to eat because I can't go near him. He attacks me every time." I said to him, "You better make sure that when you really want something, it's something that you're going to get." I called the doctor, and he said to call the Fish and Wildlife. Sure enough, they picked up the bobcat.

What's one deal you had the hardest negotiation with?

It's a general rule, when people have lived in a home for a very long time, that it's very hard for them to be objective when getting ready to sell. Often, they think the house is worth more, and the hardest thing you have to do is try not to hurt their feelings about the property they've lived in for 30 years. I've heard the saying, "Nothing is as good as the old way they used to do it." That's not true. It's true that some of the old moldings have the workmanship, and it's too expensive to do now, but the actual construction of the house is way better now than it was then. But these people don't see that. The hardest thing is to tell them that the value they've placed in their house is not there without hurting their feelings.

How do you do that?

I have to show them comparables, and I show them what it costs somebody to put windows in, to reinsulate it. When people start seeing hard costs, you're not attacking their memories of that beautiful home; you're showing them hard costs. It's much easier.

The hardest thing is when someone has to move because of illness or death, and they're crying. It's very hard, and you have to have a lot of empathy, and it has to be genuine. It's really hard when somebody goes through a divorce and one or the other person doesn't want it. It's very difficult.

I had a guy one time get mad at me because he was trying to get me to take his side, and, of course, the wife was telling her side. Finally, I said to him, "It doesn't matter who's right or wrong. I have to be fair and honest to all parties to this transaction. I'm giving a fair market value, and you may not like it, or your wife may not like it. It doesn't matter which attorney called me; I have to do a fair market value. I take no sides. I may have an opinion, but it's not relevant. You can tell me everything you need to tell me about what went on, but it doesn't matter on how I determine the value. The value is what it is. I'm not the bad guy here. I'm trying to do this for both of you. If you cooperate, it will be far easier for you. After all, this will be over and done with." I always tell people, "I've learned these three things a long time ago: You get hurt, you can get angry, and then you need to get over it." It's probably the soundest advice I could ever give anybody.

You have to do it. We all have to go through it. Everybody thinks the next person's got it better than him or her. Everybody has the same kind of problems and strife in their lives; big or small, it happens to us all.

What are some of the major lessons you've learned?

I'm a big believer in some of the old sayings. However, "the grass is always greener on the other side" is not so.

Everybody ought to work at the jobs they like. I don't care whether you're the best garbage collector, Realtor, writer, or television producer. You should do something that you like, that you have a passion for. If you're not happy, you should go do that.

People need to work at their marriage and their relationships with friends and family, just as they do a job that they like.

If you make a mistake, you do have to step up and take responsibility. You make a choice. If you make the wrong one, you have to admit it and try the other one. Sometimes, there's a reason that you don't see.

Have a good attitude about your job, your life, your family, your religion, whatever it is. As long as you're happy, whether somebody else is or not; you have to be happy in order for other people to be happy around you.

I think you have to help other people. When you help somebody, you get it back tenfold. I think I should get paid for what I do, but there are times when somebody doesn't have a lot of money, or they're heavily in debt, and I help them. I've even sold things that I haven't charged commissions for. Those people have recommended me ten times over, because I helped them. By the same token, I'm not going to let somebody take advantage of me either, because I feel that I'm still here to make money. I don't want to make it at the expense of somebody else, but if it's a fair market value, and they have the money to pay then they should pay. By the same token, every once in a while, you have to help people who don't have the money.

Agents get irritated when asked to discount their commissions.

I don't discount my commission unless there's a good reason for it. By the time they paid any commission, I have to pay a cooperating commission; if it goes on MLS, I have to pay somebody else. I've negotiated. Some people don't appreciate what you do. It doesn't hurt that people ask. You get what you pay for in this life. I tell them, "If somebody discounts their commission, they're going to discount some kind of service, whether it's advertising or something else. You can't be in business if you can't pay for the advertising." At some of the discount brokerage firms, you pick your advertising. You get either one ad a week, and none of this, or no flyers, or whatever. That's what you're paying for. You're getting what you pay for. If you want somebody's expertise, you have to pay for it.

Where do you spend your money to be the most effective?

Spend your money on the Internet because people are there: Realtor.com, ERA.com, SueFrye.com. An agent should have his or her own updated Web site. I had a Web site when it was not yet fashionable. But my husband was very smart knowing that's where the market was heading, and he, along with another young entrepreneur around here, started my Web site. People copy it. It's a compliment if they copy what you're doing. But my company, ERA, is a very forward-thing. ERA stands for Electronic Realty Association.

Our daughter's a computer engineer. I have five computers, and I don't even get on them. My husband and assistants do because I'm busy. You can get too wrapped up. I see agents who do nothing but spend all their time on the Internet; they're not out there working.

My broker matches anything that I do over and above the company. She will pay half of any advertising. If I want to put a $2500 ad in the *Big Sky Journal*, she will pay for half of it. I do some magazine ads. First is in-person, second is visual, third is phone, and fourth is mail-out. I spend very little on mail-outs; most is Internet. We have an eight-theatre complex, and it runs perhaps 900 short ads a week. I do that. You can go to the movie, and it says Sue Frye.

On Realtor.com, in certain cities, you can pay for these banners and you buy ZIP codes. We have only two ZIP codes anyway, so I have two of those ads. When somebody pulls up something on Realtor.com, my stuff comes up first. But I pay for that. It's $4,900 a year; it's not cheap.

You have to spend money to make it. A lot of people don't realize that. A lot of agents say, "I can't afford to have this." Well, you can't afford NOT to, if you want to make the money.

I don't do direct mail. Never have, and that's my choice. Maybe bigger cities need to do it. But I think you're better off getting out in your community by volunteering, being on the board, going to the Sweet Pea functions, the parades, the university, getting behind your blue and gold auction, and doing things like that. That's visual, again. You can do those, and a lot of those are free. You can volunteer your time. You can go to the old-folks home. You have to generally want to do these things. You just can't do them to do them. You might as well enjoy yourself.

An example: It all started with me selling a condo to a gal who worked as a student up at the university. She called and asked if I'd spend a little time looking at students' films. Now she's heading this huge function. It started as a teensy little thing up at the university for the film festival, and now it's turning into the second Sundance. For a little fronting, which costs me very little money, just a little time, now there is going to be a film fest. It's a big deal. They have producers and Hollywood actors coming in. Only two Realtors were invited to this function: me and one other, out of 640 Realtors. That little deal I did five or six years ago—sometimes the things you do don't reap a harvest until a few years later.

How big of a staff do you have, and when did you build it?

Until '88 or '89, I did all this by myself. But since '89, I've had at least one assistant. Since '90, I've had two. I have four children. My daughter, who's 34, started to work for me in February. I now have three assistants; one does packages, one does the closings, and my daughter does general things. I still do my own selling and listing, but I take her with me. I make sure they see all the listings I have, so they're familiar with the market. That way, if I get a phone call, they can answer questions until I can get back to somebody. I'm like a company within a company.

In the company, I have a broker. She has her executive assistant who does scheduling. We do workshops. I'm going to do one on how to overcome objections. We do little, mini seminars for our company. They might have somebody come in from an inspection company, or maybe the city planning office. We have a marketing director, a receptionist, and a relocation person, and then we have other office staff, plus our secretary who does all the commissions and checks and that kind of stuff.

You've never had a desire to go off on your own?

Never. I see agents who are really good, and once they try to be the owner, the office manager, the broker, pretty soon, what they were good at is gone down the tubes. I recognize that I'm not a good person manager. I'm the people person. I'm better off interacting. I love to sell. I like to list. I visit with people. For me to try to run an office, I'd end up making less money.

What one piece of advice would you give to other agents?

Be knowledgeable. You are selling a product, like a car salesman or a furniture salesman, only you're selling one of the most important things people ever buy. People don't know enough about the product they're selling. They ought to know about construction, about new codes, about what's going on in their town. They ought to know the trends. They ought to know what makes something important.

<u>KAREN HOBERG</u>
Independent

RANCHO MURIETA HOMES AND LAND
Rancho Murieta, California

#1 Volume Agent in 10 No. California Counties

- **Sales Volume: $57.5 M**
- **# of Units Sold: 236**
- **Gross Commission Income: $1 M**
- **# of Employees: 6**
- **www.RanchoMurietaHomesandLand.com**
- **Years in the business: 24**

What drew you to real estate?

It was totally by accident. I was in high school, and then I started college and thought I was going to be a doctor and save the world from disease. My focus was in school. Then I decided I was working a little too hard and getting too exhausted, and school was wearing me out; I would take a break. My mother suggested getting a job that would give me a break from school. I looked in the paper and found a sales job at a very small local college, which was interior design, fashion designing, merchandising, and marketing. They needed some phone help, receptionist help, sales help. I started working, believe it or not, on cold calls to get girls to come to the college. I did that for four months, and I was going nuts, sitting in a little cubicle, calling people on the phone. I decided I'd tell my boss, "I can't stand this. I have to move on. I have to find a different job. I have to go back to school right now."

Was it being enclosed in an office, or was it the cold calls?

I enjoyed the cold calls. They were kind of fun. I'm a people person. I have been since I was two. I found myself talking to strangers when I was young, being friendly to everybody, animals, people, anything. I just love people. I think it was more being stuck in this little room with these other people, rather than having the face-to-face contact. When the phone calls were going well, and when I was talking to everybody, I was pretty happy. I didn't even mind people hanging up on me. Usually, they were young high school girls, and you were calling the middle of the state, to little places liked Visalia, which probably isn't little anymore, and Happy Camp, which is a very small place, five miles from the border. They were elated to talk to anybody about college. We got pretty good results most of the time.

I was really giving them a good start to come to college, to a wonderful school. It got to me, the late hours and the phone calls. After a while, I said, "I have to get out."

My boss then said, "You're doing such a great job, and you're wonderful on the phone. We don't want to lose you."

I said, "Unless you have something else for me to do...."

She replied, "I think you're ready to go out and talk to the girls in-person." I was in fact a very shy person in school. Speaking in front of the public was not one of my better attributes at the time.

I said, "I can't do that." I was extremely uncertain.

"Don't worry. I'll set you up with a wonderful school. They are very nice. It's a Catholic school; you're going to be dealing with the nuns. They will just love you." She pushed me out the door and said, "Go."

At my first lecture, I did have a great time. I found out I loved talking to people. The young girls were very friendly. The nuns were glad to see me come in and give the girls a break, and give them a break. I brought in interior designing things, fashion designing boards. I also brought in a little bit of marketing.

For a year, I went all over the state, driving constantly and going to seminars to take the girls in to the school. That kind of honed my skills with talking to people. I went through one of every situation. I went through schools in which the teachers really didn't want to see you and thought you were being too pushy, to schools that were just elated to have you there because the teachers were inundated with kids who weren't interested.

I got them interested because I brought them in to the conversation, and I brought the boards with the interior design duties, and I had textures. I got the kids talking to me. I got them touching things. I really had a great time. Had they paid me better, I probably would have stayed with it for quite a while.

As time would have it, my dad built a new house in Sacramento. He had built some beautiful houses in southern California, before he was recalled into the military. He did a fairly expensive, dramatic house with an interior and exterior waterfall, and a watercourse that you walked over to get to the front door. It was very southern California for northern California. He decided he would have a party and invite friends and colleagues and people in the business world. I ended up giving tours of the house as people came in.

Ray Henderson, a broker and developer of Rancho Murieta, came to one of our parties. My dad was on the Boy Scouts Council with him. Dad was military at the time, with the U.S. Air National Guard. I was showing Ray around the house, and he said, "What do you do?"

I replied, "I'm going back to school. I'm going to be a doctor."

"Well, what do you do now?"

"I'm working for a little private college, and I do some lecturing."

He said, "You really should be selling real estate."

"Oh, no, I don't think I want to do that. I have to save the world. I appreciate the compliment; that was really nice."

"If you ever change your mind, come on up to Rancho Murieta." He said they would hire me.

That was the first time anybody said anything to me. At another party, I ran into a very large broker in Sacramento, who is no longer around but at the time was one of the two big brokerage companies, and he asked me the same thing. He said, "You should be selling real estate. You're really good with people." Then the broker of Jones, Brand, & Hullen, now Coldwell Banker, ran into me at another party. When the third person said I should be in real estate, I thought that maybe I should look in to this.

The next thing you know, I got my license and went to one of those quick schools where you study, study, read, read and then take your test.

Soon, my dad called Ray Henderson and said, "Karen got her real estate license. Can she come up and see you?" I headed up to Rancho Murieta and met with him. He said, "Absolutely, I want to hire you."

In the meantime, my dad bought a piece of property in Rancho Murieta, and was designing a house for us to live in.

I could have gone all these different routes. I could have gone for the big agent, the big company in Sacramento, and I could have gone with Coldwell Banker, which became one of the big companies in the country. But at the time I was 18.

Ray said, "Go on in to the project manager's office, and he'll tell you what to do." I ran in to the manager's office. I was so excited; this was my first job that I felt really good about. The project manager said, "I didn't want to hire you. You have no background in business, in real estate. You're brand new. I never hire new people. I don't think you're ever going to sell enough real estate to make it worth my while to hire you."

When this man said, "I don't think you're ever going to make it in real estate," I was just crushed. I was really excited about these wonderful company-training programs.

"I'm looking forward to the training program."

"We don't have a training program."

"What am I supposed to do?"

"Go sit out at that desk and wait for somebody, and then sell him something." He was not a happy camper because he normally did all the hiring. He was just put out that I was even there. Plus, I was 18, young, and didn't know much. But I was more excited than anybody could possibly imagine and very enthusiastic and that's what Ray obviously thought. I was really quite good with people and expressive and loved showing houses. That was my thing.

Instead of selling houses in town, I started in Rancho Murieta selling lots because of the safety factor for me at the time. At that point, that was the only thing they had to sell in Rancho Murieta. Land sales is a little more difficult than most people realize, because you're looking at a piece of ground.

My dad had a background in architecture, even though he's a retired Air Force general. He had gone to school at USC for architecture, had been recalled, and never got his architectural degree, but he designed houses in Los Angeles, Sacramento, and Rancho Murieta.

I realized I must have some kind of talent, or I've been listening, for so long over the years, to my father describing what you could put on this piece of ground, what should be on this or that side of the lot, and there's your vista. I was selling the dream home to people, rather than selling a piece of ground. I turned it in to more explaining and visualizing what people could do with the piece of ground, rather than just saying, "Here's a piece of ground. You can put a house on it."

I started to sell pretty easily because I loved my people. I loved my work. Rancho Murieta is absolutely a gorgeous place to be. You have the five lakes, the river, the environment, the rolling hills, the natural rock outcroppings on some of the lots, and these big, beautiful heritage oak trees. It was easy to sell because of how beautiful it was. The problem was that Rancho Murieta was a long way from town (Sacramento). We were out in the boondocks, as far as people thought. There was no shopping center. There was nothing here at the time. It was a slow process, selling my first lots. It was amazing how it progressed as the years went on. I had people who said, "I don't want a lot."

I said, "All I have is a lot."

"If you could find us a house, we'd buy from you." Then I got myself positioned to find a house for these buyers. I remember my very first house being a big deal.

My father had designed a house for a builder. It was kind of in the shell process: They had the walls up, but no real kitchen or cabinets had been finished. The lot was absolutely gorgeous on the golf course. The builder had not listed it, and it wasn't for sale. This attorney couple was my very first buyer on a house. They said, "We don't want to build. We don't want to go through the process. We're too busy. If you can find us a house, we'll buy it." I called the builder. I knew he wanted to move in to it. But I convinced him that he could buy another lot and build again and make some money. The next thing I knew, I had my very first listing and my very first house sale. I've sold them many houses over the years. The Brandts stayed in that house for 25 years, called me, and then moved up to the back lake. They ended up buying about 10 townhouse lots from me.

Some of those people I worked with have stayed in Rancho Murieta and move around many, many times. It's a nice community in that respect. I've sold five houses to one client in the last 10 years. I've sold another house six times in 26 years to six different couples. But it's such a small place. We have only about 4800 people and about 1800 homes. To sell as many homes as I do, I move a lot of real estate around Rancho Murieta.

I was in shock when I realized that I was in such a top position last year. I really didn't pay any attention until last year. I just cared about what I was doing and my little world. I really didn't care much about what was going on outside, because I was too busy. I was busy doing what I loved, selling. I get such a great joy out of working with my people and finding them the right house and the dream home or the dream property. I don't even know exactly how much I sold last year because the secretaries and my accountant and everybody in the office kind of watch that.

It was fascinating how I found out. At a wedding reception, a manager of one of the very, very big Lyon Real Estate offices in Sacramento came up to me and said congratulations.

I said, "Well thanks. What are you congratulating me on?"

He said, "You're number three in the county."

"Number three for what?"

"Production, of course."

"How do you know that?" It ended up, that managers of bigger real estate offices get reports from the title companies that know what's being closed and where and who's doing it.

At that point, I decided maybe we should find out where I am and who's in front of me. Who's doing more than I am? I can't believe that. Nobody can be selling more real estate than I am. Nobody's working this many hours. There were a couple of people in front of me in the beginning of the year. As the year went on, my sister-in-law looked in the MLS, because you can check all the counties. We looked at the outlying counties, just around Sacramento, and by the end of the year I was ahead of everybody in the ten-county area, except in one county.

How many hours do you work?

I work 75 to 80 hours a week, seven days a week.

What drives you to want to continue to work so hard?

It's a natural part of me. I'm born to achieve. I really do enjoy it. I absolutely love selling and working with people. What I don't enjoy, of course, is the paperwork.

That's why, over the years, I've gone from one receptionist and one assistant, doing my escrow paperwork, to now four people handling all of my paperwork. Because I am so busy, my assistants read magazines and the articles and then give me the one or two they think will be interesting. I have:

- a computer
- an MLS gal who also coordinates signs and the lock boxes
- a bookkeeper who does all the bookkeeping and comes in four days a week
- an escrow coordinator in the office

Then I have a full-time receptionist, seven days a week, because even with email, there's a chance of losing somebody because you didn't talk to them. I believe it's important to have a person who can talk to these people who are interested. A lot of real estate people and companies have voicemail, or a receptionist who's just taking a message. I have a receptionist who will find me or find another agent, or who will take care of the problem or the question. I need someone who loves the area as much as I do and can really give the company a good name and show that they understand what people need. When people call in, they need somebody to talk to, but they don't want to leave a message.

I have two agents on a salary, which is unusual, but it's also unusual because one's my brother and the other is my sister-in-law. I pay them partially as assistants, so that if I'm not there, they will handle that client who needs a tour or who needs to go in to a walk through. They're working part-time as an assistant and as an agent for themselves, and they get commission. They back me up when I'm not there.

On the weekends, I have hostesses who help me with my open houses. I still show a lot of real estate because I enjoy it. The best part is showing the real estate. I do all the negotiating and contracts. Once in a blue moon, I might be out of town, and then I have either my brother or my sister-in-law coordinate the counter-offer or something like that. But I've been doing 99 percent of all negotiations and contract work, and probably 85 percent of all the showings, my entire career.

I would rather do anything than paperwork. That's why I had to hire people to help me. That's worked well for me. I have been able to do what I love, which is selling and negotiating. I really do love negotiating and making the deal come together. It's a great joy to find houses that perhaps no one knew about, and you can put the deal together.

I'm working so much probably because I overbook. That's one of my weaknesses. I try to do too many things, because I believe I can do them all.

Delegation is always an issue for high achievers.

It's a very hard one. People want me a lot. Sometimes when I try to give people over to my brother and my sister-in-law, if they've had family that worked with me, they have to be with me. I had a client come in the other day who sat down and the first thing they said was, "We're here just to see you."

It's a little hard on you when you're trying to delegate some more of the work. But there are people who are high maintenance. It's the way life is. For the $1,250,000 house I just sold, I won't let somebody else help those people. They want to see me, they want to talk to me, and they want my expertise. If I could see everybody who came through my door, I could probably build the company to even more sales. I have come to the conclusion that I cannot physically talk to every person who comes through the door. I generate a tremendous amount of leads because I have the only real estate office in the Rancho Murieta shopping center. I was able to secure that by buying out the Century 21 office a year or two ago. I put a second little office in the same shopping center. They had a better location in the front of the shopping center, so when people would drive by, they would get walk-ins.

They were not handling their people well. They didn't have anybody staffing the office a lot of the time, and people would walk down to my office, which was much prettier, but kind of hidden behind some beautiful big redwood trees and a waterfall. We'd be picking up their leads. Unfortunately, they weren't as proficient perhaps at taking care of the clients, watching over them, and calling them back, and we would end up dealing with the same people, but we'd end up selling them.

You're almost the only one in town?

We have two little areas: the shopping center where I am, and if you keep going down the street, you go to the airport, and there's a commercial building right there. But, unless you knew someone was down there, you wouldn't go down there looking for someone.

I have an exclusive in the shopping center, which is in my lease, and that's one of the reasons I bought out the Century 21 office. I paid a lot of money for an office that didn't have any agents, for the location and the exclusivity in the shopping center.

Lyon & Associates is a huge company. If I didn't have my own company, I would probably be with Lyon. They're a great company. The local Lyon agent does all of her business out of her house.

Rancho Murieta Brokers, which is really the second largest company, has six or seven agents now, and I'm still doing twice or maybe two-thirds as much as they're doing.

How else do you market yourself?

I do a lot of advertising. When I started out with the company in 1993, I was spending about $1,600 to $2,000 a month on advertising. I'm up to $8,000 a month.

What specific type of advertising do you do?

We're doing a lot more in the local newspaper because it has a color residential section on Sundays. About two years I started to do it very consistently. One of the biggest problems with a lot of agents is that they're not consistent and don't spend the money. When the market's down, they don't spend the money. When the market's good, they think they don't have to spend the money. I find that you have to advertise more and spend more if the market is down. You want to capture those few people, because there are fewer people looking, fewer people buying. That's what I've been doing consistently for a long time.

When the market wasn't really busy, and we weren't getting that many people, I was doing little classified ads, which were pretty expensive and longer advertisements. I like to explain a lot about houses. I like to talk about the features. I like to express my feelings about the location. I would be getting calls. But you still didn't have the color. Then we set up four or five lines of color pictures, color ads. They were extremely expensive. I then had one brilliant idea. Why don't I do all six and get the top spot and really push Rancho Murieta? It's not just selling the house; for us, it's getting people to realize Rancho Murieta's not so far away. Rancho Murieta is a great community. You're selling yourself. I have a color newspaper picture of me. Then I have a blurb about Rancho Murieta in a big heading, and I have the separate houses. If I have a lot of listings, I want to sell them. I found I was getting so many more calls, and so many more people coming to the open houses when I do an open house.

A client called me and said, "We've been listed for six months, and we want you to list the house. Look at the house and tell us why it's not selling." It was a two-bedroom older house. It was in darker colors and priced pretty well. I was really surprised it hadn't sold. I sat down with them and said, "Have you ever thought about lowering the price? Did your last agent ask you to lower the price? If you haven't sold in six months, there's something wrong. You have to make a change in this house, in the price, or redo the house. We have to do something. We must get some life in to this house to get it to sell."

We went over the numbers. I found out they could take a little less. I didn't drop the price but $10,000, which really wasn't much. I did an advertisement that talked a little bit differently about the house than what their agent had done. I went on the premise of, what does somebody want who's coming up to Rancho Murieta? It's a fixer-upper. It's not a great house. I don't want to call it a fixer-upper. I want to talk about the strong points of the house.

Instead of saying, "You need new carpet; we'll give you carpet credit. It's an older house. Oh, my God, it's only two bedrooms," all the negatives, I went with everything on the positive. As I dropped it that $10,000, it also made this house the least expensive in Rancho Murieta. I had 35 people show up at the open house, which is an astronomical number of people on a Sunday. Two offers came in the next day. Two agents called me and said, "My gosh, I'm bringing you an offer; don't accept anything." We ended up with five offers in three days on this house that sat there for six months, only $10,000 over. We ended up selling it for MORE than list price. We sold it within $1,000 of where they'd been listed for six months.

It was strictly this color ad and how I wrote it. Was it on a hilltop? No. Did it have a little vista? Yes. I stretched it a little bit. I didn't say lake view, when it was 200 feet away from the lake. But I did say vista. When you're looking at a couple tops of the trees and you're above the house below you, you can do that. I just looked at it from the eyes of what is really the most important thing that I can say about this house, after the price.

Once I found out that that ad made such a big difference in this one house, I started to use it in my marketing. What I'm doing differently from other people is spending probably three to four times as much money on advertising. Sometimes it brings you the person, but sometimes it also brings you the listing. You're selling yourself when you're showing people what you can do for them that's different from someone else. The color advertising is great. So many people see it. I get people calling asking where Rancho Murieta is, which is amazing, because we've been here so long.

Things have been happening for me. Of course, after being in the business 26 years, I guess people do know about me. I had a real estate broker who does loans call me and say, "We really need somebody to talk on the radio about real estate, and, gosh, you can talk about Rancho Murieta a little bit." I said, okay, sure. It was a phone call. I didn't have to go down in-person. I didn't have to pay for it. It was nice, when I get to this point in my life where I've worked so hard that people will call me for advice, and it's nice that I get to share some of my advice.

Last year, I also was able to do a couple of spots on television—a morning show—and they wanted real estate advice. That was kind of nice. That was an advertising situation, where if I bought a certain amount of advertising, when they needed someone to talk about real estate, they called me first.

I cannot say that anyone called me because of the two television spots I did. I couldn't find a point where I could say this person called or that person called. Whereas, with the *Bee*, we can track that really easily.

I also do color advertising in *Homes and Land Magazine*. Of course, my company's called Rancho Murieta Homes and Land. So people think I own the magazine.

I've also been doing a lot of charity events: the school and the Kiwanis Club. It's something I feel really strongly about. Then I'm involved tremendously with WEAVE, which is Women Escaping a Violent Environment.

Some of it is that you have to put your face out there, and you have to be out there in the community. You have to be out there doing what you love, and then you'll run into people who also enjoy that, and eventually, they might come to you as a client. I find you have to work out there constantly and do what you like.

What made you decide to go out on your own?

I stayed with the developer, Rancho Murieta Properties/Rancho Murieta Marketing, for 15 years. It was an interesting little set-up. We had the security guard and the security gate. The developer said, "Anybody who wants to come in to the community cannot just come in; they have to stop at our office," which of course was the real estate office. Every person who wanted to go through the gate and just drive around and look at the area, unless he or she lived there or was working on something, had to come through Rancho Murieta Properties office.

Half the time people just wanted to drive around, or they'd say my aunt lives here and I want to see where she lives. If you were able to talk to the people, maybe you'd get a good lead. Sometimes you would get somebody who walked in and said, "I want to look at buying a house," or "I want to look at buying a lot." Much of it was a numbers game, how many people you talked to. It was like cold calling to a certain extent.

Then I opened up a satellite office at the country club while working for the developer. As they'd come by to go to the country club, they'd see me.

All of a sudden, the developer, because the market fell, decided they didn't want to have a real estate company anymore. They went ahead and sold it to a gal. For a couple of years we stayed in the same office, and I went ahead and stayed with her, because it was hard to make a move. I'd been with them for so long, and it was comfortable. Everybody knew where I was. Really, I was forced to make a decision because they were closing down the office.

I was pushed out of the nest—in order to open my own company. The idea of opening my own company would never have come to fruition, I don't think, except that my mother said, "Well, you could have my office." She had an antique store in the shopping center. She really wasn't doing a lot of business out of there. The shopping center was pretty much full. She said, "You could have that. You could just stay here in Rancho Murieta and do less work or do less business, but then you have your own company." I think it was the prompting of my mother and the fact that I really did not want to leave Rancho Murieta and work in Sacramento. I'm very close to my parents, to my brothers, to my niece, and my nephew, and the community is a safe haven, because we have 24-hour security. I can take a walk by myself at 10:00 at night, when I have a chance to walk.

I knew Rancho Murieta like the back of my hand. I had been here 15 years. I lived here. I loved it. It would have been a major undertaking to change my life and start over in Sacramento.

The first year was very difficult. My mother was with me from the beginning when I opened my company. She was my receptionist, because I couldn't afford to pay anybody. I had only 20 deals, and I couldn't pay my bills. I had to borrow against my credit card in order to keep my business going. It was amazing how the change progressed as the market picked up a little bit and people started to find me and I started to do more advertising.

How long was it before you were making a profit?

Two and a half, three years.

I definitely didn't make any money the first year. I think I broke even the second year. I was building a business. You can't just start out saying, "I should be selling this much, and I should be making this much." You have to put so much money out to start a business. I leased a lot of the equipment. We had one computer and a copier, and I had to have stationery. My dad designed my stationery for me because he's an artist. We have a beautiful pine tree because we're on Lone Pine Drive. I was doing beautiful finishes on my cards, embossing with the gold label, with the color pictures. It was incredibly expensive to do all the things I did.

Then, you had to start finding the clientele. That's why I had to start spending, at the time, a couple thousand dollars, which was really quite a bit of money when I didn't have it, on advertising.

I did a little bit of direct marketing when I started out. I advertised in a local color magazine, always doing at least one page. Then I started doing two pages, and then three pages, because I had more listings. That's how I was getting a lot of my listings.

I started to do color advertising locally and doing a direct mail twice a year. That would start showing how much more I was selling, as I started to sell more than everybody else. I sold only in Rancho Murieta. I focused so much, and I worked so many hours. I started to do a graph. I was doing twice as much business as any other company. I got more listings. Then I'd get more buyers because I was in the shopping center.

How do you differentiate yourself in the marketplace?

I tend to give nice gifts when people buy houses. I love art, so probably 20 years ago, I started buying a glass artist's work, paperweights and vases. I have been giving clients art glass since I opened my company.

Once in a while you give them a big piece of glass and then they go list with somebody else. How could they list with that person? I felt bad for a minute, and then I realized I sold them a house. They deserved something nice, because it made me feel good to give it. The part of the job I love the best is making people happy, finding their dream home, working out their problems, whether it's a divorce or a new marriage or they got new kids so they have to have a bigger house. Or, they're retiring and they now can enjoy themselves and play golf all the time. My people keep moving around. Some of my people are getting a really nice collection of glass.

You have to be patient with people, which is one of my best attributes. A lot of people who know me say they don't know how I can put up with what I do sometimes. I'm so patient with people, and I take a lot of time, because I care about my clients and what's best for them, rather than what's best for me. I'll sit down with them and say, "You could list with that person, and they might save you a little money on the listing, and you might end up selling your house. But you really should look at how much I've done, what I do in the business here, and the type of advertising I do. You're going to get more money for your house, you're going to sell it faster, and typically, you're going to be happier." You have to look at it as business. So, do I lose one or two? Yeah. Do I get one or two back? Absolutely. Then when the market's really good, will those agents who do one or two deals a year get some of those people from you? Sure.

People who were doing one or two deals a year were getting some of these listings because they had kids, or because they played golf, or because they went to church. That's where I've lost a little bit of the market, and I can't do a thing about it. It's just impossible.

I'm finally to the point, probably last year, when I'm finally okay with losing a deal. In the developer's office where we were selling land, there were 14 agents. If you went to the bathroom, you might lose a client. It was just awful. The competitiveness in the office and some of the backstabbing during those 15 years made you really watch your back and try not to be gone at all. That's perhaps part of the reason why I started to be even more competitive than I always was naturally, overachiever that I already was. It's like I don't want to lose that person. Gosh, I don't want to be gone. I was in the office, because I didn't want somebody else taking my clients. Unfortunately, there were a few underhanded people in the office who were let go eventually, but I had to deal with them for a while.

Do you do any type of quarterly or monthly mailings?

I did do probably quarterly mailings. I stopped that when they stopped the magazine in Rancho Murieta. When I do something, I do it perhaps a little more expensively than everybody else. I do a top-of-the-line color, I have it all set perfectly, and I make sure that it looks better, so the integrity and high-end quality comes out through the mailing. I started to get enough business. Then I bought out the Century 21, and I now do one mailing a year. I do a Christmas calendar, and then at Christmas I also give my clients, pretty much everybody that I've ever sold to, a Christmas ornament by the same artist. It's fairly pricey.

How much of your business is based on listings versus buyers?

My gut feeling is that I'm always about half-and-half. I really don't believe in doing just listings, especially in Rancho Murieta, because it's such a small community. I know a lot of agents do that; a lot of big agents just do listings. Then they have other people who turn over for buyers. You really can't know your market unless you're showing it on a regular basis, because you're getting that feedback. It's one thing that you call the agent, "What did the client say about my house, my listing?" They're not necessarily going to tell you the truth. They may not even call you back. They may not even be interested in telling you what's going on anyhow. They may be too busy, or they just don't care.

But if you're there with the client, and the client says, "Oh, my gosh, what were they thinking about, having this much furniture in that room? What were they thinking about this color? It shows so horribly. They have too many pictures on the wall. Who decorated this house?" You really get a true sense of what the value of the house is, what the problems are, and what you can do with them. If you're not showing your listings, you're hurting yourself. You're losing some of your market and some control.

For me, it's one thing to give clients to my brother and sister-in-law and for them to have clients; but, at least if I have some clients of my own and I'm showing my listings, I can speak with more authority to the sellers, when I'm changing the price or I'm having trouble selling it, or when it sells and we get an offer. I can negotiate a lot better on the buyer's behalf because I've heard more than one buyer looking at it. I've heard what they're saying and what they feel. A lot of my business, because I am a heart-based person, has to do with creating joy from my life and also creating joy for the buyer and seller. A lot of my deals have to do with what is the right thing to do, what's going to work out for everybody. I really feel I'm more a mediator than a salesman when I start negotiating. I probably give up more commission because I double-end more deals, but I put the deals together and get everybody happy. I make sure the repairs are done, and then I go on to the next deal. Long-term, I may have a little less commission on this or that deal. But I'm making more money in the long run, and I'm keeping more people happy. Eventually, when they're happy, they'll come back.

People come in to look at the new glass I have in my office. I love it. I have it at my house. I have it in one of my advertisements, because it is a signature thing that I do. It's a big local magazine, *Women in Business*. I do a whole page, instead of a little teensy square picture, and spend $5,000 instead of $400 and do a bigger splash. I've been in the Sacramento magazine for a long time, and I'm its very first picture.

I received the nicest compliment. One of my bigger houses I sold, probably $800,000, I had given the client about a $500 piece of glass. She came in and said, "Karen, I have to tell you, I was in Monterey, and I saw some more Tim Laser's glass, and you won't believe it, but a piece almost like mine was $2,000."

It's important for me to be in the office. I don't hide in a little cubicle. I'm available so people can just come in and say hello. It was 9:00 the other night, and a woman came in after exercising in the shopping center, knocked on the door, and said, "I've never met you but you sold to so-and-so, and we're thinking of maybe moving. We live on this street, and we want this and we want that." Now, I'm working with her. She might have gone somewhere else or she might have called me on the phone, but I was available and I was there, so people could see that I was working. People will stop in. Of course, I have the other clientele who stop by and say, "You're working too hard. You need to go home."

I have a new boyfriend who is a golfer. Finally, I'm getting out to golf a little bit. But it's at night, 6:30, 7:00 at night because it's summer. I'm on the putting green, and there are only three people on the putting green, my boyfriend, me, and one other person, and he comes over and asks me how much the townhouses are selling for. It doesn't matter where you are; you are "on" in a community where they know you. I love it. He actually picked up information for his brother, who might be looking for a piece of property. I don't go out to golf to pick up clients. But, you know, you don't go to the grocery story to pick up clients. But it happens anywhere you are.

People are always looking at you, judging you.

Absolutely. I had been trying to walk more. I have gotten some balance in my life by walking, hiking. We have 22 miles of trails out here and a little beach by the river. It's fantastic. I can usually go out and see no one, absolutely no one. But, lo and behold, I went by the river. I had no makeup. I had my hair pulled back. I'm in these horrible shorts. I'm thinking I don't want to see anybody. From this umbrella, where she's sitting in the sun, getting a suntan on the river, she says, "Karen Hoberg, is that you?" I said, "Don't tell anybody you saw me. I don't want anybody to know I look like this," because at that moment it was embarrassing to not be at my best. It doesn't matter where you are.
I have to tell you a quick, funny story.

Because I am in the Sacramento magazines and I have my little environment here in Rancho Murieta, I'm a celebrity here. The school really needed money, and nobody was stepping up. So I felt moved to give them $10,000. I walked in to this function and everybody was applauding. Oh, my God, this is just over the top for me. People don't usually do that to me. People have stopped me now and said thank you, and that's really fantastic. People I don't know and people I haven't worked with stop me.

For me, it's never one particular advertisement. That's where it's really, really hard to say, "Okay, should I spend $4,000 on the *Sacramento Bee* this month or should I cut back and do it here or do it there." You can't say all the people are coming from the *Sacramento Bee*. Sometimes you have to go with a gut feeling, which, in my business, has been working for me.

In the long term, I've been very lucky because I have a great family that's been very supportive. I'm in a wonderful, beautiful community. I've been blessed with an absolutely incredible memory. People will come up to me at a party and ask, "What's my house worth now, Karen?" I've been in almost every house in Rancho Murieta, and I've sold most of them once or twice, and as long as I know which lot number or what street they are, with mental focus, my mind visually goes back to that house. I could walk through a house and describe the house to somebody, even if I sold it 20 years ago. I don't know why, but I even dream about houses. You have to love the people. You have to love selling. Part of it is extending yourself and caring about people.

I really want to do the best for them. Sure, I have a listing over here that I'd like to sell, because I'll get more money. Then I have a house down the street that's the same price listed by someone else. I'm not going to force the people, push the people, or even direct the people into the other house that's my listing just because it's my listing. I honestly sell what's best for them.

I've had clients say, "It's refreshing. You care for what I want." Then they say, "Gee, we're really sorry, Karen. We don't want your listing." I say, "I'm okay with that. I'll sell my listing to someone else. I want to find what's best for you. I mean it." It's probably because of my dad being military and just the type of man he is, doing what you say you're going to do, having the integrity.

Recently, an agent called me and said, "You have a deal. My seller's accepted it. He can't sign it until tomorrow." I called my buyer and said, "We have a deal." The next morning, I didn't get the paperwork. I thought I'd give him another hour. Called him back. Oh, well, somebody else came in with more money and we sold it to them. I was appalled at that agent. I could not sleep if I did business like that. I got mad. I get madder than my clients do sometimes. That was a big thing. It was so unfair. But you know what? I'm a firm believer in karma. I'm a firm believer in what's right eventually prevailing. There has to be a reason my client didn't get that piece of property. I have to find him something better. It was so hard to see people doing business, really, the way that it shouldn't be done.

How do you keep yourself motivated?

I get two or three massages a week. I put myself under a lot of pressure just because of the type of person I am. I'm a perfectionist. I care about what's going on. I want what's right to happen. I've been very fortunate to find massage therapists who will see me in the evenings, very late. Sometimes I don't even start a massage until 10:00 at night. I do some meditation. I do take two weeks off at Christmas, my birthday. So I'm afraid I'm not as good as I should be about taking personal time and personal vacations.

Part of the way I stay motivated is actually seeing people find their happiness, their home, and a wonderful community to live in. That brings me the joy, besides accomplishing the deal. It's not as much about the money as accomplishing putting the deals together, making their dreams come true. I don't even know how much money I made last year. Some people who are looking at it as a moneymaking process are missing that the fantastic part of real estate is that it's a people business. It can be a tremendous amount of fun if you really love it. I love looking at houses.

I go on a couple of health breaks during the year. I have a natural healer. I've very conscious about my health. That really has been a very big thing in my life. I've been seeing this natural homeopath for 17 years. I go to her in Utah. I take my dad. I take my mom. I take my brother. We go on a two-day trip. Then I come back and I'm rejuvenated. That's something I do for myself that I probably should do more of.

I love to travel. This year I did a couple of day trips roughly every three months. There is a balance, and I haven't quite found it yet.

When did you really feel like you were in the big-time?

I started selling land in '78, and so '85 was probably that big deal where I sold 30 lots on the lake to one builder. Everybody was very impressed that I had a developer/builder who was going to come out and build out these 30 lots.

Selling that very first house that I told you about was a really big deal in 1979. I was inventing the deal. I enjoy finding deals that no one else could have found. That's a great joy for me. That motivates me a lot. How can I find this person a house? We don't have a house for this person. I don't know where I'm going to get this house, but will think about it. I'm going to dream about finding a house for this person.

I get that involved with my people, finding a house that wasn't for sale, getting the builder/seller to sell it, and then having the buyer be able to get in to a home without anybody else knowing about it. This is very exciting for me.

How much counseling/advice do you give your clients?

Of course, they tell us, as far as liability, not to give any advice. The Department of Real Estate and the Realtors say don't give any advice on taxes. Don't give any advice on investments. Don't give any advice on what they should do and what they shouldn't do. But, usually what I will help clients with is explaining what I have perhaps done in my investments if they're looking at investments. I have quite a few rental investment properties. I will give them more of an example, rather than saying you should do this or you should do that. I feel it's important for the client to make his or her own decision.

I will give them advice, absolutely, on location, value, how it's going to increase. I've seen the market go down. I've seen the market go up. I've seen it go soft, go strong, and depending on the market, that's what's going to drive some of the decisions on the pricing—if it's a seller's market or a buyer's market, and who's going to get the best deal. I will steer them in what I honestly feel is the best thing for them to do.

I had a client the other day who wanted to buy something, and I advised him against it. They were so on the edge of what they could afford. I said, "Why don't you wait? Why don't you get in to a rental?" Sure, I could have sold them a house if I was pushy, but it would have been the wrong thing for them to do.

You don't really want to say you're steering too much. I give them the options. "This is what I think is the best thing to do. This is your other option."

I had a client last night who I had to do that for. They were looking at two different properties. One was a fixer-upper and one was already fixed. I knew what type of people they were and what they'd been used to doing, which is always buying new houses. They were not the type of people who are going to be happy going in to a fixer-upper. Sometimes it's knowing: your client, what they have lived through, what they bought before, what their likes and dislikes are, and what their goals are. Some of them are in a position where they're trying to retire in this area. You should advise them as to what's, in the long run, going to make them the happiest and be the easiest for them.

It's a learned process in the fact that I sit and I'm patient and I talk to people and spend the time that the people need to make them feel comfortable. I find out enough about them so that I can give them a little direction. Sometimes people rush. Let's go out and look at these ten houses. Okay, which one do you want to buy? You don't get to know your client. You don't get to know what their true likes are, what their true desires are.

Watch out when you have a husband and a wife who don't agree. It makes your life more difficult. It makes you spend more time with them and find out what the common ground is. I think people don't spend enough time.

How do you negotiate the best deal for your client?

Knowing my buyer and seller really well and what their goals are and what's really important to them makes it a lot easier for me to negotiate. I usually know my buyer and my seller because I do a lot of double-ended deals. I can explain my buyer's position, how my buyer feels about the house, and how much they love it. They're going to keep this, they want to buy this piece of furniture, or they're going to put their kids' play set out in the backyard, because they're in love with it. It does not become money. It becomes them selling their dream home to another nice family. It becomes a personality of the buyer and sometimes a personality of the seller. For me, making it personal works. I'm connected to this buyer, so I have to show that same connection in what's really important to the seller. Making it more personal helps tremendously.

Sometimes it's about the money. I found that, for a lot of agents, it's just business. That's fine, if they can do their job like that. For me, it's more than business. It's finding this person a home, caring about this person and making the seller care, too. In the case of negotiating, sometimes you have to tell the buyer that this is what the seller's after. It's very hard for them to leave. They have to move close to their parents or closer to their kids. They're not here to make money. They're here to find the right person to love their house. For me and for the buyers, too, that makes a big difference.

What's the motivation? You have to get down to the bottom line. The three of us, or four of us, or six of us, however many you have involved, all have to work this out together. I negotiate so well because I mediate it, and then I make the people care about each other. It's not just paper. It's what has helped me do as much business as I do.

I can give you a quick example, the deal I just finished. I had a listing for eight months for $1,290,000—top of my market—the most expensive house that will ever sell in Rancho Murieta, at least for a long time. I've been advertising it. I've been doing a good job. We've had a couple of verbal offers, which really don't amount to anything. We had one written offer that was too low. In getting this one written offer, I found out what the bottom, bottom line was for this seller, what was really important in what they were doing.

Finally, this buyer came in and was willing to pay $1,200,000. I said, "I'm happy to write the offer up for you, but they're not going to take it. I'll do whatever you want, but that's not the number." They couldn't believe it. The seller needs a certain amount of money, or they're not going to sell. In this case, I have the buyer and the seller, and I was able to give a little advice to the buyer that, the last time a buyer wrote an offer, he didn't sell to the seller, and it made the seller mad.

My important take on this was that I wanted to make the seller happy. Yes, I want to sell their house. But I don't want this buyer, who looks like they could put this deal together, to make my seller mad again. Finally, after a couple of more weeks, and showing it to them one more time, the buyer said, "Okay, we're willing to write the offer. We're willing to pay $1,250,000." I knew at that moment that wasn't the number, but it was really close. I thought that we needed to write it up, which I did and took it to my seller, thinking my seller was going to be absolutely elated. I walked in the door, and they said, "You know, after 8½ months of trying to sell our house, this is the least likely we are to take a deal tonight, because we've been looking, and we can't find anything we can buy."

My seller said, "If we don't find a house, we're not going to sell this house. That was, absolutely, not part of our deal when we listed the house eight months ago." I was completely blown away. I decided to put the offer on hold. I said, "Let's talk about what you need." That's what really works well for me. What does the person I'm with at that moment need? I didn't even look at the offer with them. I called my buyer and told them that night that I needed a few more days. They said okay. I didn't tell them why because I figured I didn't want to get them stressed that they weren't going to get a house.

I took a deep breath, sat down, and focused on what was important to them and why they were going through this fear, because that's what it was. A lot of this stuff I do is psychology. I'm a therapist and an adviser. After talking to them for a couple of hours, I figured out what would work for them. Flexibility is very, very key.

We looked and we looked and couldn't find anything. That night I called my buyer. I told him exactly what the problem was. I said, "Remember when you weren't sure what you wanted to do? You weren't sure if you wanted to buy this house, and you kept going back and forth to other areas and other houses?" I put it in the perspective so they could understand it.

Once they understood it, they said, "Alright, we'll give them a few more days."

I said, "I appreciate it a lot. By the way, I need to show them your house. It was on the market last year. I know you took it off the market. I know your plan is to stay in this house and remodel the new one you're buying for six months. I think the person who's selling that house would like your house. Is there any chance you could possibly consider letting me show your house?" Again, I have to really be a little pushy, but nice, and honest.

They let us show it while they were having a birthday dinner party, that night, because it was the only time the wife could look. That's the house they're buying. They bought each other's houses. I had to then convince the buyer that the only way they could get this other house, which is true, would be for this seller to buy their house, and by the way, for them to move in to a rental, and move all their furniture.

What have been some of your biggest challenges?

Some of the biggest challenges are the disclosure laws. I hate to say it, but the attorneys have gotten so involved in California real estate that we have more legal issues then we used to and more disclosures. Now, I'm mediating repairs on houses that are 20 years old, and half the time I'm repairing houses for sellers/buyers. That's been a big pain in the neck.

What training should agents get?

When I started, a couple of the older brokers in the office took me under their wing and showed me how to write a contract. At the time, you usually went to a training seminar, or the big brokerage houses trained you, because when you got your real estate license, you really didn't know anything. You still don't. The real estate licenses do not prepare you for the real world. That's why you must go to some training. As you go through your life, you need to continue to train and update. Up to about five years ago, I continually went to seminars. You have to keep fresh, get fresh ideas, because you can get tired. You learn a lot from other people. You have to invest in yourself and invest in your client's life in order to make a success with this business.

CASEY MARGENAU

RE/MAX DISTINCTIVE REAL ESTATE
McLean, Virginia

#1 Gross Commission Income: RE/MAX Internationally

- Sales Volume: $136 million
- # of Units Sold: 160
- Gross Commission Income: $3.5 million
- # of Employees: 6
- www.Margenau.com
- Years in the business: 16

I'm curious, what interested you about real estate?

In the early '80s, I managed a car dealership. When I started selling automobiles, there was another guy who was the number-one salesperson in that store. I came in and became number one. He had been a real estate agent prior to that and decided to get back in to real estate because he wasn't the top dog anymore. He was successful at that time. He eventually sold me a home for $130,000. Three years later, it was worth $350,000. I sold it for a very good profit within a fairly short time. I went out to try to buy a property for $500,000.

He had always been trying to get me to come in to real estate. I thought it was a great business, but I did very well selling automobiles and felt like I had golden handcuffs, like I was tied to it and had wanted to buy a dealership and get in to that. As I got further along in the business, I realized that the small automobile dealerships were becoming a way of the past, and the mega dealerships were the ones that were doing very well. The likelihood of me being able to buy a dealership and becoming my own business and running it was probably not going to happen. In 1989, I decided that maybe I should go in to real estate. At least you have your own business there.

When you're in sales management, you're training salespeople on a day-to-day basis, so I trained and taught salespeople how to sell. That was my job. When I started looking around at real estate, I felt like the sales ability and skills of the salespeople out there were very poor. Although they lived in nice homes and drove Jaguars and Mercedes, I didn't feel like I had a lot of competition.

Since then, our industry has made leaps and bounds. We have a lot of good salespeople in the business, but, still, there are a lot of poor ones as well. I knew that I could go in to that business and compete. I was the number-one agent with our board of Realtors in my second full year in the business. That showed it could be done, that you could actually go in and do well right from the beginning, with a little sales ability.

I don't think there are any secrets to this business. There is a lot of information out about the real estate business if you want to learn it, and there are a million different ways of doing things in real estate. They all can work, whatever way you try, whatever works for you. The biggest problem is that most people have a day during which they have nothing to do, and think that's a good day to play golf, or go do something else.

The self-discipline of being able to get up every morning and figure out what work to do that day is the hardest and most difficult thing for most people to do. Many of the people in real estate are good at one thing and not good at everything. You need to build on your skills.

Most people aren't disciplined enough to get up and figure out what to do with their day?

And have a direction. I see so many people in the real estate business who get up in the morning and don't know what to do, and they spin their wheels and do things that don't sell the next home.

Also, you have to have integrity. If you really want to be successful for the long run, you have to have integrity. You have to look out for your clients' best interests before your own. I hear horror stories when buyers or sellers want me to work with and help them, but in the past, they've been burned by a real estate agent who is, most of the time, looking for his or her commission dollar, not the best interest of the client. If you're a true salesperson, you understand the meaning of that. Salespeople aren't out there trying to sell others what they want them to buy. A real salesperson helps people get what they want. Then it's a win/win situation. If you help somebody and look out for his or her interest, the money will take care of itself. It will come. I've built my business on that integrity and have looked out for my clients' best interests. That also means that you have to look out for the other real estate agent, because he or she is a customer as well, even though we don't think of it that way.

Other real estate agents are your customers when you're putting property on the market. When you keep that as your forefront and then are a smart businessperson, spending 80 percent of your time doing the things that make money for you, being in front of a buyer or a seller, you're going to be successful. Don't take too big of a step at one time, have realistic goals, and believe in what you can do.

I remember trying to break that million-dollar mark in commissions. It was very, very difficult to break, to get over that hurdle. It had nothing to do with making it. It had everything to do with believing that you could make it.

It's easy to say, "I believe I'm worth this much," but it's a whole other thing to really believe that it's there and that you can do and it's realistic. Successful people are good business people. They have the ability to wear a lot of hats and the necessary sales skills, and they get up every morning to do the job, whatever that job may be. There are no secrets and everything works. If you're good at going after For Sale By Owners, then you should be spending your time doing that. If you're good at going after expired listings, then you should be spending your time doing that. If you're good at working with new homebuilders or buyers or sellers, you should play to your strengths and work in those areas and build on those skills.

The other thing is, know your product. We have billions of dollars worth of inventory. We're the only industry in which that entire inventory is free to us. We have no floor plan, no carrying cost. The only expenses we have are the marketing and advertising for our listings and our telephones and automobiles. It's a very low-expense business. Number one: We can look out for the client's best interest because we don't own any of the stuff that's out there. Number two: We have the opportunity to sell all the property that's out there.

How does somebody determine what he or she is going to be best at?

They will have to figure that out themselves. They have to start when they're brand new, when they don't know anything. Even if you've been in the business for a year or two, you start to think you get it. After you've been in it for seven or eight years, you know you were not very bright when you started. When you begin, you have to work with people who know less than you, and the reality is that that's the lower-price range. If you go out and decide that you want to be a luxury home specialist, and you're going to sell only million-dollar homes, you're probably going to have a very hard time at it. You will compete against people like me who not only know what they're doing, but have the background and the statistics behind them. If you go to the hundred thousand dollar condo, I don't have any interest in that business, especially driving them around in my car.

Working with buyers is a very important first step. It costs less money to work with a buyer than it does to work with a seller. This would be the opposite information from what you'll get from most people. It is easier to start working with buyers, to build up a knowledge base of the market, to understand the transaction, and to understand what can happen, what can go right, what can go wrong, and where to do it, to cut your teeth, as they say, and to get experience on a lower price range person. Most of the time, it's their first home. They're first-home buyers, and they don't know as much, and ignorance is bliss when it comes to making a mistake.

How do you suggest people prioritize their time?

When I started, I had plenty of time. Today, I don't have plenty of time. I have enough time, but I don't have plenty of it. I don't waste any of it. Being a good time manager is one of the big differences between those who are at the tippy-top, and those who are just in the middle. When you start, you have enthusiasm and time.

What are the two things you need? If you find somebody who wants to buy something, you have all the time in the world to find a home for him or her. If you do the legwork and run around and find a house that matches their needs, wants, and ability to pay, which is basic sales training skills, you're going to earn the commission that you get, because you've done that. You also have to communicate with the person so they understand and appreciate what you're doing for them. You have the ability to make them a promise, and deliver on that promise, because you'll have the time to spend to find a property for them, because that's what they'll do, without any guarantee that they'll make a deal with you. That gives you the advantage over other real estate agents, because a lot of real estate agents are lazy and want the customer to find the property and then just have them write a contract.

They wonder why the fees in this industry are being cut right now, and the value of a real estate agent is going down as far as the fee he or she is being paid. This is because too many people are too lazy to do the job and do it right. They're trying to find the easy way out. When you do that, you're not worth as much.

Following up seems to be an issue.

There are two sides to that coin. I do understand it, being in the business. When I first came in and was an outsider looking in, I'd go to an open house, and I'd have either one or two types of salespeople hit me. The guy who hits me so hard, with such high pressure and bothered me, or he could care less what I was doing and wouldn't even call back or follow up. There is a possibility that the guy who doesn't call you back has enough business and doesn't need any more business right now.

I know that I can turn my business on or off when I want, just by asking the right questions when I'm talking to somebody. If I need more buyers, all I need to do is talk to them differently. I can answer somebody's question, be respectful to them, do it professionally and with integrity, and get them off the phone and not deal with them or try to do business with them, or I can turn it around and ask people for the business when I want more business. Just because I don't ask for the business on every deal doesn't necessary mean that I'm not doing a good job, because I am. I won't push for somebody who's in a price range that's below what I want.

At the beginning, when you're brand new, you need every bit of business you can get. You need to follow through and ask the right questions to everybody, whether they want to do business with you. You need to answer their questions. You don't earn the right to ask somebody to do business with you until you've done something for him or her.

I make a conscious decision whether this is somebody I want to work with or not, and I handle him or her accordingly, if they're in a price range I want. I don't work with as many buyers, and I don't work with buyers in a low-price range, unless I know them. If they're a referral to me, a past client, or a past client's kids, that type of thing, I'll work with them. But if they're looking for a $200,000 home, and I don't know them or I have no relationship to them, I'm not going to try to work with them.

What is your conversation like when you have the client you want?

Obviously, that's going to depend, and it's a flowing thing. I don't use scripts. I have the ability to talk to people and figure out what they want. In any type of sale, you have to figure out the person's needs, wants, and ability to pay. But you don't have the ability to find out personal financial information from somebody with whom you haven't built up a rapport or a trust. When you're working with somebody, at the beginning they might call you on a property, and you might talk to them about what they're looking for, finding out what they've looked at and what their price range is. When you can rattle off every house on the market that's in that price range, and talk to them about it, have seen the inside and know what it is, and know what's going on, then the person on the other end of the telephone will understand that you're a professional and know what you're talking about. Then you have value to them. So many buyers are looking in a focused price range or a focused area. They have the information, and they're out hunting for three months, six months, a year, or two years. A lot of times, they know the market better than some of the real estate agents they talk to.

How do you understand what the person really wants?

You can't short step, and you have to meet with them. You have to be face-to-face with them, to take them out with you and look at property. Through that process, you will find out what they want and what they'll accept, and you have to know the market well enough to be able to say, "We're not finding anything in this price range. We're going to need to change the parameters, either the areas you're looking at, or the price range, if you're going to get what you want." It is a natural progression.

I often compare sales to that game when we were kids, a long, long time ago, called "mouse trap." In that game, you have to line everything up right, and if you do, the ball drops and goes through its little maze and ends where it's supposed to. If you have anything off a little bit, the ball goes off the track. The sale, the closing, the contract, is a natural progression of the sales process. If you start with A, and do B, C, D, E, F, and G, you'll get to Z, no matter what. Sometimes the buyer doesn't understand the market, and he or she makes a low offer in a hot market and doesn't get the property. That's a necessary step of the process, to get him or her to make a realistic offer. Instead, a lot of real estate agents get frustrated when they want to make a low offer, or not make a decision, and lose a property. But sometimes people have to get educated by doing that. There are a million different things like that. As long as you take each person from A, and go in order, and you go through the sales process, you'll get to the end. But if you get frustrated or irritated along the way, you derail the process.

The biggest mistake people make is abandoning the client, not calling or otherwise communicating with him or her. That's where they usually lose them. Or they don't know the market, their product, or the contract. So many people are out there practicing real estate without a 100 percent grasp of what they're doing. Some have a great understanding, but a lot of them don't. That is where, if you know your stuff, you can beat your competition, take advantage of those opportunities, and be of value. If you're of value, people don't mind if you get paid. When I'm talking to a buyer who's buying a million-dollar property and he doesn't know what real estate agent he's going to pick, I'm going to tell him, "That agent will get paid $30,000 to work for you—in our area, that's pretty much the norm—and if he or she will get paid that, they better earn it and be worth it. Is the person you're thinking about using worth that much and does he or she have enough experience and knowledge to give you your money's worth? Even though you're not paying it, the seller is. Are you going to get your money's worth?"

If you do a good job with people, they don't have a problem with you making a lot of money, if you know your market, have something to say that's worthwhile and valuable, and really have a clear understanding. Agents get paid a lot these days because homes are expensive. The reality is that you make money in real estate when you buy, not when you sell. If you buy right, you do well. If you don't, it doesn't go up as much.

I recently had a lady who said, "You sold these people this house for $500,000, and now sold it for a $1.15 million. How come I bought my house at the same time for the same price and my house is only worth $890,000?"

I said, "It's because you bought it wrong. I didn't sell any of those homes in that neighborhood, when they were originally for sale, because they were overpriced compared to what you could buy." People come back to me because I make sure they make their investment a good one.

How were you able to become number one, in two years, at one of the worst times in the market?

Several reasons. I'm doing what I'm saying. People trust me because they know that I'll treat them right. I would always find the deals. There are diamonds, good values in the marketplace, and I would always find those values. I bring them to people. In those days, the banks had a lot of inventory, and that's where the deals were. I became the real estate agent for the banks. Or, the builders came in and started building new homes on lots that had been foreclosed on, so they got good deals. The new homes were good values.

I've been in this business for fifteen years; I work seven days a week. I'm on usually from nine o'clock in the morning, no matter what day of the week it is. On weekends, I'm usually done by 5:00; during the week, it's probably about 7:00, and it used to be 9:00. I take appointments at 7:00 at night all the time. I worked the other evening until 11:00; it depends. I do what's necessary to get the job done and manage my time effectively. When I want to not work, I schedule that also.

I have a different game plan. I want my work to be like an athlete's: work hard, get paid a lot of money, and then retire and not work my whole life.

At what point did you decide to bring staff on, and what roles do they play?

I hired my first administrative assistant after I had been in the business for less than 30 days. In 1989, nobody had administrative assistants. But I had been an executive and ran an automobile dealership, and I had an administrative secretary. I immediately realized it was stupidity. If I'm going to be out in my car all day driving around, I need somebody in the office to help me with paperwork and the other things that are non-income producing, but time hogs that you have to do. I hired one person. At that time, she was my closing coordinator, listing coordinator, marketing person, and administrative assistant. Now, I have one person who does just marketing, one person who's my listing coordinator, one person who's my closing coordinator, a field coordinator, and my manager who is my big administrative assistant, the one who runs everything.

You don't have any buyer's specialists?

We are getting ready to start. I did that in 1990, growing up a staff of 12 buyer's agents. I hated managing the people. I got away from selling real estate, and I had less money in my pocket. So I moved away from having buyer's agents. One of the reasons I've done so well is that everything is taken care of except for the sales; that's the part I do.

If you spend 80 percent of your time getting along well with people, negotiating, dealing with the challenges that come up during the contract process, and getting the best deal for your clients, you're going to make money.

What's your spread between buyer/seller?

Fifty/fifty.

What do you do to convince clients to work with you?

It's like anything else. If you want an attorney to handle a specific case, you find one who has handled a thousand of those same situations, rather than an attorney who might be decent but doesn't do that. Then they have to learn on your dime.

Having somebody who's an expert saves you money and time. I can take somebody who's been looking for six months or a year for a property and narrow down what he or she wants and find a property, only meeting a couple of times. Obviously, there has to be a property available. But for the most part, I can find 10 very good properties that will match his or her parameters, very easily and quickly, and streamline the process. I am a human GPS. My clients have a lot of confidence because I know where I'm going. I show them pluses and minuses and know how to take them through the process so they feel confident about what they're doing and are able to make a decision.

How much marketing do you do?

I do a lot of advertising and marketing. Every year or two, I do some type of personal marketing campaign. I did more of it at the beginning of my business than I do now. I meet enough buyers and sellers through doing business, like I'll meet somebody here who talks to me about this property, and he or she has that property to sell and wants to buy a property like this. I wind up doing the transaction and becoming the real estate agent to do everything that he or she is going to do.

I don't spend my time advertising and marketing for me. I do spend an awful lot of money selling property through marketing and advertising my properties. That makes the phone ring and gives me the opportunity to talk to people who are in the business of buying or selling or both. Because I have a lot of advertising out there, other people will see that and say, "Hey, this guy does a lot of advertising and marketing for his properties. I'll want him to sell my house as well." I help probably 75 percent of the people I work with sell their home and buy another home. That's partly because of the price range I deal with, and they are not first-time homebuyers.

Are there times when you don't want to take a client?

In fact, I had a guy who wanted to buy a $10 million property. I didn't want to deal with him. I could tell that he was not the kind of person who I wanted to try to deal with. If they're not going to be loyal to me, I don't want them. I don't spend a weekend away from my family showing somebody homes and then have them go out and buy something else. I really care about the time I take away from my family, or from somebody else who would be loyal to me.

What type of marketing do you do?

I have a marketing plan: where we spend our money, and what we do. I advertise in the local newspaper and the big papers: the *Washington Post* and the *Washington Times*. I advertise in the little books you get, and then there are other magazines, luxury home-type magazines on a local, national, and international basis that I advertise in, consistently. That's why they come to me. I'll spend the money. I did it even when I was at the beginning, because you have to make the phone ring. If the phone doesn't ring, you're out of business.

What about doing business only by referral?

If you're willing to take that little bit of business, because only a certain percentage of people are going to do business with you on a referral basis. If that's enough for you to be happy, then by all means, that's a very good way of doing business. In the real world, however, if you want to do big-dollar business, that's not going to be enough.

Are you still in a scarcity market?

It's a good, solid market. It's not so frantic that houses are not on the market at all. There is inventory. Homes are selling quickly if they're priced low. They're doing okay if they're priced right. If they're priced too high, they don't sell.

What's your average market time?

Right now, we're at 60 to 90 days on the market in the higher-priced bracket. There are parts of the market where, as you go up in the price range, it's 200 days on the market. As you go down, it's three minutes, three days, whatever.

You get first access to these deals in the marketplace.

You can't buy every deal, and if you buy all the deals, you're not giving them to your customers. If you're not giving them to your customers, you're not going to have any return business. You don't just go and find good deals for you. You have to find good deals for everybody.

Have you always been with RE/MAX?

Yes. As cocky as I was, this was how it worked. I went in and said, "I want to work with a high-end company because I want to get in the high-end business." I interviewed with some of the bigger firms around here, and they wanted to split the commission 50/50. I said, "Wait a second. You want 50 percent of the money I earn? No. I don't think that's a good idea. I don't like that."

I accidentally went to this boutique broker, who asked me to stay for their sales meeting. Being a salesperson, trainer, and sales manager, I sat there and listened to this joker. Then we drove around with these agents and looked at the menus to decide which houses they were going to tour, went to these multi-million dollar homes, and they're never going to sell them anyway. They're looking for the best lunches because they needed the free lunch. It was a waste of time.

I interviewed with this other small company, and they were 100 percent concepts. They kept saying, "We're 100 percent concept, just like RE/MAX," and so on, but it was chinchy, and everything about them did not have the image that I wanted. Then I interviewed with RE/MAX. I said, "This is what I want." Then I interviewed a bunch of different RE/MAX companies until I found the one I wanted. I could afford to pay the fee monthly. I knew I was going to do well. I knew I was going to make sales and wasn't concerned about making money. I wasn't concerned about paying my way, paying all the different fees to RE/MAX that you had to whether you sell one house or 100 houses.

You pay RE/MAX a flat monthly fee?

Yes. Then you're your own business. That means you pay for all of your own advertising, all of your marketing, every single copy that you make.

You're paying RE/MAX to use its name? What else is it providing you?

That's about it. National advertising. Name awareness. There is camaraderie among real estate agents who are all within the same company. That's the "rah-rah" factor, as you say, which is all good. The reality is that RE/MAX agents have a reputation of being some of the best. The reason being that not very many people are going to pay $3,000 a month to be part of an organization unless they're making enough commission so the $3,000 a month that they're paying is better than the 50/50 split.

Did you have a first big deal where you said, "Okay, I have this down"?

When I got started, I didn't know where I wanted to go. I didn't know if I wanted to go commercial, industrial, residential, whatever. I chose to go into residential because at that time there was less competition in residential. In the commercial and industrial business there were a lot of good people. I did a little bit of everything, but I also talked to people doing commercial real estate. They worked two-three years on a major, mega deal—it would blow up, and they'd spent all that time and didn't make anything. I liked the residential business because I can do a ton of medium-sized or smaller deals in their scheme of the world. If something blows up, at least your income doesn't.

One of the biggest problems with real estate agents is that they work on a deal, it's made, and then they work on getting it closed. Then they have no business. They have to go out and find some business. Their income goes up and down because they're working to get the business, but once they get it, they're working on trying to make it happen and trying to get it settled. That's the other reason why you should have administrative help in this business, so that you have somebody who's working on those things.

In '89, I met a real estate agent who had 30-36 listings at the time. He was making $20,000 a year. He had all these listings. What is wrong with your business? I helped him analyze it. He was spending all his time on everything but selling his property because he was just trying to maintain all these properties. I never get too many properties at one time. That's why I don't necessarily go after and try to get every single listing in the world. I want them priced right, to be good properties, and to be the type of properties I handle so that I can focus on my core business.

Did you have a mentor or coach?

No. When I got in this business, I made a conscious decision not to. I wanted to do it differently, to run the business from a completely different set of understandings and skills. I thought the business was run in a way that was from the '50s and '60s, the way the whole industry worked, and to some degree, still does. I didn't invent anything, but most of the things I implemented at those times are the norm now.

How did you establish a brand?

You must exude confidence. Your actions and your aggressiveness can get you in the door. But, ultimately, you have to deliver. A lot of people don't. When you do, people know it and want to do business with you. There are a lot of things I don't have control over. If I want more listings, they just come. I just say I want them and they come. There are people upstairs who look out for me and make sure I get taken care of, because I take care of a lot of other people. I don't take 100 percent credit.

In the short run, you can brand anything you want. But in the long run, there's only reputation.

We use a slogan—"Experience is everything." The reality of being the number-one agent for RE/MAX internationally is very powerful because people want to align themselves with success. They know that, if you're the top person, you have something going for you. I am confident in what I know and can do, and I know that I do a better job than anybody else, given the same set of circumstances.

Have you had situations in which the clients have walked away from you?

Not buyers—except, many years ago, during the winter with snow on the ground, I was driving around showing this guy million dollar homes. He didn't call me back to go out the next weekend, after spending a couple of weekends with him. I wondered what was going on. I finally reached the guy, and found out that his cousin was a real estate agent, and he wanted to give him a break and let him make the commission. His cousin hadn't sold anything over $90,000 in his life, and he was going to trust him with a million-dollar transaction.

How do you negotiate the best deal for your clients?

There are certain things I can't talk about.

I'm paid not for the deal I make but for all the deals you don't make, all the times when you show somebody and don't buy it. I'm getting paid for that, as much as I am for the one person who comes along and buys it.

Negotiations are an art. Like the sales process, the negotiations start at the very beginning. Obviously, it depends on what side of the transaction you're on, whether you're working for the buyer or you're working for the seller. I have a good example right now: There are three houses that sold in this one neighborhood, on the same street, and they're the same model. They all sold this year, within a short time of each other. A real estate agent, who was a moron in my opinion, listed the first house. The market, at that price range, didn't sell as fast as it should have—he was impatient on it. He had the property priced at $1.15

million, which is too high for the property in its current condition. It did not have a finished basement, and a couple of other things. It was just an okay lot. He lowered the price to under $1.1 million, which was a very good price. It didn't sell, and two weeks later he lowered it to $995,000 and took $960,000. He didn't understand his market.   He only understood price. He did a disservice to his clients.

When it was under contract, the sign was still on the property. I listed the same model, on a better lot, with a finished basement and professionally decorated, for $1.25 million. In the first weekend, I sold my property, because of my negotiating skills. I had only one offer. I sold mine for almost $300,000 over the other one.

The third house—the same model and the same street was listed for $1.26 million—I'm representing the buyer in the transaction and bring them an offer, and negotiate the deal for $1.15 million. My other property's sign's still up, it hadn't settled yet, and I get a deal for my buyer $110,000 less then what I sold that property for.

What that other agent doesn't realize is that he will lose other business because of the way he handled his client. And he discredits the real estate business by not knowing his market.

How did you explain that in the negotiation?

I knew what the first one sold for, and I was the only one who knew what the second one sold for. I was in the unique position of having all the cards in my hand and coming in and giving them an offer and being able to talk to them about condition and everything else. Knowledge is power.

What knowledge did you use?

The next one had a finished basement, but I was able to use both properties as comparables. The person didn't know whether the property I had sold was at full price or not.

Negotiations are knowing what to do and how things can come apart, just as important as how much and when to grind, when not to grind, and when to make an offer. Sometimes that higher offer is better. If you come in with too low an offer, another person says no, they don't feel like they lost anything. If you give them an offer that's just a little bit below what they were expecting, it's very hard for them to turn it down, because they don't want to lose the deal.

I believe that circumstances determine what you're going to do or not do in every transaction. Let's say a guy comes in and makes us an offer. We have so much interest in the property, and it looks like we're going to get a bunch of different offers. I might treat him differently from an offer after we've had the house on the market for a while. Foremost is an understanding of what the market value is compared to what the offer is. If I get an offer that's $5,000 off, but the property is worth full price every day of the week, then I don't have to worry about losing something over some small negotiation because there will always be somebody else to buy it. On the other hand, if I have a property that's hard to sell, I don't take the luxury of being able to negotiate some of the finer points.

My homes sell at 99.7 percent of the asking price. My major competition is at around 96.3 percent of their asking price. I look at their deals and find that, most of the time, their preference would be just to make a deal, and my preference is doing the right thing by my customer. If you're a real estate agent who wants to get the deal done, and there's a deal there and you can convince your people to take it, then you can convince them to take it whether it's in their best interest or not. With $10,000 or $20,000 more, three percent of that's not very much.

If the money and the property are there, it's a lot harder to negotiate a transaction correctly and properly and not lose it, of course, because that would not be very good either. Part of the negotiation is what your client wants, but part of it is what the real estate agent wants as well, and educating your client on all the possibilities of what he or she should be doing and valuing. If clients put their trust in your hands, you have to be right by them. If you don't give advice, and you don't have an expert opinion, why should you be paid the dollars you'll be making?

Do you allow the buyer's agent to meet with the seller?

No.

Do you insist upon it if you're on the opposite end?

No, but if they give it to me, I'll take it. In this area, at least, if you're working with the buyer, you normally don't get the opportunity to meet the seller. That's just how the business is done around here.

Do you ask?

Of course.

When I started, that's how it was done. When you had a contract, you met with the seller and the other real estate agent and you did the deal. I immediately realized that that was the dumbest thing in the world on my listings. I'm one of the forefront people who started having offers faxed in to me and then I dealt with them with my client. When I started it, it was unheard-of and not understood. It was common sense to me. It didn't make sense the way the industry was run, and I checked into other ways of doing business. I believe other people felt the same way or had the same ideas at the same time. Smart people figure it out and do it that way.

The reality is that, if you had sat across from a buyer, your position of negotiation would be compromised. You're going to negotiate differently than you would when you had the opportunity to think about it and to talk about it with a competent real estate agent who understands and can educate you on all the ifs, ands, or buts. You also don't have the ability to talk to them about other potential offers, or the ability to negotiate more than one transaction at the same time. There are a lot of things like that.

What did you learn from your mistakes?

Mistakes are just part of doing business. My granddaddy always taught me that, if you make a mistake and learned from it, it paid. If you don't learn from it, you're a fool.

I tried to grow my business the way I did at the beginning. I got burned out on one thing, doing something different. It was okay. But when I look back on it, I was trailblazing into an area that had never been done before, with the buyer's agents and this whole team-concept thing. It was hard to do it at that time, before everyone else did it, and I wasted a lot of money. I try lots of things all the time to see if they work. Some work; some don't. If they don't work, they're a mistake.

I'm willing to learn and try new things all the time. Some are good; some are bad. You make mistakes on everything. Mistakes are part of life. You have to get over it and go forward. If I make a mistake, I try to make amends. I try not to make mistakes that cost somebody else money. I don't mind making a mistake that cost me money. It's really bad if you make a mistake that costs somebody else money.

Hiring people was where I made my biggest mistakes. I've had people steal money, all kinds of things like that. If I thought about it, I'm positive I could find some advertising and marketing mistakes that I've made. I made a mistake today, writing something. I read it and spell corrected it. I saw that it was corrected to the wrong word. I meant to go back and change it. They have a letter that says "weather" like the temperature outside, instead of "whether or not." I made a mistake. Big deal.

I get English teachers who send me stuff back. We're getting it back in the mail with circles and grammar, and some people love to find those mistakes and bust your chops over them. One of my weaknesses is English. A spelling error in a brochure is not going to make or break the deal. The house has to sell itself. It's good to have spelling correct, but it's not going to make a difference in selling it or not. They're going to buy it based on the house, not based on if you have a word mistyped in your brochure, or a grammar mistake, which is usually the case.

Have you ever had a client get upset about that?

Of course. I talk to them. I get it straight. We get it fixed. People get bent out of shape on a million things. Buying a home is not a logical decision: It's an emotional decision. Anytime you're selling or buying something, and it's heavily emotional, things are going to bother you that don't have any meaning or anything. Our job is to make those concerns important to us and handle them, calmly.

How do you deal with the changes in the marketplace?

Just change with them. I don't care what the market does. I'm an individual salesperson. Whatever the market conditions, you just deal with them. One of my most important quotes is, "An individual can always outperform the market."

How have you kept up with your education?

I pick and choose what I like and don't like. I talk with other people who are earning and investing, and doing the same type of things.

Make sure that you understand the market. The biggest problem that everybody seems to have is that they don't really have a thorough understanding of the market, where it's going, what's happening with it, and what is and isn't a good value.

What do you do to work *on* the business instead of *in* the business?

We're changing constantly and hearing new things, to get new ideas, to do different things, and to see what other people do. I meet with my staff twice a week, and we figure out directions on what we're doing on a weekly basis, not just doing the business every day. It's something that I do naturally, especially on the down times of the business. During the doldrums of summer, we work on business. In the middle of winter, we work on business, so that we're not trying to work on business in the middle of the spring or fall markets. The opportunities present themselves. Although that is one of the problems of this business, you do get caught up in the doing, not always having the time, and working on the business goes to the back burner.

Any last words of wisdom you'd like to share?

There are no "tricks" to real estate. It is working diligently, consistently doing a good job for people, and working on understanding the marketplace: hard work. In the real estate business, you have every job there is. So many facets and different things happen that you really have to be a top person. I don't say talented, but you have to be multifaceted, and you have to be able to do many things at the same time. You must juggle and understand them. You're wearing a lot of hats all the time. It's not for everybody because the business is very, very difficult. There are so many different parts to it. It's not as easy as it looks from the outside. But, if you have the temperament and ability, it's one of the greatest businesses in the world.

You get to help people. There is nothing in anything you have to do that would ever harm anybody. You can do things honorably, and that's a wonderful way to be. You're helping people do something they really, really want to do. You're helping them become more financially successful. You're helping them have a home, not just a house. You're helping families. It's very rewarding, a great business, but also very stressful. It's retail, and if you're not prepared for the retail business, don't get in it, at least at the sales level. It is nights and weekends, and at the beginning, you will work them all. I love the people in this industry today who say that we should make it a five-day-a-week business and make people do things on our time, and so on. Once you're successful and you want to do those things, that's your power.

But, in reality, this is a 100-percent retail business. You have to be there for the customers when they want you. You spend all this time with the customers, but then next weekend, you just don't feel like working. That might be when they find the right house and they don't buy it with you.

MIKE McCANN

PRUDENTIAL FOX AND LOACH
Philadelphia, Pennsylvania

#1 Gross Commission Income—Fox and Roach
#2 Gross Commission Income—Prudential

- Sales Volume: $122 M
- # of Units Sold: 604
- Gross Commission Income: $3.75 M
- # of Employees: 12
- www.McCannTeam.com
- Certified Residential Specialist (CRS)
- Years in the business:18

What were you doing before real estate?

I was a banquet waiter and in room service at a Hilton Hotel.

Two friends of mine decided to take a course to buy real estate. Their fathers had businesses, and they had a lot more money than I did back in '84, '85. I said, "I can't afford any real estate. I'm just making ends meet. But, I'll take the course with you, just to learn." I took the course, and right away, within the first class or two, I said, "You know what, I can do this".

I always have had a good work ethic from when I was very young. My father was a college professor at a Catholic university. He didn't make a whole lot of money. He got paid every two weeks, and we didn't have a whole lot of food by the end of the second week. My parents would say, "You can have whatever you want; we just can't buy it for you." All my friends had nice bikes, mini-bikes, and dirt bikes. I had to learn to get what I wanted by myself. I learned how to work early on.

From age 18 to 21½, I sold Kirby vacuum cleaners door-to-door. That's where I got my sales experience and tenacity. Unfortunately, at that point, I was very successful, very young. I cancelled college because I was making so much money in the summer. The gentleman I worked for became a multimillionaire selling vacuum cleaners. He did it while he was going to law school to make money. He ended up getting his law degree, but never became a lawyer because he became an entrepreneur. James B. Marion, III, was one of the mentors in my life.

When I went on an interview for a summer job, I didn't know it was selling vacuum cleaners. They showed you this motivational movie, and they didn't say it was selling vacuums. It just said, "You can have the American dream; the harder you work, the more you can make." I always said, "I don't know what I want to do, but I just hope I can get a job where the harder I work, the more I can make." And that happened with selling vacuums. Unfortunately, at age 22, I burned out. We had opened our own franchise, with a partner, and that didn't work. Then I went back into the restaurant business, which I had been in from 8th grade up until my senior year in high school. I found myself going back into the hotel industry/restaurant business until I figured out what I wanted to do when I grew up.

Your friends said they were going to take this real estate course and you thought why not?

Yes, I thought why not, just to learn how they were doing it. But I didn't have any money to invest in real estate. We took Real Estate 101. I didn't want to be in the hotel business my whole life, even though I was doing pretty well there. I liked the holidays and weekends and evenings off. If I could take the success I had in selling vacuum cleaners door to door, but with a much bigger product, real estate, I thought I could probably do well.

Where did you come up with the money to pay for the real estate course?

I had the extra money. I was a bachelor, and I was doing pretty well at the hotel. The course was only $400 or $500.

I had become an entrepreneur within the hotel, doing coffee breaks, end room service, and banquets, and I was the third highest paid at the hotel. I did very well. It irked the bosses, but I took things that other people weren't doing properly and did them. I worked like a machine at the hotel. But I didn't want to do that 90-100 hours a week for the rest of my life. So, I took this course.

A friend told me about another friend who had just opened up a real estate company. As soon as I finished the course and passed the test, and while I was still working for the hotel, I interviewed with this gentleman who said, "You can make a lot of money. I'll hire you." So, he hired me.

This broker, did the two of you work well together?

Yes. He didn't actually sell real estate. I didn't know that. He was a property manager; he managed people's buildings. We live in historic, two hundred-year-old Center City, Philadelphia, so it's an urban environment. There are a lot of universities, Penn, Drexel, and Temple, and there's a big demand for apartment rentals and stuff. I didn't realize that I should interview with other people, so I took the job. He gave me a phone and a desk. Zero training.

I had my license at that point. He said, "Here's a phone book. Call on these people and see if they want to sell their house." I immediately took another course at Temple Real Estate, in the evening. I worked at the hotel from 6:00 A.M. until about 10:00 A.M., and I still worked on weekends while I was establishing myself in real estate.

But from 10-10:30 A.M., until 7:00, 8:00, or 9:00 at night, I was trying to do this thing called real estate. I was taking a course once a week, joined the Philadelphia Board of Realtors, and started to read all the materials out there.

I learned on my own, through the Board of Realtors, through the school, and just reading everything about real estate. Of course, I got every book that was out and read everything: how to market and list real estate, how to get expired listings. My first year was pretty much teaching myself.

Fortunately, I got my first sale about three months after being hired. I sold a property for $180,000; in 1986 that was big dollars. That pumped me up.

It was slow, but it was steady. I was a sponge; I was taking everything in and trying every day. I started to go to the board functions and just networked and talked to people. I said, "If other people can do it, I can do it." That's what James B. Marion, III, taught me. He said to look at the best people and find out what they are doing right.

I got married in January 1987, and bought a home a month after that.

Did you have written goals?

I did not have any written goals. I knew I wanted to be an entrepreneur. What I liked (and still like) about real estate was the entrepreneurial spirit. The harder I worked, the better I could do. I was in a professional atmosphere, a professional business, but I wasn't just sitting at a desk; I was out on the street meeting people. I like people. As I was educating myself, it was exciting to see the effects of giving people the confidence, the direction, and guidance to help them reach their goals.

Back then, I would go after a lot of properties that were expired listings, listings that other agents could not sell. I would focus and get them sold, and would build off of each little sale I had.

What advice would you give new real estate people?

It was a little bit different when I got started—if you made $25,000 or $30,000 the first year, you were very successful. Now, I see new people making $60,000 or $70,000 the first year. A new agent should have enough money not to worry for at least six months in the business. And a new agent has to give the business at least one year to know whether he or she can make it or not. Within a year, if you haven't made some money then real estate is not for you. But you should not gauge yourself in six months. We have people who get a bunch of sales in the first two, three, or four months, and then they go stagnant. Three months down the road, they've lost it because they had early success without learning how to work. It takes two to three years before you really know what you're doing, and you start to become very successful. You have to enjoy it, first and foremost.

In my 18 years in the business, I have always built on the previous year. Even when the market went dead and many agents left the business between '89, '90, and '92, my income increased every year.

New agents need to like people, and want to help them. Many of the people I sell to don't always know exactly what they want. They rely on me for direction, guidance, and confidence. Someone says, "I can't do X because of Y." I say, "Did you consider Z?" I work hard to overcome objections and obstacles to help clients, through my knowledge, to reach their goals.

Every transaction has different things involved. I'm involved in every aspect: the conveyance of the property, inspections, title insurance, and soup to nuts. Attorneys don't handle our sales. We handle them.

What made you different from everybody else?

First, I would say having a positive attitude. Second, I honestly enjoy people. That means finding the good things in people and identifying with them. I can hang out with a truck driver, or I can converse with the top executives.

Is that something you learned, or did you have it naturally?

Believe it or not, you learn how to tweak that. I can identify with people; it is a natural gift that was God-given to me, finding the good things in people and being interested in them, whatever their background is.

We hear about positive attitude all the time, but what does it mean?

James B. Marion, III, embedded this in me: "Can't means won't." If you say you can't do something, it means you won't do it. I employed this belief from early on. I would list properties that an established agent with a big company couldn't sell. I would say, "I will sell this property," having the confidence to make that happen. A positive attitude means I won't let anything get me down. I might get down for a couple of minutes, but I bounce back and find a way to overcome the problem. I don't have bad days. I have bad moments.

So it's managing your mind.

That's a great one. That's it exactly!

What happened after your first big deal?

Our market, between 1986 and 1989, was steadily growing, but I was with a small company, and I was unknown.

Our market changed dramatically when real estate prices collapsed in '89/'90, and the high-end market died. Many agents left the business. But, luckily, I was very active. My niche was first-time buyers, families, single females and males, just out of med school or law school, dock workers, and young blue-collar professionals, buying their first property on the perimeter of the city.

But I worked my way up. I really did not have a big deal until I made the move to Prudential in 1993. I didn't hit a sale over $500,000 until probably 1996.

What made you decide to make that move?

By 1988, I received the Top Selling Awards in the city for number of units, not gross commission income, or dollar amount. Prudential, which was Merrill Lynch at the time, and other companies solicited me to move with them, but at that point, I felt I was pretty established and starting to get a following. However, May Acker, the manager at Prudential Preferred, was tenacious and worked me from 1988 until 1993, when I finally made the commitment to move to Prudential.

That's how you found the ideal broker?

Yes. Prudential was one of the top three in the marketplace. Now, I was scared. I worked so hard from '86 to '88. I was starting to get these Top Selling Awards, and starting to do pretty well financially, but I wasn't moving. I was a big fish in a little pond. I didn't want to be a little fish in this big pond. I thought all those agents would steal my leads. But that manager said, "Listen, Mike, I know, from all my agents, that you have a great reputation and everybody respects you. If you come to Prudential, you will get higher clientele. Your average transaction will probably double."

Did you have staff, before you went over to Prudential?

Yes. In 1988, my wife Cyndi came in a couple of hours a day, two or three days a week, to help me out. She helped me create checklists, and organize the office work. She helped me systemize what I did. I was sales and my wife was details. She helped me tremendously. I was like the Eveready Bunny, and I still am. I'm out there meeting clients, negotiating the deals, and directing what I need to have done. When I was starting, anything I wanted done, I had to do myself—and I was finding myself doing all this voluminous paperwork. So I hired someone to do that.

In 1989, I hired my first full-time assistant, a neighbor, whose kids were all in school, and she was getting back in to the work force. No one in our marketplace had done that. But some of the top agents in California, New York, and other places had hired assistants to do the things they themselves didn't have time to do: write letters, make phone calls, set appointments up, and things of that nature.

By the time I came to Prudential, in 1993, I had my own computer system and two full-time assistants. No one had his or her own computer.

There was one computer for the whole office of 40-45 agents.

When should you hire an assistant?

I believe that, once you're grossing about $50,000 to $60,000, you should hire an assistant.

This was a learning experience for me. My first assistant was an $8/hour. Her clerical skills were not high-end; she was someone to answer the phone. I paid her maybe $20,000 for the year. But that year, I made an additional $35,000.

Now, I hire a higher-level person; I can afford to. I know that the return is so much better. For example, if someone hired somebody and paid him $30,000, it would probably generate an additional $50,000. Plus, I won't be doing the things I don't want to do, the clerical work that I am not skilled at. I enjoy my life more because I'm doing what I am good at, and I'm not doing things that someone else can do for me. I make money from that person. Every time I've hired an assistant, and I have four full-time secretaries right now, my income has gone up.

When you made the move to Prudential, did you have access to bigger deals?

That is correct. Now that I was with a broker who had a good reputation, in a more prominent area, all of a sudden I got higher-end leads. One client said to me, "Oh, good, now you can sell my house in Society Hill." I could have before! But he wouldn't list with me because I wasn't with a highly visible, reputable company. I built on that name recognition with the company. My now-established resume and success started to generate more business.

It seems like you have challenges to deal with every day.

I love challenges!! Around 1994, there was this four-unit apartment building, in a good location, and the client wanted to buy and subdivide it. I took the offer to the other brokerage, an 80-year-old established company, and it said, "You can't subdivide that; you'll never have that approved." From my knowledge and established contacts, I already had all my ducks in line. I knew who could have it approved. I had it all approved and set within 30 days. I remember walking in to that office and delivering the approved documents, and the whole office clapped for me, because no one thought I could do this.

At what point did you start taking weekends off?

I stopped working Sundays in 1996.

In 1996, as I became more successful, I hired my first buyer specialist because I had so many leads coming in. The key thing to me is to get the listings. If you have the properties to sell, the buyers come to you. The theory is that, if you have the property for sale, you control the market, and that's what I learned to focus on.

I was getting more listings, working 12-14 hours, seven days a week. I thought, "I can't keep doing this. It's been 10 years; I've been working seven days a week. This is crazy." So I hired a buyer's specialist.

It was immediately obvious that I made the right decision. I got a phone call while away at my cabin in the Poconos, regarding a $600,000 house, which was a big deal in 1996. The buyer said, "I'm in town from Connecticut, and I want to see this house today." I paged one of my new buyer's specialists, and he showed him the house. That night we had an offer on this $600,000 house! This was unbelievable for me because I was on vacation for the July 4th weekend. Because I had my buyer's specialist available to show my property, we sold it. That was really rewarding.

My buyer's specialists help with all the buyers calling my office to see my properties, so that I can take weekends off.

That was about 10 years in.

Yes. I stopped Saturdays in probably 1998 or 1999. From Friday night until Monday morning, I will not meet a client.

I will still be available on the phone; I'll still negotiate a deal. About every two hours I'll check my voicemail. But any buyer leads will go to my buyer's agents. They sit the open houses now. I am still available, but I don't physically meet with clients or my agents. I have a wife and three children, so every weekend I have soccer games, dance classes, football games, church, and breakfast on Sunday. I hang out. That's my kids' time.

How did you get your family to support working that much?

My wife understands the business, participates in my success, helps me, and listens to me in the morning when we're having coffee, or at night.

I will not miss a parent/teacher conference, a school function, any of my children's activities. They get blocked out in my calendar, no matter what. My daughter's a cheerleader, my son plays football, and my other daughter dances. I put in my book every single function, and I will not miss any of them. I have a very good relationship with my children. They eat breakfast, and I have coffee. I cherish the time I catch with them during the week, either at bedtime, or early morning.

In 1994, we moved outside our marketplace. I used to go home for lunch or dinner. Now, I am 20 miles from where I work, so I can't go home. I won't eat fast food or restaurant foods. My wife packs me celery, carrots, fruit, and sandwiches. I credit that 100 percent for keeping me healthy. She claims she is protecting her investment! And I can eat when I want to; most of the time it's in-between appointments in my car. I come in the office only two to four hours a day, throughout the 12-hour day. Monday through Thursday, I'm out of the house about 8:15 in the morning, and I really won't be back until 8:00 or 9:00 or 10:00 at night.

But on the weekend, I'm all theirs. I don't use the phone when I'm with them, either on the weekend or when I'm with them at a function. I think phone etiquette is very important. I don't talk about my business in front of them. It's not like dad's here but he's on the phone. When I'm with a client, my phone does not go off. That's very important. Today, you're showing a property and the people's phones are going off. I have listings because the agent's have taken phone calls—the people are interviewing agents, and the agents are talking on the phone. You have to give people the attention. I don't want to stress them out, so my phones are off when I'm with them.

In 1988, when I started to get some success, I bought a little cabin in the Poconos, about two hours from our house. Every third or fourth weekend, I'd go up there. I would burn out if I didn't do that. I would work myself to death. My family really bonds when we retreat to the cabin.

How do you keep yourself motivated?

An agent said this to me recently: "You've been selling real estate for over 15 years, and remember how you felt when you started in the business and got your first deal, or your second deal, and you were all enthusiastic and excited? You're still the same way!" Whether I'm handling a $65,000 property, or I show a million-dollar property, I don't treat either one any differently. I still work just as hard. And I love it.

My enthusiasm comes from the drive of getting results. I'm always challenged. With every property I put up for sale, I try to give them the confidence and direction so that everything goes smoothly, and I give my clients realistic expectations. By helping them out and getting it done, and hearing their thanks, that's really the reward.

My initial motivation to be an entrepreneur was probably to have money and wealth. That definitely changed. Once I had a family, that immense responsibility, I was going to make sure my family was taken care of. My family is a big motivating factor. I don't look at the money at all, and I haven't for years. I don't look at "next year I'm going to do 10 percent more, 20 percent more." I just really enjoy helping people, and I do what I like. I want people happy and work to keep people happy.

I get energized from the confidence that people put in me, the trust. I go out of my way to make sure that they are completely informed, and I do the complete best for them, not for me.

I remember when the market was going down in 1989-1990. I would say to people, "Now is not the best time to sell. Your home is worth less than one sold nine months ago." Clients said to me, "Don't you get paid if you sell?" I replied, "Yes. If you want to sell it, I'd be glad to sell it, but it's probably only worth this now. If I were you, I'd try to hold on for a year or two, and see what the market does."

I look at the client's goals first, over my personal goals, and that comes back to me tenfold. Even when I didn't sell property to someone, they'd say, "You have to call Mike McCann. Mike's the best." They don't just say their agent was good; they're advocates of me. They all trust me. I never misuse it. That makes me work harder for them.

How do you stay up on the market changes?

I go to the Prudential and NAR conventions and to our company retreat once a year. I might pick up another course, and I read all the trade magazines, *NAR*, and *Pennsylvania Association of Realtors* magazine.

By the time trends get in the paper, I've been experiencing them for two to four months already because my hand's on the pulse. At least in my marketplace, I feel the trend. I keep my eye on every transaction in the marketplace. You have the most knowledge of the marketplace by reading everything, staying on top of everything, and being out there day to day. If the market's changing, I will tell people, "Look at all these properties that have been on the market for four months now. We've always had a lot of showings, but there's no action on it, there are no offers on it, and there's a bunch of others that are on the market. If you want to sell it, we can do two things: We can pull it off the market, wait until the spring, and see how the market is then, or we should probably adjust the price now if you want to sell it. As this new inventory comes on, and the old ones aren't selling, prices are going to be pushed down."

If I see properties are selling swiftly, I advise, "This property down the street sold really fast, and there were multiple offers on it. That agent's probably pretty low. I think we can get another 20 percent." I'll assess that.

At our office meetings, we're communicating about what's going on and what the buyers are saying. I get feedback on all my properties from agents that show them. Staying in touch with buyers and sellers really keeps me in touch with what's going on in the market.

What tactics do you use to get people to list with you?

To have people hire you to sell their property takes name recognition. One thing that has been incredibly effective for me is "Mike McCann, the Real Estate Man." That is on all my signs, all my advertising. It's fun. That tagline makes me very recognizable in the community. When people see me, they say Mike McCann, the Real Estate Man. A while back, a congressman called our office, and the receptionist said, "Tom is looking for the Real Estate Man." It wasn't even Mike McCann; it was the Real Estate Man. So that name recognition, that unique positioning, has been really effective.

When I get the appointment to go in to a house, it usually takes me about an hour and a half to two hours to review the listing. I take longer than most people. I establish a relationship, and I walk through the house and take all my notes. I sit down with the sellers, and I go over what I will do to sell the property, and a little bit about my company, my team, and me. This is when I really bond, connect with the people, and really inform and educate them. There is so much to go over. I try to keep it simple and answer their questions.

In our marketplace, you can have properties on the same block where one sells for $200,000 and another one sells for $600,000. So pricing is very difficult. Our houses are mostly between 100 and 250 years old. They've all been renovated, but some of them have not been updated in 40 years. I review:

- the recent sales, and where I feel the value is
- any recommendations I have to make the home more marketable
- where the seller is going, and what their timeframe is
- how it all works—paperwork, responsibilities,
- what the costs will be for the seller

I really connect, because a lot of people interview two or three people. I plan for two hours.

I believe sellers choose me because I am a professional. I am organized, I know my market, and I am confident that I will sell the property. I also have a great reputation for getting the seller through settlement.

To be successful in residential real estate, you have to treat it as a business. Probably 70 percent of the agents just sell a property. I work from a checklist. My secretaries work from checklists of what I do for each property, each thing that occurs. For example, for each listing I get, 100 postcards go out, a virtual tour is scheduled, agents are notified, and a business plan is generated.

Probably six times a year, we send out mass mailings— Thanksgiving cards, Fourth of July cards, and magnets for the New Year for past buyers and sellers. We mail a settlement sheet to every buyer in January for their taxes, because often they can't find it for April 15th!

I have an action plan for each listing and for each settled property. I have a contract with the paper to do my ad. When I go in to a listing, I'm prepared. I have a listing booklet, a contract complete, my tip sheet, pictures of my ads, and my virtual tours, showing how many people come on my Web site. I'm on time and professional.

The part that's not business is an emotional decision for buyers or sellers. They're only going to buy or sell with someone whom they can identify with, who cares about them. It's not a business to them. This is a big thing, a big investment, where they're going to live and whether they're going to sell.

Our industry, really, is two businesses. There's a listing end. It's a totally different animal from the buyer's end. I'm pretty much a listing specialist, a listing machine. I have my buyer's specialists to work the buyers. I don't work many buyers because my time is all focused on getting the inventory to come in and listing the properties for sale. Like doctors, we've divided the work, so that I list properties, and then I have a support team that will work for the buyers and show them our properties, as well as other properties.

What made you decide to do that?

For years, I was probably 60-70 percent buyers and 30-40 percent listings, but as I got established, I started to get more and more listings. I couldn't handle all of the leads as personally as I wanted to. So I hired a buyer's specialist to work more buyers, which sold more of my listings, which got me more listings. Then I hired another buyer's specialist.

That enables my sellers to be serviced, so someone's always available from my team to show their property. I spend my time making sure that property is marketed, so the phone does ring on that property. I am generating new business.

It's not easier doing listings; it's a different talent. But once they sign a contract with you, they're committed to you. You don't mind investing more energy.

What kind of "different talent"?

You need to have more real estate knowledge including:

- how to market the property

- to whom to market the property
- what things to do to market the property, for example, virtual tours
- who receives emails about the property
- the fax lists for networking the property, including not only your buyers, but the real estate community

I have engaging ads and do brokers' luncheons and schedule open houses. Once you have a signed listing, your focus is marketing, getting the information out to those who want to buy.

When you're working the buyer, in contrast, you're searching the computer, calling five or 10 different agents to show their properties, and running out to view homes with the buyer. You're getting them pre-qualified for financing. It really is a totally different animal.

What made you decide to stay with Fox & Roach?

I'm a conservative guy. I waited it out, listened, and met with the owners.

The company has an unbelievable market share. You're big if you have a 33 percent market share; my company has a 67 percent market share in our marketplace. It's unheard of. Prudential Fox & Roach in Philadelphia was formed from a merger of three companies: Prudential Preferred Properties, Jackson Cross, and Midtown. My business has gone up dramatically as a result of that. We have a great mortgage and title company.

The networking among all the agencies is unbelievable. It has worked. I was devastated when Fox & Roach bought our company, which was called Prudential Preferred Properties. I was very committed to the owner I had worked for since 1993, who sold out his interest. I really cried. Everyone in the company was looking to me to see if I was going to leave.

It was hard to work with our competition. But, they ended up being even better than our previous company. They invest in the business. They're into the technology. They're looking 10 years down the road and have great training. They make sure that the new agents are trained, and they match them with mentors. It's unbelievable.

The owner, Larry Flick, received Broker of the Year from Prudential

Real Estate Affiliates, which boasts about 60,000 agents. Prudential is a franchise, so we're not owned by Prudential. We're owned by Fox & Roach. My company has approximately 40 offices and 3,500 agents in the tri-state area, which is Pennsylvania, New Jersey, and Delaware. The company has grown and innovated. We're really like a family-owned company with that Prudential affiliation, which gets us awesome relocation business and great resources. It's kind of the best of both worlds.

How do you network a property?

I network it by emailing, faxing, distributing, and snail mailing to all the agents in the marketplace. My properties have a weekly sheet that goes out on my new listings. I return phone calls right away. Agents call me at 9:00 at night; they know they'll get a call back by 9:30, keeping them posted.

Networking is also made easier because I have the best reputation in the marketplace among my peers. I coach and help a lot of people, both new agents and experienced agents. It doesn't matter whether they're with our company or they're with any other company. Agents like to cooperate with me because I will give them direction and help them out. You would not believe all the calls I get from agents. I have been doing that my whole career.

A lot of agents, especially successful agents, will give new people the snub, but I coach them, help them out. Having the best reputation among agents has been key for me. And I learned that from being with that small company because there were no peers to communicate with. I cooperate with all the agents from all the other companies, and I learned that that's good. People will sometimes call my office and say, "I have a buyer in the $300,000-$400,000 price range. Mike, what do you have available for sale?"

That's been going on for years. I tell my team that we service the real estate community. I tell my clients when I list their properties, "One of the key things I do is make sure that this property is networked, not just to our buyers, but to the real estate community."

How do you use negotiation skills?

I always try to create a sense of urgency when I'm marketing my sellers' properties. Sometimes, I'll put their property up on Wednesday, but the first showing won't be until the Sunday open house, so it creates a sense of urgency. The agents and the buyers who go in there see a bunch of other people excited about the house.

Creating a sense of urgency is key. If I take buyers out and show them 5, 10, or 15 houses, and I see one that I feel is good, I'll say, "Listen, you've seen what's out there. How do you feel about this? What do you think? This is a nice house. This house probably won't be around in a week or two. If you want to buy a house, this is probably as good as we're going to get." Of course, this is if I really feel that way. I don't create false things.

An agent will call me saying, "Mike, my buyer liked that property, but it's $499,000, and they're thinking about offering $450,000. They thought it was priced a little bit high." If I don't have an offer on the property, I will never tell them that. Instead I'll coach an agent to ask his seller, "My people liked your property, but have you had any offers turned down?" I keep track and get feedback from every showing. "Keep me posted. They're not ready to make an offer now." I will let the agent know that. I'll say, "There is some interest; I don't have any offers on it now," trying to create a sense of urgency.

When I get an offer from another agent, I review it before I call the seller. I do most of my communication over the phone. I've established a relationship with my clients, so I will give them a call and discuss the offer with them. I will sometimes drop it off, sometimes meet with them, and sometimes fax it to them, depending on their situation. I deal with a lot of busy professionals, and they're looking for my direction and guidance. I would say only 5 to 10 percent want to read every word on the contract, and most want me to tell them what the highlights are. I communicate at the pace and at the level that people want to communicate at. Some don't even want to see the agreement until it's physically agreed upon, with me outlining all the contingencies, the costs.

I review the agreement thoroughly, and communicate that to the seller. I look at what the feedback has been, what the showings are, and the time on the market, and I discuss it with them. After I've made them thoroughly understand all the contingencies, the settlement date, the inspection contingencies, and the mortgage, and they're pre-qualified and everything is in line, I'll go back to the buyers with the counterproposal on the property.

Also, if someone has shown the property in the past week or so, and there was some degree of interest, I will communicate to that agent. "I know you showed this property last week and said there is some interest. I wanted you to know that I got an offer on the property." Sometimes that will generate additional offers. More times than not, when someone wants it, other people do, too. That will create a sense of urgency.

How do you respond to an agent who says $490,000 is too high, and they may offer $450,000?

I will say to them, "I don't know what they'll take, but if your people are interested, have them give me a written offer." I will never tell them not to present me with an offer. I find a lot of agents are lazy. They don't want to put the agreement in writing. But in real estate, everything has to be in writing. If you want to present the offer, please put it in writing and get it to me.

I find that buyers tell agents one thing. Half the time they end up doing something totally different from what they're telling the buyer's agent because they don't always know what they want. The buyer doesn't even know what they want. They really don't. I'll get people who say to me, "I want three bedrooms, two baths with a garage," and they end up buying a two bedroom, 1½ bath with no garage.

Is it asking the right questions up-front, or is it learning as you go?

Buyers get a feeling for what's out there in the marketplace. What they think they want, in our marketplace, and what is really out there, may be totally different things. So I believe the buyers learn as they go.

It's really a function of supply and demand. For example, buyers may think they can spend $500,000 and get everything they want. Then, they see that, for that price, they're going to need a fixer-upper in order to get the space they want.

So, that buyer's agent could say to their client, "This is it. This is all I'm going to do, and I really mean that." The buyer's agent really believes it because he or she was sincere. But, I've found from experience that you get a little hook and slowly reel the buyers in.

When the agent spends an hour preparing the offer, then spends an hour or two going over the offer, he or she starts to get connected to the property emotionally.

Some transactions work really fast, and some work really slowly. I always do get the direction from my sellers, to make sure that they agree with how I recommended it to be handled, and they agree with that position.

Have you ever said to somebody, "You can put that in writing to me, but my feeling is that the client will not accept the offer"?

I never do that. Never. You never know what your seller will accept. If I did that, I would probably sell 10 or 20 percent fewer transactions per year.

Seller's situations, like their moods, constantly change, throughout the day and week. I've learned that from experience. I've had people who said, "Mike, we can't sell the house unless we get $400,000, and we're not getting $400,000." Three months later, somebody makes an offer for $380,000 and they take it, because their situation changed.

So you never know. I will never, ever take the shortcut. My clients' situation could have changed. The buyers can change. It can change while we're negotiating the offer. I check the hot sheet every day, and I see what properties settled.

For example, I saw one that was listed for $420,000 and settled at $380,000. One of my buyers said, "Man, I would have paid $380,000 for that!"

"You didn't make an offer."

"Well, I didn't know they would take that." You never know what they're going to take, no matter what the buyer says, no matter what the seller says, no matter what the other agent says. You put it in writing, and you take the extra step.

How much control do the agents have on the outcome of the deal?

The level of control depends on the agent, and a good agent has a lot of control. Control is really preconditioning and educating the buyer or seller on the steps and the process.

Agents like to deal with me because my sellers are educated about the offer, the building inspection, the property, and potential issues after the inspection. My sellers are conditioned with the realistic expectations. A lot of agents might sign a deal, and it's FHA, and they don't tell the sellers that FHA is going to call for repairs on the house. They don't explain to them that the buyer has ten days to do a building inspection and can cancel or ask for repairs. Then, the buyer does the building inspection, and asks them for these repairs to be fixed. The agent says, "My seller's not doing that. They didn't agree to that."

The top agents have a very big effect on the seller's decisions. Some sellers will have their ideas: I want this price, or I want this date, and so on, and that should be communicated to the listing agent. But, when I'm dealing with an experienced agent on the end of the transaction, it goes smoothly. That's probably where they have the most influence.

If I'm the listing side, a good agent will coach the buyer on how long a property has been on the market and get back with a reasonable response. It might take a week or two; it might take a day or two. But, a strong agent has a very big influence on the transaction getting done: explaining what a good offer is, what's not a good offer, what are good terms, and what are good conditions. I have a very big effect. That's why I do 600 deals a year, and the average agent does 30.

The better agent will know what the better deals are in the marketplace. You're not going to get anybody to do something he or she doesn't want to do. When a buyer comes to me, I'll know the best values in the marketplace. Agents who are not as committed won't know that. They'll just show them houses. That's the importance of a good buyer's specialist.

An agent with control will keep the people focused on the big picture. I try to keep my clients calm and levelheaded. Being calm and having a soothing voice through a storm has a big effect. I'm constantly refocusing them. Inspections are a pain in the neck in our marketplace. People renovate hundred-year-old houses over time. Home inspectors find $20,000-$40,000 worth of work that they think should be done. Usually, the house is really okay. I always condition my sellers and buyers that, when the home inspector goes through, they're going to say it needs numerous repairs. If they're all major defects, we're going to have to address them. I tell them, "We are not obligated to do anything. But, if we don't negotiate this repair, or fix this repair, we will have to disclose it."

A good agent is that calming, reassuring, confident, and knowledgeable person who keeps them levelheaded and the same thing with the other agent. If I'm the listing agent, I give that buyer's agent tools to close his buyer on my counter proposal. I put the words in his mouth. Many agents welcome that, because they don't know how to give their clients the reasons why they should take this offer. That is absolutely crucial.

People ask me, "Mike, why do you do so many more sales than anybody else?" I tell them that it's because, as the most-respected agent in the marketplace, everybody knows when my properties are listed. They know that my listings are good. They believe everything I say. We'll give them the information. We help people.

What have been some of your major challenges?

Managing my time. Making sure I'm efficient. Get things done, but not cutting people short. I normally can get my point across pretty fast, and I'm on or off the phone in three to five minutes. Multitasking and knowing how to get things done, because I handle 100 or 200 phone calls a day.

How did you learn to be most effective in managing your time?

My assistants have been with me between two and 10 years. I take care of them, so they stay with me. I have excellent support people who know how I do things, and I delegate a lot of tasks so that I can look at the bigger picture. I take care of my people; I appreciate them every day, both monetarily and verbally. I make sure that everybody around me is taken care of.

I had to learn how to let go and delegate. That was a great challenge that no one thought I would be able to do. But I trust my staff, and it doesn't let me down.

I have been blessed in life and in this business. No one gave it to me, but I haven't had anything adverse ever happen to me. My biggest challenge is learning how to continue to grow my business and yet have some time for my life. I'm really a results-oriented, get-to-the-bottom, get-to-the-business person, but I still cherish that emotional connection. People have to feel that you care about them, or you won't be able to be results-oriented. You have to have that bond and that trust and know how to get things done.

My vendors put me first, and save me time searching for help. I have helped several get started in their own business. I've sent work to them, and other agents would follow. When a new business is starting, and they're good, I say, "Listen, when you become super-successful, remember, when I call you, you come out to me first." They have great respect, and they'll jump and do anything for me, because of loyalty.

Every vendor I've encouraged seems to become very successful, because agents follow what I do. For example, I had some properties that weren't selling; I got the seller to decorate them. The buyers said, "Mike, we could do better decorating of your properties. We're thinking about starting a business." I encouraged them, and employed them. Now they come in to an empty house and decorate and furnish it. It costs my sellers about $3,500-5,000, but I get $20,000-40,000 more for that house. And now many other agents use them, and their business is a success.

In closing, is there anything else you'd like to share?

To me, an important key to success is to differentiate yourself. Allan Domb, who is a top agent in my marketplace and who was number one in the country last year from NAR, once said, "Mike, the most effective marketing tool you have is that 'Mike McCann, the Real Estate Man.' Everyone knows that." If you differentiate yourself and market that, people will remember you.

Remember that old saying, "It takes money to make money." You do not need to do all these different programs and all this fancy stuff. Pick four or five basic things and do them. I am still working the checklist my wife created in 1988; we've added a few things, like virtual tours and

Internet, but we keep the organization. I do the basics consistently.

Try to have the best reputation in your marketplace, within the industry. If you're a doctor, you want to have the best reputation, so other doctors will send people to you. I sell a lot of other Realtors' properties; they hire me to sell their own home. That's how strong a reputation I have.

Be a good listener. Have enthusiasm, high energy, and tenacity. Learn how to delegate and hire a good assistant or two. Take care of them. As you grow, they have to grow with you. Invest in yourself. Continue your education.

No one can believe the volume I do, and not working weekends is unbelievable for a Realtor. Having control of your life is very, very important.

Mike McCann, the Real Estate Man, was kind enough to share some of his tools for success, which are included in the Appendix. He walks his talk.

PAUL MORAD

COLDWELL BANKER GUNDAKER
St. Louis, Missouri

#1 Unit Producer: Coldwell Banker

- Sales Volume: $25M
- # of Units Sold: 504
- Gross Commission Income: $800,000
- # of Employees: 12-15
- www.CBGundaker.com
- Years in the business: 26

What brought you in to real estate?

I emigrated from Iran in 1969, when I was 22 years old. I had a thousand dollars in my pocket, and spoke very poor English. The only person I knew was my cousin. I went to English school for two months. In the fall I went to college. I worked at night and went to school during the day. When I graduated from college, my cousin was in the building business. I started with him, and then I decided I didn't want to be just building new homes. I decided to sell houses. I went to Gundacker Real Estate Companies in St. Louis. It was one of the biggest ones here. Two years ago, it was sold to Coldwell Banker.

You had to get your real estate license to sell new homes?

I didn't have to, but I got it. They could hire you to sit at the new homes and sell.

What made you decide to do new-home sales?

It's a start, a new kind of experience. I was interested in how they built the home, how they started all that. When I started real estate, I knew houses, how they are, what their problems are. I would help the seller and buyer. It helped me a lot.

Why did you decide to change to retail?

I just wanted a change. I thought dealing with different people was challenging. It's more challenging than just sitting in new homes and people coming in.

How did you pick the real estate office to work with?

I picked this office because it was close to where I live. I knew some people here. You started, you knew some people, you had some contacts, and someone helped you out. I've been at this office for 23 years. I didn't move around. If I went to another office, I might have been more successful, but I didn't, because some other offices sell bigger area, bigger homes. Now, thinking about it, I should have.

I started selling houses. I was on the phone all the time. I work seven days a week, sometimes 7-10 hours a day, just constantly calling the people.

Now I do bank foreclosures, all different kinds of properties. I do the whole St. Louis area.

Did you interview with the broker?

I interviewed with the broker. She hired me right away. She knew me. As soon as I walked in, she said, "You have the job."

What was it like for you when you started out?

In new homes, they come in to see. They don't call anybody. You don't have to do anything. But when you come to retail, you have to have contacts. I didn't have that many contacts. I had to create some business. Call people. Open houses. Do all kinds of things to create business.

As my manager was telling me, "Paul, you're on the phone constantly calling these people." She's still saying that. What I learned was that anyone can make it in this country. There is opportunity for everyone. It just requires hard work.

Who were you calling?

Clients. Calling different people, asking for business.

You're still working 8-10 hours a day, seven days a week?

Normally. I have assistants, but still I'm available. If you call me at 2:00 in the morning, I will answer my phone. I transfer it to my cell phone. That's the reason most of my clients like me. They say, "You answer your phone in the middle of the night." They call at 2:00 in the morning, "Oh, we were going to leave a voicemail." I say, "No, I answer the phone."

When I'm out of town or something, I do a lot of conferences. Then my assistant Jason answers the phone.

What kind of conferences do you go to?

I go to Coldwell Banker conferences—bank conferences, foreclosure conferences—they invite me. I go all over the country.

Tell me a little bit about how you built your business.

First thing, really, you have to be honest and consistent and ask for referrals and do a service. Treat everybody just like your own. When I hire people, I tell them, "Just treat them like your own, nothing different."

At what point did you bring somebody on and start getting some help?

About two years later, my wife got a license, and she was helping me. She did all the paperwork, and I was doing the selling, going out and stuff. Five years ago, we got divorced. My business picked up. I started hiring. Right now, I have seven or eight people. With the clean-up crews, I have 12-15 people working for me.

How long were you in the business before you hired someone to work with you?

It was 16-17 years because real estate wasn't that big, like 10-12 years ago. You didn't see any top agents doing a lot of business. Really the last twelve years or so, it's been like that.

How did you decide to get in to foreclosures?

I contacted RTC, a savings & loan that ended up going bankrupt. I sold a few properties for it. Finally, I got involved with GE Capital, and I did a few properties. After a couple of years, I quit foreclosures. Then I went back to it. All over the country, they know me and they call me, or email me, and send me business.

What made you decide to get out of foreclosures?

I got out of foreclosures because there weren't that many foreclosures after RTC went out of business. In 1989, '90, it picked up, and then I went back in to it again. Then I became really active in '92, '93.

How do you deal emotionally with foreclosing on people?

Well, the bank forecloses on it and then emails me or faxes me. It says that this house is foreclosed. You check to see if it is vacant or not. If the house is vacant, we change the locks. If it's not, we give them a letter telling them the bank foreclosed on it. Then if it's occupied, we just tell the bank that it's occupied. It starts the eviction. I feel bad about it; it's sad. But, if I didn't do it, somebody else would. I don't have anything to do with the eviction and all that. Most of the houses are vacant.

What percentage of time is the house vacant?

I'd say 50/50.

It's really hard to get people out!

They usually have their own attorney. I don't have anything to do with that. The bank handles the entire thing.

What is the bank looking for you to do?

Just market the property for the bank. I'm its agent.

You take the property and clean it up. Are you getting a percentage of the sale?

Yes. I list it and get a commission, three percent. Then if I sell it, I get the whole thing, six percent.

Does the bank pay you to fix the place up?

Sometimes if it wants to fix the property, yes it does. It hires a contractor who gives me a bid, which I send to the bank. The bank fixes the place. Sometimes it sells the property and then fixes it up.

Do you turn these directly to investors, or to another agent?

Yes, investors. Most of them know me in town and contact me. I show them the list. Right now, I have 70 listings. If they're interested, they call me. Say we want to put a contract on this property. I contact the bank and send it the contract. We negotiate, finalize, and close.

What types of negotiations do you do?

We send the offer to the bank. It comes back and says that the mortgage is okay. For example, we listed this house for $110, and this person offers $95 or $100. I came back and said, "We want $108." The buyer said, "No, I want to go $104." That's negotiation back and forth. We negotiated and sold the house for $104.

You have a relationship with these different banks.

Oh, I do. They love me. They all love my business. If they didn't, they wouldn't give it to me. There are a lot of agents here. The banks contact them. They're looking for business. If you do one thing not right for them, you won't work for them again. They want everything to go smoothly, the way they want it.

What enabled you to establish those kinds of relationships?

I did three or four deals with them, and they saw how smoothly it went. I have to check the buyer's background. A lot of people put in a contract and they don't have the financing available. Make sure this property's going to close, because the banks don't have time to get one contract, and another contract, and another. Some of them have 5000-6,000 properties all over the United States. Each house may take four to five contracts. Then they go to the next one.

You have to screen it very carefully to make sure this property is going to close. They like me because I screen. When they call me, they say, "Paul, are you sure this is going to go?" I say yes, and it's closed.

How much negotiation do you do, on the bank side?

I let the banks decide. They tell me. They email me. They say, "Okay, this is the bottom line we're going to take." I tell the person that this is the bottom line, and that's it. "You take it, or I'll take my seller to somebody else."

There is not much negotiation?

No, I don't make decisions for them. They want only to make sure the buyer's good. Sometimes they don't know the market there, and they put the price too high. They ask me, and I will tell them, "Honestly, this is too high. You have to keep reducing it." When you list it, the bank won't take a low offer. The bank will take something close to the asking price. For example, I estimate the house will sell for $125. The bank lists it for $170, and then you have to take three to four months to reduce that to get to $125 to sell it. If the bank gets a firm appraisal at $175, and it gets $130 from me, they go with the higher price, because the appraiser gave it to them. After three months, they realize, oh, yeah, Paul, you were right. Reduce it to sell it.

You'd think it would behoove them to get rid of that property earlier.

Yes. Does an appraiser have more knowledge than a real estate agent? But that's not true. Most appraisers call us and ask me what I think this property could sell for.

What type of negotiation do you do when you're representing the buyer?

I go back to the buyer. I say, "Look here, this is the price the bank wants." For example, if the bank wants $110,000 and the buyer is negotiating for $104,000, I tell the buyer, "They want $110. Why don't you split the $6,000? You could go $106 or $107." Then I tell the bank, let's split this to get it sold.

I just talk to the buyer. I say, "Really if you want the house, let's negotiate. If you don't want it, you're just wasting your time. This is the price they want."

Then the buyer says, "I want it."

I say, "Okay, let's negotiate. You go to six. I'll go to the bank, and tell them we came up two more. Sometimes, the bank says no. This is the bottom line we're going to take. We can't take less than $110. They have to wait another month, and then they sell it at $106. Sometimes they have a bottom line they could take.

It seems like the banks are a little shortsighted sometimes.

They are. Sometimes, for example, I list it for $125. I bring in an offer for $110 or $115. They won't sell it. Three months later, or five months later, they end up selling it for $105. But those are their policies. That's the way they work.

The people at the bank don't have any real estate background?

They do have, but what happens sometimes is, in the last few years, there has been so much fraud. For example, somebody has a $145-$150 loan on a house worth $110. The bank wants to capture the loss. They think it might be worth that much, but they end up losing. They recoup, but they can't, most of the time.

What keeps you involved with foreclosures?

It's fun. It's challenging. You meet different people. You go to these conferences. Another thing, most of the people who buy have financing lined up or cash. Usually, you don't make that much money. If I did that much business in retail, I'd be making $100 million. I just like it. I travel. I like the foreclosures better than retail.

What makes it more challenging?

The negotiation with the bank and with the buyers. You try to get more property sold.

Do you have employees, contractors?

Yes. They work in my office. Foreclosures have a lot of paperwork. I do repairs for some of them. I was doing repairs, selling for the bank. I started that first, repairing it and then selling it. Then they got so many properties. I guess they couldn't handle it. They sold it as is.

The last six or seven years, the foreclosure numbers were so high, they couldn't handle it. It would be too difficult for them to fix all the 6,000 properties and sell them. Some of these properties are in bad areas. When you fix it at night, put in a sink or cabinet, the next day it's gone. I wouldn't fix it, because if we do, every day we have to put back cabinets or sinks or dishwashers. Actually, 30 percent of these properties are in rough areas.

You brought on the people you have working for you as the paperwork increased?

As the number of units increased, so did the paperwork.

I have some cleaning people. Some people cut grass. I have 15 people working for me. I have seven employees and eight contractors.

Does it require a different skill-set to do regular residential property versus foreclosures?

That's right. We are very different. Banks wouldn't give deals to new people, because they have a form you have to fill out, and you have to know how to do it, to price it. A lot of times, they have what they call drive-by. For example, we told them a house was worth $30,000. Somebody did a drive-by and said it was $90,000. The bank called and started laughing. Have you seen the picture? We had this drive-by. Somebody said it was $90,000. You had to send another one, a third opinion, to see what it was worth. They would look at it, come back, and say, "Yeah, you were right." This guy drove by and just made a price. It's not something reasonable.

You have to know what you're doing. You have to do it right away. You have to have knowledge to sell property. You have to have knowledge about cost and fixing and all that.

You have to have the knowledge of fixing things up. They look at the house. What are they going to do? They will look at the house next door. The house, for example, was $200,000 and this house was $150,000. They figure this house was probably worth $180,000,

$190,000, but that's not true. $125,000, $130,000 is what it's worth. You have to take a look at that. Plus, because it's a foreclosure, it's not going to sell like a retail house, because retail houses are fixed up. People live in a nice place. People want to walk in and buy, rather than buying some houses sitting in the market. The bank won't give it to you.

What does it take to be number one in foreclosures?

You have to be consistent, honest. You have to work hard. Some of these companies want you for 24 hours. You check the house out and see that it's vacant. I let them know and send a bill. We call it BPO. If it's vacant, you have to change the locks, clean it up, and take a picture. You have to send it within 48 hours. Some agents don't do that. They take a week. If you send it in a week, they won't take that property. They'll give it to somebody else.

If it's occupied, you have to let them know within 24 hours. Sometimes it takes me two hours. They call me, and in two hours I call them back, I tell them this property is either occupied or vacant. They're shocked. They say, "Paul, how do you do that? Two hours, three hours, you let us know." The calls transfer to my cell phone. Sometimes, I say, "I'll let you know in 30 minutes. I'm in this area."

You actually peak in people's windows?

Sometimes. Now, mostly my assistant does. The person changed the lock. We just knock on the door. Ask the neighbors. Look for furniture. See if the grass is nice. You can tell. A car sitting in the driveway. This is occupied. We check weekly to see if it's still occupied.

I used to do it myself. It's not that bad. You go and check. You check them out and let them know. Also, they call me, saying, "We have this property, Paul, and it's not a good area. Do you want to take it?" I say, "Don't tell me that. I take them all, or I take none." That's the reason they like me. They know I don't discriminate. I take the bad and the good. You have to take that. If you don't do that, they won't give it to you. They think you only want the good easy ones.

Is there anything else about being great in foreclosure?

If you make a mistake, call and tell them you made a mistake. I call the bank and say, "I'm sorry on this one. I made a mistake. Would you change this?"

They say, "Okay, Paul, no problem." If you don't do it, and they find out, they'll come back and ask, "Why you didn't tell us?" Be honest, consistent, and do the work. Do what they ask. Then they'll give you the work. Be very responsive.

What kind of mistakes did you make?

I made a lot of mistakes. My assistant made a mistake once on a property that was occupied. He put it on the sheet as vacant. They didn't find out until two or three weeks later that it was occupied. They got upset. They wanted to know why I didn't let them know. We lost that company. The mistake was just an error in typing. We were working on it to evict them.

How do you hire good help?

I get to know them. I sit down and talk to them. I tell them what I'm looking for and find out what they are looking for. I let them do their own thing. I don't control them or anything. I tell them, "This is your job." They do it. If they have any questions, they're to ask me. You have to treat them like me. This is my own. They know everything like me. Give them responsibility.

What do you do to invest in yourself?

At the conferences, I learn and then I come back and tell my staff. I meet a lot of new people. All these banks come to the conferences. They bring the foreclosure people. Attorneys and judges come and they talk about different things: how they want it done; how they want to handle the mold, clean up, repairs, evictions, and the house. I pick up some new companies. I introduce myself. I sometimes sponsor lunches and dinner for the staff, the crew. Sometimes, about 1500 people come by. So I do some advertising.

What type of advertising do you do?

For my foreclosures I have a Web site, and then I use newspapers. Sometimes we call around to investors. Sometimes we get property, and we can't sell it. We just keep calling them, telling them to reduce the price.

So you have a list of investors whom you work with on a regular basis?

Yes.

How often do you advertise the property?

Every other week.

What is your average turnover time?

When representing the bank, I usually sell 60 percent of my foreclosures the first month, and the rest in about another thirty days. I sell about 30 percent of my own properties.

Are there more legal issues around foreclosures than other real estate?

Yes, especially in bankruptcy.

How do you handle a bankruptcy foreclosure?

Attorneys handle it. For instance, this lady took six or eight months to get out of there. She was filing bankruptcy and then never went through with it. Every time they go to evict her, she files bankruptcy. When you file bankruptcy, they can't touch you. Six times she did that. Then the judge said, "That's it. You can't do it any more. You have to get out."

This person gets free rent for eight months.

Eight months no rent. The mortgage was foreclosed for six months, with some of them a year.

How does the legal system allow that to happen?

They have so many properties. A lot of times it takes a year to get them out of there. They file bankruptcy, and you can't touch them. You have to go to bankruptcy court, take that back, and then foreclose on it. It takes four or five months to get paid, and then you figure up to two months to foreclose. Then they file bankruptcy again. You figure up another three or four months for bankruptcy. For almost 10 to 12 months they stay there for free.

Fifteen years ago, all the banks came back at the person to get their losses. Now they have so many of them, they just forget about it. They won't go after them. Some banks have 8,000 properties all over the United States. How are you going to go after people? They don't have the money. A lot of them don't have a job.

What type of marketing do you do?

I have a farm area. I send them a letter, flyers. I do some open houses.

Are you holding the open houses?

Not myself.

One of the people working for you?

Yes.

What advice would you give agentss who want to be more successful?

Be consistent and honest, work hard, and treat the people's properties just like your own. Don't give up. If somebody says no, just wait a month or so and call him or her back or send a letter or something. Eventually, you're going to get it. Some day they're going to come back and say, "We need you."

Just do a good job, the best you can, and be available to people all the time. If they call you, you can return the call. Just don't ignore them. Return people's calls.

What advice would you give about establishing relationships with the banks?

Do a good job for them. Be consistent and timely in getting back to them.

Are there any specific tools you use that have enabled you to be so successful?

I do some advertising. I made a color glossy brochure and flyer about myself. I send or email it to the banks or seller. I give them referrals they could call if they have questions. I have a picture of all my assistants and me, and information about what each one does. It's impressive. People like it.

GREGG NEUMAN

PRUDENTIAL—Neuman & Neuman
San Diego, California

#1 Gross Commission Income: Prudential

- Sales Volume: $152 M
- # of Units Sold: 323
- Gross Commission Income: $4 M
- # of Employees: 16
- www.SellSanDiego.com
- Years in the business: 23

How did you get interested in real estate?

I wanted to make more money, and there's more money in sales than there is in anything else. It doesn't take 12 years and a degree. I assumed that, in sales, the bigger the item, the more dollars you make. I said, "Okay, I'll sell real estate."

I was a bartender for 15 years before I got in to real estate. I tended bar and worked real estate for the first two years. I would rush to the bar at 6:00 P.M., tend bar until 2:00 A.M., and then go in to the office at 8:00 A.M. and work till 5:30 P.M. I did that for a year. I'd ask everybody who came in if they wanted to buy a house, and they'd say no. I said, "Okay, how about a cocktail?"

Two years later, I was rushing to write an offer before going down to tend bar. I said, "Wait a minute, I'm going to make $30,000 on this transaction, and I'm hurrying and rushing to make $150 a night tending bar? This is it." I gave them my notice.

Was that your first big deal that you were working on?

That was the first deal, a million dollar deal in 1981.

How did you happen to get that deal?

It came from one of the builders who drank in the bar. I told him I knew about some vacant lots, and I asked him if he was interested in buying them. He said sure.

Every time I would go down to the bar, I would meet somebody who would buy something. I worked waitresses and bartenders, people who are traditionally left out of the home buying experience, and taught them how to buy. It's like hairstylists; they're not usually sought after. But there's a way for people who want to buy to buy. I would talk to people. The very first time I said to a guy, "Do you want to buy a house or to buy a drink?" He said, "I don't want to buy a house, but I want to sell mine." I said, "You're kidding me." "No, I'm serious." I went to his house, during the day, of course, because I had to work nights, and signed him up. While I was signing him up, he said, "By the way, I know a woman who wants to buy my house." I went to her, and she said, "Yes, I do, but I have to sell my house." I ended up doing five sides of a six-legged transaction for my first deal. I made $18,000 on my first deal.

It took a lot to put that deal together.

It took an awful lot. The minute I got my real estate license on February 28th, the real estate market interest rates went to their all-time high of 17 to 21 percent and to compound that, I bought a real estate office April 1st.

What made you decide to do that?

I knew if I didn't spend the money to buy an office, I wouldn't be able to make the commitment to work two jobs, because it's too easy not to succeed unless you push yourself. I took all the money I had, which was $25,000 at the time, and bought the office for $10,000, no money down. She let me use her broker's license. None of that set off an alarm and warned me that she just wanted out desperately. I had to learn an awful lot because it really put me in the spot where, all of a sudden, I've been in the business a week and people are asking questions on how do you do this, how do you do that, and I had to get answers. It was a very, very good way to get in the business.

Sink or swim. By putting yourself in that position, you knew you were going to do whatever it took to swim.

To save my money. That's exactly right. Because it took me a long time to come up with $25,000 tending bar.

Plus you had your $18,000 from your first close to use, right?

That didn't happen right away. I sold my first house in April, but it didn't close until June or July. It was an excellent opportunity, and it taught me that all you have to do is apply yourself and you can do almost anything. As long as you have the physical and mental capabilities, I don't believe there's anything you can't do.

You bought the office and you were still working in the bar?

In the bar every night.

What did your agents think about that?

I didn't tell them. I just said that I had an appointment. Clients would call in and ask, "Can you come by and list my house this evening?" I said, "I'm sorry, I have listing appointments every night this week, but I could certainly come by on Saturday or Tuesday afternoon. I'm certain you could take a little time off during the day to let me see your house. If you go in to the doctor's, you take off from work. You go to your doctor's for one of your most-valuable possessions: you. And your second most-valuable possession would be your house. I think you need to take the time off so that I can see the house in the same light and time during which buyers are going to come and see it. That way I'll be able to advise you accurately as to what the price should be."

You really sounded that good when you were brand new?

I think so. One of the advantages of being a bartender for 15 years is that you learn to talk to people, all different kinds, and all different walks of life. In the restaurant I worked at, doctors and judges and attorneys and truck drivers would come in. So you learn to converse articulately with different types of people. You don't become intimidated. You find that, just because the person's a judge, it doesn't make him any smarter than you, especially when he's drinking!

You did that for two years.

I cut back a couple of days after the first year. I was working four nights a week. Then I cut back after two years, and then I just completely quit and went full-time into real estate.

Did you have actual staff besides the independent agents?

Debbie, my partner, who was my wife at that time, became the administrative assistant before she got her license. She worked the office. In the Red Carpet, the real estate franchise I bought, there was one secretary who worked in that building. We just kept her on.

When would you recommend to bring staff on?

I think you'd bring staff on the minute you have more than five transactions open on a consistent basis. What happens is that, once you have five transactions open on a consistent basis, you're going to spend more time handling those transactions. Then your business is going to start going in spurts because you will be busy working those five deals, and then you have nothing, and you have to rush and get some more.

Once you get to the five constant transactions, it becomes worth your while to bring somebody on. It makes you far more productive. Doing that stuff is $10 or $13 an hour. Absolutely not worth it.

What about before they can afford to bring somebody on?

They would be better off at that point to use a transaction coordinator, where the company has somebody you pay, like, $300 a transaction to oversee most of the paperwork. They're doing the major paperwork, and you're handling the negotiations, the repairs, and the challenges that come up in a transaction, rather than the day-to-day paper shuffle. I find new agents are too reluctant to spend even the $300.

They seem to be very reluctant to spend any money and yet, consistently, I've heard that it takes money to make money.

Right. And you have to invest in yourself. When I started, I spent probably 30 percent of my earnings on advertising and marketing. Now, I'm to the point where I generally spend 10 percent. It could drop as you do more and more business. Ten percent of $4 million gross income—I'm still spending $400,000 a year marketing myself.

When you started, what type of advertising/marketing did you do?

We did postcards, Just Listeds and Just Solds. We did little mailers that we made up. We picked a little farm area, and it had 350 houses in it. We mailed to them twice a month. We bought the little gimmicky gifts that we put in: sponges, rulers, and notepads. In 1981, that was still good.

I remember one year, we were in a gasoline crunch, and we sent out little things that hold your gas nozzle open. We sent out all of that, and we did it every week, week-in and week-out. We called it *Neuman's News*. We just sent out information, talking about what happened in the neighborhood, little postcards telling them where we are and what was happening to the market.

We began to dominate the market area. It's getting your face in front of the clients over and over and over. That's the most consistent thing. Most agents don't recognize that farming, which is what that mailing is, is just that. You don't get instant gratification from it; you have to do it for six or seven months, and then the results start, and it builds and builds.

When we start now, we always mail once a week, for the first three months, then three for three months, and then get to two times. And I've had people, after three months, say, "Boy, I've been getting your stuff for years." They haven't. It just seems like it. All it is is branding my name in their minds on the way to the trashcan.

In branding, did you use a special logo or tagline?

We built our logo very early, which was Neuman & Neuman, the power of teamwork. And we took the two Ns and made it into a lightning bolt going through the N. We still use that trademark. We've stayed with it consistently. We didn't use pictures for a long time. I still don't have pictures on my business cards. I found that that has been very successful. It's name recognition. It doesn't matter as an agent whether you're with Century 21, Prudential, RE/MAX, Coldwell Banker, or any of the large franchises. It's the agent who makes the difference. If you rely on your broker or your franchiser to build your name, they're not going to do it; they're going to build their name.

What is one of the best ways of building your name?

Farming, advertising, and referrals are the only ways I know to build it.

Signs, of course, help when you have them in the neighborhood. If I were a brand-new agent, I would pick an area where I wanted to work, find a house in that area, and see if I could hold it open. I'd hold it open early in the evenings, especially during the summer months, like 4:00 to 7:00, when people are on the way home. Pick one that's fairly easy to get to and put out 25 signs so that people see those signs everywhere. As they drive through, they're on every corner, going to this house. Most agents put out three, maybe four, and they hate to do it. But I used to put out 20-25 because the people would see those signs all over the neighborhood, and they'd think that guy's doing everything. It wasn't even my listing.

What is the secret to holding a great open house?

The main reasons for open houses are really to collect clients and to make the seller think you're doing something. The main thing is to make sure you have some way to collect and then work the names. Find out the people who are really interested in buying. Separate them from those who came to get decorating tips, and continually work them. Most times, agents try to get the name on the way in. I always liked to get the name on the way out. Rather than getting them to sign in, you let people look at the house, you're courteous, and you kind of keep an eye on them. But then, as you're done, you talk to them, and say, "Now I'd really appreciate it if you'd sign here so I can let the seller know how many were really here." Talk to them, and most of the time they're a little more willing to give information, particularly if they have any interest in buying a house. You say, "How did it work for you?" "Well, it won't work for me because it has only three bedrooms." "Terrific, I know of three houses in this neighborhood that have four bedrooms." You have to go there, be prepared, know the neighborhood, and know the inventory in the neighborhood. I don't care what they buy from me. I just want them to buy. I get paid whether it's two, three, four, or five bedrooms. If you know the inventory and if you're ready and prepared, then you can have a good open house.

Do you put cookies in the oven?

No, typically, the easier thing to do is put a little vanilla in a cup of water and put that in the oven on simmer, and it smells like you're baking, and you don't have to clean up the mess. It just smells fresh-baked. People say it smells like grandma's house.

How did your advertising/marketing transform over the years?

I think I made the same mistakes that probably 85 percent of the agents make when they advertise. I would advertise and say, "Three bedrooms, two baths, 1700 square feet, San Carlos house, $56,000," and wait for the phone to ring. Then I began to realize, if you give them all the information, why are they going to call you? They know where it's located, they know how much it is, and it's three bedrooms. What if I need four? I don't call on any three bedrooms.

My advertising has changed now to the point where I don't give bedrooms, baths, square footage, or price in any of my ads. You have to call to get that information. I use the Interactive Voice Response (IVR) system. It's a system with which you could call every one of my ads with an 800 number. Then each house is assigned a four-digit extension. The first three digits of the extension tell me what house it is. The fourth digit tells me what advertising medium they're calling on so I know which ads that I'm running are drawing the calls.

When they call the 800 number, we give them all the information on the house except the address. However, because it's an 800 number, I call-capture your number. You cannot call-block an 800 number. We call back and say, "Hi, I notice that you just called on this house on Scripps Ranch. What time would be good for me to set up a private showing for you?"

"Well, that house won't work for us. It has only three bedrooms."

"Terrific, are you aware of the ones that have four bedrooms or more?"

"Well, no." And there you go.

Or, if I don't know if you're working with someone, I start out, "Hi, I noticed you called."

"Yes."

"May I ask if you are looking to buy a home?"

"Yes, I am."

"Are you working with an agent?"

"Yes."

"Oh, you are? May I ask you a question? If you're working with an agent, why are you making these calls? Isn't it your agent's job to inform you about houses that are for sale? Let me tell you how we work." Then we go in to the pitch on how we work. "Once we have your parameters, we put you on this special system that automatically notifies you of any house the minute it comes on the MLS. A lot of ads have to be put in three weeks early, and by the time you call on the house, it has been long sold. Let me spare you that frustration. Let me spare you doing what the agent's supposed to do to get paid. Let me show you how we work." And then we go from there. That's the start of a showing appointment.

I get the client to come in and sit down, and I get them pre-qualified. Typically, at that point, we try to make almost all our clients sign a buyer/broker agreement where they agree to work with us exclusively, even if it's only for thirty days. I tell them, "You don't shop doctors. We're not going to shop real estate agents. You're going to go with me. One of the things you need to understand is the way I work. I do such a thorough job that I have the ability to work with five buyers at one time. The good news for you is I just put a buyer into escrow, so I am presently interviewing people to fill that fifth position. If you'd like the opportunity to be one of those people, then let's sit down and meet, and let me see how I can help you with your needs."

Obviously, you must be valuable if you're interviewing people to work with you.

Exactly. Everybody else says, "I'll show you." We call it pop-tarting, where they jump out of the toaster to go show people when they have no idea if they qualify or can afford to buy, and don't even know if it's safe. I discourage that. If the people are not willing to come in, meet you, or get qualified, they may be buyers but they're not buyers for me.

Once we start, we fill out their wants and needs. We fill out what you want, and then we talk about what you need. You want a fireplace, but if I found the perfect house and it didn't have a fireplace, would you be willing to give up the fireplace? Of course, most people would say yes. That's how you narrow it down to what they really, really need.

The first thing we do is sit you in the conference room and have you fill out the questionnaire. Just like when you go to the doctor's, you do consultations. I'm trying to create that air of professionalism. Now you recognize you are really with somebody who knows what they're doing.

The conference room has trophies and different things that appeal to different people. We use the DiSC® system for clients. We have a *D* wall and *I*, *S*, and *C* walls. Usually, we say, "Sit anywhere you'd like," and they almost always sit and face the wall that's their behavioral type. We have things that show charities that we work with on one wall. We have kudos on another wall. We have pictures with famous people on a third wall. And then we have bullet information on the fourth wall, so there's something that appeals to each of the behavioral types.

They just stand there for a minute, looking around the room, and then they automatically pick the one that tends to fit their behavior?

Almost always. It's pretty astounding how often they do. I'll say, "Let me get us some water or coffee, and here's a little questionnaire we'd like you to complete. Look around and then have a seat." When I come back, if they're facing the bullet wall, that's the *D*. I know it's a person who's pretty much a no-nonsense guy, so I know how to treat him. Boom, boom, boom. If it's a guy who's facing the wall with the photos of all the famous people who I've been fortunate enough to meet in my career, I know that he's the *I* behavior type, and he's going to be driven by what his friends think; he's very impressionable. He probably wears designer clothes. If I start to work with him, I'll close him completely different from an *S* personality. An *S*, of course, is a socializer, a person whose family is more important to him or her than anything else.

We use the same system in listings. I look for these signs in their house so I can determine what their behavioral style is. It changes the close. When you're showing the same house, you'd show it to an *S* by saying, "Isn't this just what you need for your family? It's on a cul-de-sac

---

® DiSC is a registered trademark of Inscape Publishing, Inc.

and has a big yard. It's a nice place, safe to play, and your family's going to love it here."

If it's an *I*, I say, "Do you know how much your friends are going to be jealous with you living in this cul-de-sac with this big backyard for having parties? You are going to be so excited!"

If it's a *C*, the analytical type, like engineers and CPAs, you have to answer, "Okay, now, we've done our analysis, and here's what it is, price for square foot. This is what it should bring. If I added this for the yard, I have to add that." You give them all the information.

And *D* said it's a great buy, buy it. How long do we have to walk around looking at this thing? We want the house. Sign it. Time is important to him or her.

We do the same thing when we go on a listing appointment. You walk around looking for those things on the walls. An *I* will almost always have pictures on the wall, and he or she is in every one of them.

An *S* is very rarely in the photos. He or she has a lot of them, but isn't in them. This is the person who always says, "Okay, come on everybody, I'll take a picture of you."

With a *D*, there's very little around the house. Of course, when there are two behavioral types, husband and wife, they're mixed. It's not always as easy to tell. But it's pretty good. And then you know how to deal with them. You have to slow your voice down; you have to talk slower to an *S*. You have to make him or her feel comfortable. You can't apply pressure. With a *D*, it's boom, boom, boom.

You're combining the DiSC behavioral styles with language styles to establish rapport deeply and quickly with your clients.

Exactly. And making them feel comfortable with me. We try to teach a lot of that to the people who work for us.

What is a listing appointment like?

The first thing we do is prepare a prelisting package and have it delivered to your house.

On my team I have a full-time courier. I have the courier deliver the prelisting package. It's very extensive: it's about 45 pages with lots of information. It's designed for all personality types. It has bullets for the *Ds*, a table of contents, charts and graphs for the *Cs*, lots of photographs of famous people and testimonials for the *Is*, and it has warm fuzzy photos and charitable information for the *Ss,* like grandkids, dogs, and so on. The competitive market analysis is included. I like them to have it in advance so they can have some sort of feeling for what the market is, assuming they even look at it before I get there. Some do, some don't.

Sometimes it's easy to get overwhelmed with a 45-page package.

We've learned a lot of things to do to get people to look at it. If you want them to look at one or two pages, you take a red stamp and put *confidential* on those. That guarantees that they will read those pages. A lot of times, we'll stamp the CMA *confidential*; they'll look at that. At least it gives them the idea of what we do. We also put "Neuman and Neuman Exclusive Marketing Services," and we stamp that *confidential* so that they think that it's very important and read it. It gives them an idea of what we do. We found that that works very effectively to get them to read those pages. They have that in advance.

We used to, but don't as often now, send a little package of popcorn with it and a little bag. We'd say, "Take a few minutes, look at this, have a little popcorn, and relax while you read it." We also included a 20-minute video from David Knox on preparing your home for marketing. But we haven't done that as often lately, because in the present market, it's so difficult to get listings at all that you have to work harder at them.

Always arrive at the appointment on time. It astounds me that agents show up late. What I will do a lot of the time, even though I know I'm going to be on time, is to have somebody from my office call and say, "Mr. Neuman's running into a little traffic. He may be a few minutes late, and he asked me to apologize to you." And I still arrive on time anyway. But it gets them in the feeling already that here's a man who cares. And, not only that, he has staff. I know some of the stuff people think it's deceptive, but it sets me apart a little bit from other people.

When we arrive, I typically ask the clients to show me the house. I spend the time going around looking, with them, at the house and talking about the different things I see, trying to build a little rapport. If I see a whole bunch of pictures of soccer teams up there, oh, terrific, my sister used to be a soccer coach, or whatever. Anything I can do that will build a rapport with them, I try to do.

Then, while you're walking around, you ask them questions: Why are they selling? Do they have any idea what their home is worth? You try to get a feel for how realistic they're going to be. Typically, I have a pretty good idea of what I think it will be worth before I get there. Based on condition, of course, if I get there and it's a rat hole, it's going to be worth a lot less. Or I get in there and it's been dramatically improved. Those are things you can't see just by looking at an analysis.

Then we sit down and I ask them, "You've looked through the package. Do you have any questions on it?" If they have, they'll say yes and I'll answer one or two questions. Then we go into the meat of the listing presentation. "Are you prepared for me to sell your home?" A lot of times they'll say that they're ready. Sometimes, they'll say no. I'll say, "What would it take for you to want to hire me to sell your home?" And you overcome every objection they have, or attempt to. If you're going on multiple listings, most agents try to go last. I always try to go first. I feel if I'm really good, I am the last one.

I'll ask, "The question I have for you is what have you not heard from me that would make you want to list?"

"Well, I haven't had a chance to talk to anybody."

"What do you think they could possibly tell you they can do that's more than I am?"

"Nothing that I know of."

"Terrific. Why don't I do you a favor? You don't want to have to go through this three more times. It's a waste of your time. I have buyers; I'm ready to get marketing. Why don't I contact these three other agents you were planning on interviewing? I know a couple of them. A couple of them are very good agents; they have a lot of buyers. I'll tell them what I've listed the house for. I'll even do you a special favor: If one of these people brings a buyer in the first week, I'll cut the commission on my side to 2½ percent, so you can actually save some money, and we can take advantage of the buyers these agents may have and still get my marketing. Now, wouldn't that work for you?"

How did you get that education?

Unfortunately, when I started in the real estate business, there weren't a lot of trainers. There were only two I knew of at the time. I did learn one thing from Tommy Hopkins: When people ask how the real estate business is, you always say unbelievable. I listened to him and Danielle Kennedy.

I don't think I really got good at teaching until I hooked up with two people. One was Howard Brinton with his STAR POWER® club. Howard's been very good because what he teaches is what he gathers from when he interviews top stars around the country. What his system does: These top stars, once a month, share what they do and their techniques and closes. I learned what people in Georgia, Texas, and Maine are doing, and I then tweaked it or changed it so it would apply in my field. Some of it does work, and some of it doesn't work. He doesn't believe that there's a right way or a wrong way at all. He just feels this works, so take what you think is worthwhile out of this and go from there. That's where I was first introduced to the IVR system.

I can remember doing $28 million in 1996, when I first discovered the IVR system; I put it in in January. The next year, I did $58 million. It doubled my business just because it increased the volume of calls, and gave me more people to talk to.

I've always believed that contacts are like strawberries; they have a very, very short shelf life, and if you don't work them quickly, they're gone. It's who's persistent who will get them.

When starting out, what's the best use of your time?

I think there are only three things in the business that are worthwhile: being in front of a buyer, being in front of a seller, or being educated. Of course, that's not to say that being in front of your sphere of influence, whether it's getting involved with the Kiwanis or whatever you are, is not worthwhile, because that's being in front of clients. Those are the things you have to focus on. You have to set yourself up to make sure that you're doing one of those three things as often as possible, or attempting to do that. Anything else is just a waste of time.

What happens with most agents is that they come in to the office, hang around, and talk to the other agents, and none of those agents is going to buy anything from them. But they seem to think that there's this camaraderie if you're back having coffee, and you're talking about how your transaction went sideways, and theirs went sideways, and you feel better about the fact that you're having challenges. But it doesn't do any good at all. You have to pull yourself out of that and focus on trying to reach buyers and sellers.

I think Mike Ferry's a great coach. He has this system I don't particularly care for, that he's a prospector where you call, call, call, call, day-in and day-out. I mean all you do is contact. But what I do like about Mike is that he taught me to focus on my bottom line and not just to make a lot of money, but be profitable.

I know people who make probably less money than I do and net more. But I try to get better at that every year. This year our business is down a little bit, but our profitability is up. What I'm focusing on now at all times is making sure the profitability increases every year.

What types of things are you doing?

Using the IVR system is a very good way because I can find out what ads work. I can track what ads people call on. Sometimes you'd think that these ads work very well, and you get no calls. If I'm sending out a 5,000-piece mailer, I'll send 2,500 with one message on them and 2,500 with another message that's tweaked. I put a different four-digit code on each of them, so I'd know which of the two mailers worked the best. I constantly monitor, track, and tweak my advertising to make it better and better so that I know I'm getting the most bang for what I'm spending.

I also try to become more efficient as far as what I buy and spend, fighting for my commission dollar, particularly in this marketplace where people are taking a listing for one percent, two percent. I hold the line on commission. I believe that I'm worth what I get paid, and if you want my services, you're going to pay what I'm worth. I try to explain to people all the time, "The house is probably the most important asset that you have in your life. If you needed brain surgery, would the question of how much it cost even come out? Is that how you would shop for a brain surgeon? I don't think it would be, and you know you wouldn't. So if we're going to talk about your most valuable asset, shouldn't we talk about who has the ability to bring you the most money for it and make a smooth transaction in the least amount of time?" And that's what I offer. That's worth it to me. There are other agents who will do it cheaper, but they know what their services are worth. They'll probably bring you less money in the long run.

How often do sellers buy in to that?

Most of the time. I don't get them all. Nobody gets all the listings they go on. But, then you have to sit down, to show them the differences. Right now, you have to show them the difference your marketing will do. You have to know all your areas of expertise, and that all your listings sell within 98 percent of list price. You have to know your average market time. My average market time over the past 10 years is 36 days. I can compare it with the MLS, which is 78 days. I'm more than 50 percent faster.

How do you deal with the changes in the market?

The most important thing is anticipating the market. If I have one strong point, it's that I anticipate the market rather than react to it. I could tell that the market was heating up in 1996/97, and it really started to get going in '98. That's when I added buyer's agents to my team because I knew it was going to become difficult to get listings, but there would be a lot of buyers. So I had buyer's agents on the team who were ready, willing to go work all the buyers I couldn't.

The market slowed dramatically in 1991, like somebody had turned off the faucet, but I knew that was coming. I developed a builder trade-in program. I went to the builders and said, "Look, it doesn't do you any good to keep lowering the price of your house; it will eventually sell. The first thing you're doing is destroying your neighborhood because the people who bought from you for $300K are going to have a heart attack when you sell a model similar to theirs for $250K. We both know that, if I walked in to the market today to buy your house, you'd probably give me a $25,000 discount if I could close in 30 days."

They said, "That's true."

"But that discount doesn't help Mrs. Smith if she has a house that she has to sell but can't sell in this marketplace. Here's what we're going to do. Mrs. Smith is going to come in; she's going to buy your house for $300,000. You're going to guarantee to buy her house for $200,000, because that's the value of it. That $25,000 you were prepared to offer her, if she could close in 30 days, you're going to give me to discount the $200,000 house." Now, a $200,000 house, at $175,000, I'll have multiple offers on it. So it does three things for the builder: (1) He doesn't use any more money then he would have used for concession; (2) it maintains his values in his neighborhood; and (3) it moves the house that the contingent buyer has to sell—all for the same amount of money. I got 550 of those from 1991 through 1996 because it really helped the builders, and it was something they needed.

Frankly, I'm getting it tuned up again, because I think, probably early next spring, we'll be in a similar market—it won't be as bad as it was in 1991, but it won't be the robust market that we've had for a long time. Most agents are yet absolutely unaware of the market turning.

You're going to have to be a salesperson, to spend money to market the house, to have merchandise, to know how to do scripts to work price reductions, and to counsel people to get houses priced accurately. This is where the people will start to vanish. Most of them, especially the ones who have been doing the discounted brokerage, don't have the money to market. It will take a lot more than putting it in the MLS and an ad in the paper to sell the house.

It will have to be staged. There will be negotiations done. You will have to counsel your client, to help your client make the right decision when the offers come, rather than say, "Well, we didn't get our full price today; we'll wait until tomorrow."

About 93 percent of the houses today are sold by seven percent of the agents. I think the California Association of Realtors says that the average agent is licensed five years. They're on the way through. They just don't know it. They're leaving the business.

In my real estate programs, it is surprising the number of people who don't feel they have the obligation and responsibility to counsel their clients. They're like paper pushers.

That's what they are. They're glorified scribes, rather than agents. My job is to educate you. My job is to tell you, "I hate to bring this to you, but based on what's happened in the market, I think this is probably a pretty good offer. My feeling is that, if you don't take this offer, with a few changes that we need to make to make it safer for you, in 60 days, you're going to be angry with me. Now, if you elect not to take it, I have no problem with that. I want this to be your decision." When you go to an attorney, you don't have him say, "Well, this can happen." You say, "What should I do?" And I think agents fail to advise. Lack of confidence is probably the reason.

I've always believed that there are two ways to do things. There's the right way and the wrong way. I do the right things for two reasons: (1) It's the right thing, and (2) someday I may have to explain why I did it. I look at every transaction in that way. What would I say if I had to defend this before the judge? It makes the decision really easy because there's no amount of commission that's worth going through the aggravation of being sued. I've closed over 3600 transactions in my career. I've been involved in seven lawsuits, which is minimal. I've won every one of them because we did the right thing. We counseled our clients. We got all the paperwork signed. We had proof that we had all the paperwork signed. And we did a good paper trail for them and for us. Even more than that, I've saved sellers money because I've been able to prove they disclosed things, and they provided that information to the buyers because we saw that they did do that. I think that's critical.

What's the impact when working with an agent who isn't good?

You know you're going to have to do both sides. It's been very beneficial for me over the years because I've picked up a lot of agents' clients. I've had agents' clients say to me, "Boy, we watched you represent the seller. And we asked, 'Why isn't our agent working like that?'"

What types of things do you do?

We're always very forthright and knowledgeable. We send all the information out. We make sure that every piece of paper is sent to them and followed-up to be signed. We detail it. We stay in contact with both the buyers and the sellers of a property. If I'm representing a seller, and you bring the buyer, at the close of escrow I send the buyer a nice letter. I say, "We're really thrilled that you bought this house. We hope that you're going to be as happy as Mr. & Mrs. Smith were. What I'd like to do is offer the opportunity, if anything occurs that you need some information regarding the house, to feel free to contact me, because I probably know the house as well as anybody except the sellers. I'll be here." Then we call them after three days. Most agents hate to call after three days. After three days, something's gone wrong, something didn't work out, they didn't get their garage door opener, or something, and we take care of it. That's no problem. "Here's what I want you to do. Sears is the manufacturer of this. Call them and order one. You send me the bill. I'll take care of it." For $38, I picked up a client.

They probably never heard from their agent again.

We call them orphans because that's what they are. I have a handyman who does a lot of work for us. A lot of times I'll say, "Let me send my handyman over. I'll give you two hours of free work from him. If you want something hung, the washing machine hooked up, or something taken care of, he'll do those things for you. He has the tools. Welcome to the neighborhood, and let us know if we can help you in any way."

Over the years, 3600 clients, and I may have half again that much because I have the buyers.

Did you put them on your mailing list?

Yes. With most of the agents leaving the industry, they're not going to be there. If they don't leave the industry, they change companies and jobs. They don't track who their buyers and sellers are. They don't stay in contact with them. Their brokers are at least trying to do that now. But they're my clients, so I mail them all.

What have you learned about negotiation skills?

The biggest thing that we've learned is that everything in the funnel is important. There's no detail that's too small. An awful lot of agents send us contracts that are missing sections filled out, don't have basic information, or have too-specific information. Like a contract will come in with a 60-day escrow, and it'll say interest not to exceed 5¾. I'm never going to let that contract go through because 5¾ is too low an interest rate. I'll counter back at the interest rate, and the buyer's new loan is to be 8 percent. If there's a tick up or a hiccup in the market, as long as the buyer still qualifies for the loan, he's locked in to the transaction. I try to make sure that all the loopholes are gone. If something is due, something has to be removed within 17 days, then in 17 days it needs to be removed, or we have to start hounding the agent to provide it. It becomes very, very important that you make sure that all the details and all the things of the contract are followed through exactly.

The second thing in negotiating skills is counseling the client. The seller typically gets less than he wants for the house. The buyer typically has to pay more for the house than he wants. You have to make both parties understand that, even though neither obtained exactly what they want, it's really a good deal for both of them. That's what I said: It's really a lose/lose situation. Everybody loses a little bit. Mr. Buyer, you're going to pay a little more for this house than you really wanted, and you're not getting his widescreen TV. Mr. Seller, now you understand that you may not get every dollar that you want, you can't sell it as is, and you will have to do the termite clearance, but this is what you have to do. If somebody comes in and offers you more money for it, he or she will come back after you and want you to do those things. You have to negotiate back and forth to make sure that that's exactly what happens.

Do you set people up with these kinds of expectations?

You're doing it both at the listing and at the buyer meeting. You have to let them know, "This is the range in which I think your home is going to sell. But, you need to be aware that the market will speak to us. If we don't have an offer within a certain amount of time, and after a certain amount of showings, we will probably have to adjust our price, or you may have to do something." I'm a great believer in telling sellers that I do not want them to advertise the property "as-is" because, when you do that, it creates a fear in the buyer's mind that there's really something more wrong.

I also counsel them to do things to make the house sell better. I hate it when an agent says, "We'll give you a carpet allowance." Mr. Buyer thinks it's going to take Kurdistan Carpet at $35/yard. Mr. Seller is planning on putting indoor/outdoor carpeting.

I tell the seller, "Let's put in a good, what I call, real estate beige; it's a decent looking carpet. It'll last a couple of years. It will look good. We'll upgrade the pad. It'll feel plush, and we don't have to negotiate." There are many things that sellers can do that are "one-for-ones," as I put it. If you install carpet and paint, and you put some reasonable window coverings in, you'll get that money back, one or two dollars for every one you spent.

There are other items that I won't let them spend on. I won't let them put in a bathroom because adding a bathroom won't bring the price. Changing the countertops won't bring them the price. But those minor, cosmetic repairs do because they set the stage. You have to be honest with them; you have to tell them when their house actually stinks. They may not even notice the pet or cooking odors.

Do they accept that?

If you phrase it right. "We have dogs. One of the things that people have pointed out to me, in my home, is that the dogs have their own smell, and the house begins to get that odor. We've lived with them so long, we don't even notice it." Of course, I don't have dogs, but maybe my cats stink.

You tell them that anyway?

You have to make it acceptable. I've had to tell people, "One of the things you're going to have to do is lay off of the cabbage. You can't be cooking cabbage here every day. It will create an offensive odor in the house, either coming or going. And we will have to make sure that the house smells and looks its best." I tell them to buy plug-ins, clean up, weed, and do whatever needs to be done. You spend the time and teach them why it will be important for them. They're almost always willing to do it. I have to tell the "you" benefit. "Here's what will happen. If you carpet a 1500 square-foot house, it'll cost up to $2500. If you paint, it's going to cost $1,500. For that $4,000, my expectation is you'll probably get at least $4K and maybe $5 or $6,000 more and it will probably sell faster. Now, isn't that worth it to you?" Yes. "Okay, let's sign this listing agreement, and I'll give you the names of a couple of painters. I'll give you the names of the carpet guy, and we'll get this taken care of for you."

Let's say you're representing the buyer side. Do you normally ask for everything you want, initially, as long as it's reasonable?

When I represent buyers, I always ask for the washer, dryer, and refrigerator. They can counter out that or agree and buy newer appliances. It gives them something to say no to. "You can't have my washing machine," but they may give my buyers the price. It depends on the market, of course. If it's the market where there are 17 offers, you have to be very careful. There are ways to position your buyer to get a house, particularly in multiple offers.

One of the very first things you have to do is to have a fully approved buyer. The buyer has to be approved by a lender. You have to go in with a pre-approval letter.

The second, very, very effective thing we do is to have the buyers write a letter. The buyers write a letter to the seller telling about themselves. "Dear seller, what you need to know is that my wife and I are thrilled with the house. We have two small children who just love the big backyard. They can't wait to go to school and get to know the kids in the neighborhood. We hope that we can keep this house up as well as you have."

There are times when I've had clients get a house for less money than somebody else has offered because of the letters they write. Sellers are selling houses, but a lot of times, they're selling homes. More than anything else, they want to sell their home to somebody who's going to care about and like it.

Now, that's not to say that the people don't come and bulldoze it the day after the close.

Clients write better letters, and they sound a little more sincere. If they have little kids, they'll have them draw a picture of their dog. Or, I'll tell their kids, "You're going to be looking at a couple of houses. If your mom and dad see a house you like, why don't you draw me a little picture of either the pet, if they have a pet, or something that you like about the house." When it's older people moving out of their house and they get this little 8½ × 11 drawing of some little kid, who obviously doesn't have any clue what he's drawing, and it's a picture of the swing in their backyard, that's very emotional to them. That's very important.

Agents don't take the time to do those things. I would say 90 percent of the offers I get are faxed or emailed to me. They send a cover letter: hope to see you in escrow. How impersonal is a fax? If I have any opportunity, I always present the offer in person, first off because I'm better than most agents. When I get there with the seller, I can do a good presentation. I can make the seller feel comfortable that the transaction is going to close. I can make the seller aware that at least there's one person now who knows what they're doing.

I always call the agent before I write an offer because I try to find out things that are important. How long an escrow do your sellers need? When are your sellers moving? What are their plans? Are there things that they want to leave and things that they don't want to leave? What are they willing to do and not willing to do? I can write an offer that is as appealing to the seller as possible without ever getting their price.

A lot of people are fussy about their decks. They don't want to do a termite inspection on a detached deck that's in the backyard. I ask the agent how his seller feels about the deck. I may have to tell the buyer, "We're not getting termite clearance on this deck. We have a better chance in multiple offer situations if we don't ask for it, than if we ask for all these things."

How you handle the transaction depends upon the market. If the market's red hot, you have to beg, give me an opportunity. But if the market's slower, you can put a lot more things in or ask for fewer things and come down on price. When I present the offer, unless it's full price, price is the last thing I talk about. "I want to tell you about my clients, Barbara and her husband John. He's a new teacher. She's been working for five years as a nurse practitioner. They have one child who's two years old and another that's one, and she's pregnant again, which is why they're looking for a new house. They're really excited about raising their family in your home, and they love the colors and the drapes."

The whole time they're getting more and more interested in the people. Then I say, "By the way, they've offered $175,000." "We're asking $180." "Yes, I know, but they've done all the research, and it really wouldn't do us any good to bring it in at $180, if it doesn't appraise. Then we have your expectations up for money that you're probably not getting anyway. We know it's probably going to appraise at $175. I'm comfortable, and I think your agent's comfortable. Aren't you, Mary?"

Mary would say, "Of course."

"Terrific. Both Mary and I feel it's going to appraise for $175. We have this lovely young couple that wants to buy your home. Wouldn't it feel good tonight to know that you have somebody?"

I also have a little cover thing that we put on our offer that says:

Our buyers have been counseled. We know that when they have a physical inspection that the terms of the physical inspection are strictly to find things in the house that are safety or health hazards. We're not going to be nitpicking you for paint touch-up, for a leaky faucet, or something like that. We're here to make this move as smooth as possible for you.

Those are all good things that get sellers turned around, even when you're working the buyer, to get them thinking that these are reasonable people. We have a chance to put this together. It's going to close.

Sometimes you'll get an agent who won't let you talk to his or her people. Then you have to type a good letter and do your analysis. The agent has to sit down and do this rationale for what the price is going to be, and why you've done it. You have to do that. California law says that, unless they say it in writing, the agent has the right to present the offer. A lot of times agents say, "Oh, no, no."

"Fine, do you have that in writing?" Most of them will say no. "Good. Why don't I just come over? I'll only take 15 minutes to present it. There will be eight offers, and I'll be the only agent who shows up."

And you're the one who gets the deal.

Almost always. And you bring them all the things that make the offer seem like a real offer. I get offers faxed to me every day that don't have the clients' pre-approval letter or any information on the buyer. I don't even know if the buyer has the money.

Agents tell me they've been working with a client for quite a while and then they go work with someone else. Why does that happen?

Did you sign a buyer/broker agreement? Were they committed to you? If you don't do those things, you don't have a lot of chance to get that. I'm always amazed at people who don't do that. I tell them, "You need to understand that, if at any time you're unhappy with my services, or you feel I'm not doing the job, I'll cancel. I have no problem. I'll release you from this listing. I want protection on everybody I've brought through, but I'll release you on the listing." Maybe one in every 400-500 asks to get out, and most of the time it's because his or her circumstances changed. He or she is no longer going to sell or can't get the expected money. I won't work with people who won't commit to me, so I won't expect them to hire me unless I'm agreeable to commit to them.

How many hours do you normally work in a week?

The good thing about working with my ex-wife is that we split weekends. I work a four-day week, Monday through Thursday, the first and third week of the month. And I work a six-day week on the second and fourth. I have Friday, Saturday, and Sunday. It gets you really refreshed. I get up at 5:00 in the morning; I take Pilates (exercise class) at 6:00 every day. I'm down at my office at 7:00. I built a shower in here, so I take a shower, and I'm at my desk at 7:30. I typically work until 6:30, unless I have an appointment at night. I try to do very few appointments at night. So I average a 60-hour week, probably.

Did you use to work more?

Yes, because I would go on more night appointments, until I got better at making those people take the time off during the day.

That was a close I learned probably in 1997 or '98 from Phyllis Wolborsky, and I've never forgotten it. I use it all the time. People think that it makes perfect sense.

How do you balance your life, especially with children?

I have found that you have to book time off.

If I were flying in from Chicago to buy a house from you this weekend, and I told you I'm going to be here on Friday, I'd expect that you and I are going to look at houses all day Friday and all day Saturday. You would book those two days completely for me. And you wouldn't show anything else.

So somebody else says I want to see houses at 10:00 Saturday. You say, "I can't. I have this guy in from Chicago, so how about I show you on Thursday." That appointment from Chicago is you, your wife, and your family. And you book it, and you don't change it. You just say, "I'm sorry I have somebody coming in from out of town on Thursday, and I can't do that."

My answering machine at home says, "If it's Monday through Saturday, from 7:00 A.M. to 7:00 P.M., please call my office. If it's Sunday, I do not work on Sunday. Feel free to leave a message here, but I won't call you until Monday."

How big a staff do you have?

Right now, I have five. I have a full-time listing coordinator, two full-time escrow coordinators who are handling the transactions, a full-time courier, and a full-time receptionist.

Do you have buyer's agents?

I have some buyer's agents, but I don't call them staff. Right now, I have six buyer's agents. They're independent brokers. I don't pay them. They get paid only if they sell.

I work very few buyers anymore. Buyers are the least effective method of working with clients because you can only sell them when they're sitting beside you in a car. Listing works for you 24 hours a day, and there are 10,000 other agents to help you sell it.

How else do you keep yourself motivated? Do you listen to tapes, read books?

I read a lot of books about real estate. I think those are very effective for me. I like to read how other people are successful. I read biographies. I really like reading because you can think only about what you're reading, while you're reading. It completely shuts my mind down about whatever I'm thinking about at work almost instantly. If I want to read a casual novel, I just sit down and read for an hour or an hour-and-a-half or read the newspaper or whatever, and that immediately takes me out of work.

I'm also a gardener. It's very easy for me.

I've learned to departmentalize. I've learned to take the peaks and valleys out of real estate. I think it's the peaks and valleys that burn real estate agents up. They sell a million-dollar house, they're all excited—I'm going to make all this money—then it falls out. Then they're all depressed that they didn't get the sale.

I know if I have enough listings and sales going at all times, I'll make a great living, and I don't get excited when the big ones sell. I don't get excited when they fall out. I don't get excited at any time. I know it's just inventory. As long as I merchandise my inventory, as long as I don't take inventory that will not sell, I will do a good job, and I will make money.

A lot of agents forget that that's really all we are. We're merchants. If I take houses that are overpriced, or houses that are poorly designed, or won't sell and don't get them priced right, then I've wasted my money and time, and dealt with sellers whom I don't want to deal with because they're the most demanding sellers. It's the guy who won't fix the house up. Or, it's the owner of a four-bedroom, one-bath house with a converted garage who's more demanding of your time than anybody, and he's going to call you every two days to see what you've done. I've gotten to the point now where I fire sellers. I'll just say, "No, thanks. I'm sorry; I don't think you and I are going to work well. You're already making too many demands of my time. I'm going to suggest you take your business somewhere else." And just let him go.

Most agents hang in with somebody like that, with the hopes that they just make it through.

That uses up more of their time and energy than if they let that person go. They let go of the outcome and say, "Oh, if I could only sell this house." Forget it. That person will drive you to distraction and keep you from doing other business. You'll find yourself spending far more time than you'll ever make on that thing, assuming it does sell. Firing a difficult buyer or seller is one of the most rewarding feelings in real estate.

You could potentially find two clients with whom you would spend the same amount of time as you would have with this one client.

You may even like the people.

What have you learned along your path?

The biggest thing I've learned is letting go of the outcome, not getting caught up in it. Another thing that's very important is that we have no problems in my office. We only have challenges. When you have a problem, it's almost always assigned to somebody. If I come to you and say there's a problem, it's your problem or it's my problem. If I say that we have a challenge, it becomes something that we can work together to overcome. That slight change in vocabulary has changed the way I've been able to interact with clients, staff, and other agents. There's less finger pointing and more problem solving or challenge solving when it's phrased that way.

What I don't understand about real estate today is that agents have become very confrontational. They try to make this a battle. All we've done is hurt both of our clients. Your buyer wants to buy and my seller wants to sell. It shouldn't be you and me pitted against each other. It should be, okay, we have a common goal to sell this property. How do we solve that? How do we work toward that issue? I see that so much. Maybe it's an overflow of road rage, or whatever it is. I call it agent rage, where the agents are so competitive with each other that they lose sight of their job, which is to help our clients buy or sell or both. The clients lose when we battle. It's very hard to get them past that. Agents need to be a little more civil to each other and make those calls first, before they do things. How do we want to solve this before I take this to my client? Do you have a solution? Do you have something we can do? The ability to do those kinds of things has taken my business to a higher level.

Let's say you have the buyer, and the seller wants $500,000. Your client doesn't want to spend any more than $450. Assuming it's not a scarcity market, how do you negotiate the difference?

That's a big difference. If the client doesn't want to spend more than $450,000, I shouldn't be showing him $500,000 houses anyway. But let's assume that I did. More often than not, I have to find out what the house is really worth. Let's say, in my analysis of this hypothetical house based the comps, it is probably between $470 and $480.

Then I have to convince the seller that he's going to come down to $470, and I have to get the buyer up. I do the buyer in many different ways. It's usually the easiest to move the buyers, because you can reduce it to the ridiculous. "Where we stand right now: We think this house is really worth $470, so we're only $20,000 apart. With today's mortgage rates, $6 per thousand, so we're $120 apart in this transaction. Based on the fact that we're $120-a-month apart, what do you think that equates to? Dan, I know your wife wants this house, probably a little more than you do. Dan, are you prepared to give up one latte a day to give your wife this house at $470? If you're willing to make that sacrifice for her, I think we can get the seller down to $470 to put you in a house that you want." That's where you have to go, and sometimes it takes two or three moves to get them there.

If the client isn't insulted by the offer, it seems most agents will counter with $490, and the other one goes to $460. Then we go to $470, and you end up in the middle.

A lot of times it depends. I'll call an agent and say, "Tell me about your client. Does your client like to dance? A lot of cultures really like the negotiation. If that's the case, then we're going to dance. If they're not, I can get my people to make what I think will be their best and final offer. I'm certainly willing to do that to save you and your client time. Do you want that? Do you want us to come back?" If they tell my client to negotiate, we're going to come back at $455. You're going to come back at $485, and it will take us to 12 counteroffers to get there. But I also tell the buyers that all this negotiation is stressful on both parties. The quicker you can arrive at a transaction where you've agreed on price, the easier the escrow's going to be. If you have 12 counters, by the time we get to the end of the transaction, the seller's going to think that you are a real grinder. The seller is not going to be willing to do anything for you. When we find a window that has a failed seal, and we ask them to repair it, he will remember that you ground him to death, and he'll say no.

A lot of times I'll tell them, "Here's what I want you to do. Give me a number and tell me, 'Gregg, if you come to me tomorrow and tell me that somebody paid $471 for that house and, even though I offered only $470, that I would be perfectly willing to say terrific, I'm glad, it's not worth that to me.' If we've reached the point where a thousand dollars is more than you would pay for the home, then I have no problem. We'll make that offer, and we'll go on to the next house if you don't get it. But I don't want you feeling bad that you would have really gone to $475 or $472.5. We don't have to go there now, but I need to know where that number is."

You need to educate them on what the market is. If you're educating the buyer in today's market, and they're thinking that they should negotiate, you're doing them and yourself a disservice. They'll lose three or four houses before they realize that they have to be making full-price offers, or they have to be making very good offers.

When the market turns, you have to tell the seller, "Look, typically the first offer we get is going to be our best offer. We have to look at it if it's a number we can live with, and this is where we have to go."

I do like value range market. It's not popular in a lot of places. It's very effective. Interestingly enough, in the MLS in San Diego County, there are now more houses for sale using the variable range than there are not. Basically, you're saying that the seller will entertain offers in between. Often, buyers don't know where to begin in a negotiation. All it says is, I will entertain any offer that's between these two ranges. I'll approve it, disapprove it, or counter it.

Why would anybody make an offer above the bottom range, unless we were in a scarcity market?

Interestingly enough, 60 percent of the houses have sold in value range, and this goes back to before the market was scarce, where it's 60 percent or higher. The range does a lot of good things. It helps bridge the gap between what I think it's going to sell for and what you think it's going to sell for. I can say, "Fine. I think your house will sell for $470, and you think it's going to do $500. Terrific. We'll put in a value range between $475 and $525. We'll see. If it sells in the first couple of days, you and I both know it will have to be at the $525 range. But we know, if it's 60 days in, 30 days in, it's going to be at the bottom range, or slightly below the range, and you have to be willing to accept that."

Weaker agents don't have to get price reductions either, because you built a price reduction in. It's an ironic tool. I think a lot of people have done it for years without recognizing it. Builders sell new homes starting from $400,000. It is confusing to some people, but a lot of people get it. To show their good faith they come in a little bit over the bottom range.

How do you become a great agent?

Work hard. Be honest. Invest in yourself. Those are the three things that most great agents do. They work long and hard, particularly starting out. They're ethical and do good real estate and then they spend money to continue to grow their market until they get as big as they want to be.

And yet, there are so few people making a lot of money in this business.

I think the average agent in the United States makes less than $24,000 a year, which is probably what they'd make if they worked at 7-11. Most of them don't get it. But most of them don't do anything. They don't work it. They don't try to drum up new business. They don't go talk to people. I talk about real estate to everybody I know. People are always interested in real estate. They either own it or they want to. It's a very easy conversation. It's something that everybody is willing to talk about. I've sold to grocery clerks, because I've talked about it and asked, "Do you own a house?" "No." "Well, you should. Here's my card." If they say, "Sure do," ask, "Ready for a bigger one, yet?"

You can ask, "Do you own the home of your dreams?"

That's a great line. I'll have to remember that one. If the answer is no, you say, "Let's move you closer to it."

What advice would you give agents to be more successful?

Nobody knows how little you know. If you're a brand-new agent, you already know more than most people, because you passed the test. Go out there and act competent, act like you know what you're doing, and dress well. Agents don't dress well. You go to a guy in a million-dollar house and you show up at his house in a t-shirt. If I walked in to a law office and the attorney was sitting there in a t-shirt, I'd probably leave. You have to look, act, and talk professional. You have to get educated and then get out and interact with the public. Get out and talk to them. Get out and make them want to meet you.

Do you rely only on referrals now?

Absolutely not. Every time somebody moves out of town, I have one less client. Every time somebody dies, I have one less client.

You have to continue to advertise, build your market and grow. I moved my business downtown because downtown San Diego's a whole new market. I moved here specifically with the goal of trying to capture a good portion of that market. I thought, why not, it's here to be taken.

It will take somebody who's willing to spend the money. I'm looking forward to the market, because the market's slowing down. Now all 4,000 of those agents who have one deal are going to be gone from the market because they can't stay in. They won't be able to hang on. The market's going to open up for good agents who do good business. I expand my business always when the market gets slower.

CREIG NORTHROP

LONG & FOSTER REAL ESTATE, INC.
Clarksville, Maryland

#1 Gross Commission Income: Long & Foster Real Estate, Inc.
#1 Agent in the State of Maryland

- Sales Volume: $231 million
- # of Units Sold: 550
- # of Employees: 31
- www.NorthropTeam.com
- Years in the business: 17

What interested you about real estate and how did you get started?

I grew up with it. My mother has been in business for 30+ years. I had always been exposed to it, been around it. I definitely knew or had expectations of what I was getting in to. Then, I fell in to it because I was a natural.

And how did you know you were a natural?

Usually when your parents are in a business, you want to get away from the business, because it sometimes can take your parents away from you. It's almost that progression, where you don't like the business, where you don't get to see your parents so much. But in this situation, ironically, I just love sales, I love people, and I loved that part of it. Through college, I owned video stores. I learned business aspects which helped in real estate later.

How did you start owning video stores?

I went to the University of Maryland and worked at the video store. I went right to the head guy, and was made manager in two months. I learned the business. I opened my first store probably about six months later. Then I opened up five stores. Then the economy changed with the videos. Blockbuster started coming and everything else. So I got out of that business and said, "You know what, I'm sick of selling myself for $2 when I could be selling myself for $200,000." I found that was a much better way and, watching my mother being as successful as she was, I jumped right in, too. I started selling land first, and then got in to the residential part of it.

Did your mother spend time with you and give you advice?

Yes. My mother is one of the most positive people you're ever going to meet in the world. She is always saying you can reach whatever you want to reach. That's part of it, being around her, and then, of course, hearing her on the phone and then her jumping in, teaching me certain things. Certainly, she was my mentor.

What were some of the key elements she taught you?

Her philosophy is if you can conceive it, you can believe it, you can achieve it—pretty strong words.

When you left doing the video stores you went to work for?

At that time, it was Coldwell Banker.

Were you a team together?

In marketing, my ultimate goal was to get in a position where we were seen equally. In the marketing part of it, it was Elaine Northrop and Creig Northrop. That's where my marketing aggressiveness started. But the other part of it was that I did everything from running signs to contracts. I started from the ground up, which I think everyone must do. I preach that to all my people, because that's where you learn the most—running contracts and getting initials done on contracts and all the paperwork, and things like that. That's really where I started. She had me, a secretary, and, I believe, one other person, and that was the first team created in our area.

How many hours were you putting in then?

When I started in video, I would open and close the store, which was 10- or 12-hour days. I was already accustomed to that. When you own a store, you are the store. I always said, in my life, or in my businesses, whatever I owned, I wanted to be big enough to maximize potential, but small enough to close the doors at any time and check my inventory, to be able to have "hands on" on everything I do. In the beginning, between the two businesses, if I wasn't working one, I was thinking about the other, pretty in-depth. I'd say it was at least 80 hours.

I always believed that, if I could get as many hours in as possible in my younger years, I could relax in my older years.

Has that held to be true?

The question is when's the older years? The problem with that goal was it was 40, and now the question is, is it 40 or 45? My wife wants it to be 37!

She says now would be a good time to slow down?

She would like to slow down and enjoy the time with our four kids. We work together, because in this business it's hard not to work with your spouse, because either (a) you don't see him or her, or (b) you don't understand when he or she comes home upset, or talking about things that are kind of not in English.

What was driving you so hard?

Driving me, traditionally, is just to be the best, at whatever I go after. When it was land, it was that we don't have a lot of nice neighborhoods, so I paired up with a builder who was Southern Living Builder, and he really had the same goals, to create more neighborhoods. We have a lot of little piece-meal—a street here, a street there—where I wanted more communities. In order to create it, I had to develop it, and I developed a couple of neighborhoods in the area that I'm proud to go by.

You wanted to make more money than your mother?

It was never really a money issue. I worked from a standpoint of volume, or how could I help the most clients in the least time, with the most efficiency and make them the happiest. The money will come to anybody who has a vision and is focused and knows what he or she wants. That's secondary to me.

You opened your own office?

Right before our division of Coldwell Banker was bought out by Long and Foster, I chose to go on my own. Wes Foster is the owner of our company. What I really love about the company is that we have an official owner. He's a real person. It's not some big company owner whom you never meet. He came to me personally, and my mother, and said, "Here's what I'm going to do for you. You can call me anytime." I like that. I like the guy who has the same visions I did. I immediately joined his company. I went on my own and my mother went on her own, but we were still in the same Long and Foster company. It was just that I had one office, while she had another office.

Were you in the same building?

Yes. It was always interesting when you start talking about whose space is where? I would say I lived in a cracker box for a while. I was not looking for the big office down the hall to make a statement. My goal was not to make a statement. I consistently learned it; I gained the knowledge. I knew every street of every price range. If I walked in to anybody's house, I knew the value. I knew what you were competing with. I always said, knowledge is confidence, confidence is trust, trust is a sale. About a year after Long and Foster bought us out, I took over being the number-one producer of sales.

How did you build your name and separate yourself from your mother?

The first challenge is to get your name out there. I'm very aggressive in my marketing. I found areas outside of the market she was not concentrating on, like where the market is going next. I targeted the markets where they're going next and where their higher-end properties are and where people think they're getting a deal if they buy in to this county. I went outside the county to market, to bring them in to our county, whereas she was more focused on just the county itself.

What type of marketing did you do?

I did everything. I had a little more technology background, so I got in to virtual tours. I got an in-house printing company. I did beautiful brochures for every property. I got all the magazines—in any one you pick up that has to do with Howard County, I have the first three pages, let's say, of every book. You can't pick up a Howard County book without going through my listings. I fought for that. I went in and decided that every book, here's where I wanted to be. I started that working, and working, and working, and being patient enough to get where I needed to be.

My mother was known for the high-end, the million-dollar properties. I, fortunately, said, "Wait a minute. Her market thinks she sells only high-end. Guess what I'm going to do? Large or small, I sell them all."

Was that one of your slogans?

Absolutely. I went after the whole market and tried not to fight off the high-end market, because in a market that's not selling as well, the low-end sells a lot faster. I picked up much more volume. My transaction count doubled because of that marketing. The townhouse buyers became single-family buyers, and then the single-family buyers became million dollar buyers, that kind of step-up approach.

That's where I started. I also began going in to universities, like the University of Maryland. I went back to my college and created relationships with its sports programs. I created community service with all the schools. I started getting myself out there, around the whole community.

Was that positioning yourself so when they were ready to buy, they would think of you?

Yes. I went in for a listing one time and got in the door, and I said, "Hi, how are you?" He said, "My son, who's only seven, wants to show you something." I said, "Great." We walked upstairs and went in to his room, and it had a beautiful painted mural. In this corner, there was a little turtle, which is the mascot for the University of Maryland. The father said, "He wanted to show you this turtle because he thinks of you when he sees the turtle." That marketing works. I hit such a huge chord with the sports, with the college—from college kids, to the young kids, to the adults. That was a very successful part of meshing the community with college. College promotes success.

Without consistent advertising, how are others ever going to succeed?

I didn't hold anything back. I always say, "I'm just getting warmed up." Everybody else is scared about the dollar. I'm not worried about the dollar, because the way I look at it, if I get myself out there enough, they will find me and my properties and I'm going to sell them. The more repetitiveness, the more successful you become. If I was cold, starting from scratch, I'd say it'd be a little bit harder to mass-market yourself. I am not taking anything away from that. I already had some sales under my belt and things like that prior to me doing that.

Your psychology and business degree gave you a good solid background to know how to run this as a business.

This is what I believe in, and I felt, before I went on my own, that I would create the IBM business approach to real estate. My model: Let's break up what real estate transactions are about and put it in different categories and then create a team that focuses on each part of that transaction. That's what they're good at. That's where I started.

I never wrote them down. I knew. I had a vision of where my team would be today, and I just put it together. When I found the people who I felt fit the positions, my wife and I put them together. My wife's a huge part of that, because she has a lot of that intuition. My team has grown probably in the last six or seven years.

Take me from your small office, a whole in the wall at Long and Foster. What transpired from there?

About four years in the business, I decided I needed to get an assistant, so I got an assistant. I realized I didn't want to be doing all the paperwork. I didn't enjoy it bogging me down. I'd rather pay somebody to do it. I enjoyed meeting people, talking to them, things like that. That's what I was good at, what I knew, my markets, and where I wanted to be. In order for me to be successful, I had to be there. I'm not successful when I'm sitting there doing paperwork.

Then I realized I'm getting a lot of calls in, because now I'm doing a lot more marketing, and I get my first buyer's agent, who's there to help with my buyers. It grew from there. I think I took on one more buyers agent and brought a marketing specialist in, the best marketer I could find. She wasn't doing marketing for real estate; she was doing marketing for a newspaper. I was so impressed. I said, "I want to give you a job. Here are my goals." She shared the goals, and we expanded our marketing even further. At that point, I had a marketer, a secretarial/administrative assistant, and I had two buyer's agents. About that time, probably seven years in the business, my volume started exceeding my mother's.

Now it's started doing really well. In order to keep selling and maintaining the level of customer service I wanted to provide, I realized you needed people to do that. That's where my goal really started expanding. I think it kind of burst, and I started finding different people for different positions.

Right around then, I found my wife, which is the best part of my life. She helped me see things that I didn't see before. We created a team. At this point, I have departments for listings, sales, marketing, and customer service. And I have a buyer bullpen agency, where my buyer agents are. I divided them into sections.

Working that many hours, how did you meet your wife?

It's funny. I wanted to buy a house. I said here's what I want: a cul-de-sac, brick-front house, and to back up to some parkland or some open space. That's all I wanted. I went in to a house, around midnight, and didn't even really look at it. I said I'll take it, and I bought it. I realized when I settled on it that it was a baby blue all-over, and it had five bedrooms. Here's a bachelor buying a five-bedroom house. I was too busy through the summer, and couldn't get anything really fixed up, and it was getting toward the tail end of the summer. I recommend a lot of contractors to fix up things, so I brought them all in my family room and said, "Look, I recommend you to other people. I'm going to give you thirty days to fix this house up. You fix this house up, and we'll have a huge party." I get this bachelor pad all spic and span and it's fantastic. As a matter of fact, at 6:00 A.M., the guy's still drilling the bar downstairs.

That night, my future wife—I never met her before—shows up at that party, and it was just amazing. She has two kids, and I do, too. What bachelor would ever buy a five-bedroom house? That part of it was just meant to be. She actually had a law background and that really helped me, because you need to have that semi-background to protect us. She complemented me, and finally we realized she was best being with me in the business.

How much do you think your knowledge in legal issues and finance has to do with your ability to be highly successful in this business?

In success, you have probably a thousand eyes looking at you every day. In everything you do, you have to make sure that they are curtailed to every aspect of any rules, regulations, or whatever. My wife is very good at making sure that, before we release anything, it is very professional and matches all the guidelines, everything else. The minute it does, anything wrong with it, believe me, we'll know about it within an hour.

What's interesting is I really love it. I've always said that you should be able to go in to any supermarket anywhere and never have to hide your face. That's when you do good business. I'll go anywhere, and kids from four years old, to teenagers, to adults know who I am. They'll say, "Hi, Creig, how are you? Love the commercial." I do commercials and stuff like that.

I've done TV, radio, and a lot of media stuff. That part of it is very rewarding in a sense that they recognize me, almost like a celebrity. I know them, and I appreciate it. I don't abuse it. I just keep doing what I do, the best I can.

Do you get special perks because of that celebrity status?

I don't take advantage of any perks, that's my answer. I don't abuse my power. I don't chose to. Do I get invited to functions because of that? Certainly. But I don't get any other special privileges. If anything, it causes the people to ask you for more.

I create programs. About three years ago, I sponsored one of the most successful programs called the Unsung Hero program for the high schools. That's not new in the sense of the word, but it's new in the

Howard County area. Each school puts them in the paper. I find the top person who's helping the nursing homes and charity functions and stuff like that. We have a nomination committee, and we have written essays and then we do a banquet. It's really neat.

The newest thing is a state-of-the-art soccer field. They wanted and needed money for the field, so I gave them a contribution. Now it's called Northrop Field at Covenant Park.

That's the kind of stuff where the community sees that I'm giving back. I'm not here to just take it from the community and not reward the community. I want the schools to be top notch, because that's what drives the prices up.

I wholeheartedly believe that, the more you give, the more you get. I'll give the schools computer labs and things like that. I'm a very big part of giving back to the community. I gave all the high schools lights for the football field they never had. I just think, you live there, so you want to be happy. I was born and raised here.

What do you think makes you just a little notch higher?

Are you ready for this? I think the most powerful ingredient I have, and not everybody has it, is energy and how I'm able to expose it to the world. Energy is amazingly powerful. If you're given that energy and you're able to form it into your business, into your life, it's going to create success for you. I believe in energy.

How does the energy show up in the business?

Through excitement. If I'm walking through your house and I tell you, "It's okay, and the market's pretty bad. We might sell it in a month or two." Certainly, you're going to be down with me. You will feel the way I feel.

I come in with excitement and say what's great about the hard wood floors, and how that's going to make it even more enhanced. "By the way, here are the market conditions and they're looking fantastic. Here's what we're going to do to figure out how to sell successfully." There's a big difference in the energy we have in this property.

In a buyer's market, you're still going to use that same approach?

Sure. My ultimate goal is, if you price your house right in any market, I don't care what market it is, it's going to sell. If I get to more people quicker, it will sell quicker, if it's priced realistically.

What percentage of your budget is for marketing and advertising?

I would say probably a good 20 percent of my business is marketing, at least.

How big is your team now?

I have 31 people. I have 12 to 14 buyer agents, who do some listings, but I do the primary listings. I have two professional stagers, two virtual tour specialists, my marketing person who takes care of all my ads, three listing coordinators, three settlement coordinators, and two customer service people.

I believe in what they call ownership. In order to be successful, you have to own what you want. I always felt that you could be successful by owning everything that you could want. If you like to watch movies, own a video store. I enjoy real estate and land; therefore, I sell real estate and buy and sell it, too. I own it.

I try to get the people who work for me to own it. I handpicked every one of them. I don't believe in taking on other organizations, other Realtors. Certainly, if you can grow up or live around it, you'll learn the way we do it, not the way you think it should be done.

First of all, all my team is dressed professionally every day. If you're going to be a professional, you better act like a professional. There are a lot of agents who let that go by the wayside. They dress in jeans and stuff like that. I don't work like that. All the men wear a suit and tie. All the women are dressed professionally.

Every other Saturday morning at 8:00 A.M., I have an hour of power with my team to train it. In order to be on my team, you must have a laptop, because you want to be tech savvy and have knowledge in your hand if you don't have it in your brain. We do team meetings. It's almost like a family group. That's really a fun atmosphere.

We had a goal last year of $200 million. We ended up doing $231 million. I told them that, if we got that goal, we would go to the Ritz Carlton in Cancun on the Concierge level. The way they treat us is the way that I want to do my business in real estate. They learn how it felt for people to make them feel that way. That's what I wanted them to do with my clientele. I want them to feel like they're in the Ritz Carlton buying real estate from Creig Northrop & the Northrop Team.

What do you do to deliver that type of service?

There are specific things, from the full color brochures to the virtual tours, and consistent communication on a consistent basis. Everybody knows they can get to me anytime. I'm not one of those step-out owners. I'm in it. I'm with them. If their house is on the market and it's not selling, it's my house not selling. I own it.

What is it you enjoy about doing the listings yourself?

I enjoy the challenge of meeting with the seller, coming up with the determination of how we're going to market your property effectively, sell it within a reasonable time, and get you the most money. I enjoy getting letters thanking me for how great a job I've done because I do what I say I'm going to do.

The customer service part of any business is taken for granted. It gets harder, as you build your business, to contain that, to keep that. That's why I needed to build a team. My weakness could be that I have a big team. My strength is that I have a big team to service my clients better.

I have all the control over it. Here's the Northrop team mission: It is our mission to be the leader in the real estate marketplace, using the highest degree of professionalism and expertise to meet and exceed the needs of our clientele.

I always say that our focus is responsive and reliable, open and honest, communication at all time, the highest caliber of professional real estate services, and the latest real estate technology. I have computer guys to make sure that when you go on any search engine you're going to find me first. You go to any real estate book that has to do with my county, and you will go through my listings first. Superior knowledge of Maryland real estate rules and regulations and teamwork, with one ultimate goal: 100-percent customer satisfaction.

What percentage of listings do you close?

I'd say probably 90 percent of them.

How do you make such a successful listing presentation?

The energy, the knowledge, and the enthusiasm. First, I always go to your house. There are agents who list houses from their office. Their home is what you're listing, so go to their home. I introduce my team, intimately through pictures, to the people and let them know what we're about, giving them a sense of what we've done in the past, and things like that. I go through my credentials, all my accomplishments.

But really it comes down to my marketing; I will market your house to 20.5 million people in 30 days. I don't cut corners. I don't care if your house sells in a day, a week, or a month. I will do the same marketing, regardless of how long I feel your house is going to be on the market. That's an amazing statement that no one else can make. I have six trucks right now that I use to help people move. It's a little more common with the top producers. They like moving trucks with their face on them. That's a little perk.

Then, really, it comes down to giving them what they want, which is ultimately what the price is. Show them how to get it, and then give them what they need, what it costs, what's involved, and how we do it. But ultimately what you have to make them understand is that you're there to represent their interest. That's why they're hiring you. That's how a very successful presentation should be done.

How do you stay ahead of the market?

I was the first one to come out with full-color brochures of the inside and outside of the properties. I started the virtual tours here. I put 50 pictures online because I knew online was coming. You find areas that are going to be hot, not hot now, but later. Here, schools are a big priority, so you should get involved with all the school activities in the community so that you're tied to the schools, along with people.

I know that, when I'm slowing down, the market's slowing down. When things aren't selling as high as they should, it tells me the market's changing.

I'm always trying to find different markets. I just opened another office in Carroll County, the county next to me and cheaper than the county I'm in, that everybody's moving to. You can get more for your money there. I always use this Wayne Gretsky quotation: "Skate to where the puck is going, not where it's been." I've always kept that in my mind, because my goal is to be ahead of where the market's going.

How much counseling, advice, and input do you give to your clients?

As much as they need. I've been their therapist, psychologist, and marriage counselor, whatever it takes, meaning, ultimately, to get that offer or more and whatever is in the best interest of my client. My goal for my client is to get them the most money I possibly can.

How do you do that?

You have to create urgency in the marketplace. If you create urgency, it creates price increases. If a buyer feels they're going to lose the house, they will spend more money. You have to create that urgency in them. That's the ultimate goal.

Preparation is just as important as the presentation in your houses. It's very important that they show to the best of their ability. That's why we spend so much time making sure we prep them.

How do you convince sellers to invest more money in their house?

I tell them we have a professional stager on my staff who will come out and spend some time with them and give them the best advice. They don't have to do it; it's up to them. But it will help in the marketability of their home.

How do you best represent your seller with another agent?

First, the conversation that goes on is only between my client and me. My client's interest is the only thing we talk about. How can we make this offer the best, what else is out there that could be even better, and what time frames do we have to make this decision? That means that, if you need me to sell it in a week, I don't have as much time as I would if you give me 30 days. It's that kind of timing that we're going to base our decisions on; what kind of motivation you have to take what type of offers.

How do you get the most for your clients?

I market so much for my clients that they have multiple offers on, I'd say, a majority of them in a great market. In a good market, we have a couple of offers. In an okay market, we have one or two offers. It depends on which market we're talking about.

How do you deal with multiple offers?

I outline each one of the offers before I meet my sellers. I get all the financials out of the way, everything done. When I meet with them, I outline the positives of and my concerns for each one. They share their concerns. We go through them and then we decide which ones would maximize the dollar and the timing and financial credibility that works best for them. The client ultimately makes the decision. My goal is to guide them. That's where I think a lot of people get in the way. Ultimately, you want to guide them, but you don't want to tell them what to do.

How does the other agent affect the negotiation?

Outside of our county, they all want to try to be there for the offers, but I don't let them be there. They like to present their own offers. I never want any agents with me when I'm presenting to my seller. My sellers have the trust and confidence in me, and I want to uphold that. As for the agents who are writing the offers, there are agents I know who have been in business a lot longer than others, but that doesn't influence it. It's the offer and the quality of the offer that really make the difference.

Do they normally just fax you over an offer?

A majority of them do fax and some are hand-delivered.

Do you intimidate other agents?

I try not to create that personification, but has that happened? I believe it does. There are times when I get listings over others, and it always creates that competitiveness.

And people always say I want Creig Northrop's sign up there because I know (a) it's going to get sold, and (b) it's going to get sold for the highest-priced dollar. I have that reputation. People know, in my industry at least, I'm not looking to negotiate the offer. If I negotiate, I negotiate up. I price my houses so they sell. Here are the terms my sellers are looking for. We make that happen. Let's go on. If not, I will find another buyer who will work for these situations. I will sell it to somebody else.

At what point did you have the confidence to take that attitude?

I guess when most of the sellers got confidence in me.

What advice would you give other agents?

Create a professional image, using every avenue of marketing, with attention to design and detail. That's very important. I don't let anything go on the street until it's fully approved by my marketing department and my wife. Everything is very professional. We have a lot of agents, discount agents, all kinds of different agents, but I maintain the professionalism. When you ask who's your top professional agent in this area, they'll say Creig Northrop. Maybe how we present ourselves in the marketplace has made me the number-one Realtor.

One of my unique business strategies is demonstrating the ability to maximize the team concept. The team is where I grew up in sports and things like that. That does make a difference—depending on others. One person can't do the business anymore. It's too dynamic, too many different avenues. We also use a strong team of individuals to serve the clients' needs. But each one is specialized in order to ensure that no detail's overlooked.

If somebody really wants it badly enough, the first thing you have to do is gain the knowledge. Without knowledge, you have nothing. I wouldn't want to go to a lawyer who doesn't know my case. I wouldn't go to a Realtor who doesn't know, in my price range, what a house looks like and is not familiar with the price ranges. If you feel intimidated by a price range, go see all those houses within that price range and learn them. Then you won't become intimidated by them anymore.

What other ways have you invested in yourself to become this great?

I'm a more hands-on learner. I believe in hands-on rather than somebody teaching you.

I believe I bring the team up to the strength I have. I put back in to the team, teach them, have classes with them, and learn more from them than I do from any seminar or anything else. They're the ones who are seeing and doing it every day, in my marketplace.

Do you have this level of energy all the time?

That's the level I have all the time. My wife says she has never met a more motivational speaker—with my team, I just get them really pumped up to get going. My goal is to deliver that energy to every one of my clients through my team members. That energy level is just amazing.

When you started, how did you learn to allocate your time most effectively?

You have to figure out where your talents lie. I work smarter, not harder. It's challenging because, when a buyer wants to buy or a seller wants to list, they don't want to wait. I'm very responsive to the timely needs of the client. You make it around your schedule, but you want to be courteous to their schedule, also. In our business, you can't say you don't ever work evenings. It's almost impossible to get a husband and wife home during the day, and list their property. I pick an evening when I have to work, because you certainly have to work around the families.

Find out what your strengths are. Is it in listing, or in dealing with buyers? I had land interest, so I went in to land a little bit. In which one do you want to prioritize your time? I chose listing houses and selling land. They were my two choices. They were my time commitments. Then, I got assistants to do everything else that would take time away from that. There is no question that, right out of the chute, it's very hard to time manage until you know what you're managing.

How can you make a decision you're going to focus on buyers if the philosophy really is list to live?

Well, the way I look at it, every buyer's a seller. So if every buyer's a seller, then you certainly have to start somewhere. Unless you have a reputation or some type of credentials, they trust you're going to sell the property for the most money and in the least time, sellers aren't going to list with you. That's, truthfully, the goal. Buyers are traditionally where everybody starts. It's hard to start with listings, because what are you starting? You start with buyers to learn the inventory, to learn what they're looking for so that, when you are with a seller, you know what buyers are looking for—the qualities of the house, what price range, and things like that.

Teams are the only way of the future because you can't do everything. Time management is taking things that you don't want to do and enabling others to do that.

There are people who believe in doing business "by referral only."

Go back to the statement that you have to eat, drink, and sleep the business. My principle is that you'd better be talking about the business if you want to be successful at it.

By referral only—good luck. I appreciate that referrals are good enough to live on and that's fine, but that means you're willing to put a limit on what you can achieve. I don't do that. I'll go in to a football game and talk about real estate, because the conversation is about real estate, and they know I represent real estate. I have the ability to have that conversation every day. You have to create that conversation. Everyone is a buyer and a seller, whether that's today, tomorrow, or yesterday. You have to bring that conversation out. Fortunately, they know who I am, so their conversation gets brought out from that.

What major lessons have you learned along your path?

Honesty and integrity, and I'm sure that consistent behavior will get you a lot farther in life than anything else. There are no shortcuts. You have to have the motivation, the organization, the negotiation, and the positive attitude, along with the endless energy. This is what has put me where I am today. If I had to do it again, the only difference would be that I would have started the team earlier. I recommend that agents get a mentor. Jump on to a team, or at least get with an agent who will mentor with you.

How do you negotiate the best deal?

Negotiation is interesting. In order to be a good negotiator, you have to feel both sides of the fence—ultimately feel and think like the buyer's thinking. But you have to keep in mind whom you're representing. I have to know my sellers well enough to know what they're thinking and what's going to make them satisfied at the end of the day. To do that, I have to get involved with them. What is their passion? What is the most important thing to them—is it money? Sometimes it's not money. Sometimes it's security. Sometimes they want to know the deal's going to be done.

People consistently think negotiation is all about money, and they're the ones who aren't good negotiators, because it's not all about money. It has to do with many different elements that take into account the person you're negotiating with. I can't tell you that one deal is going to be the same as they negotiate the next deal because I have different emotions in one deal than I do the other. Sometimes I have to tell them to detach themselves from the house and create it as a business instead of a personal object in order to negotiate the deal. But you have to do that, because in that situation, it becomes a business.

Psychology is definitely a big part of seeing how far the buyer will stretch, knowing when I've stretched them too far. That also is a big part of negotiation, knowing how far you can stretch it. Patience and silence are the two most successful things to negotiation. People tend to talk too much.

In closing, can you think of anything else you'd like to share?

Use an in-house training program. An hour training session keeps my team ahead of the changes in the marketplace: new and useful techniques, presentation strategies, ideas, directions, answers to questions and concerns, and ways to promote professionalism and offer buyer and seller services.

My number-one career goal is gaining each of my client's trust by giving extraordinary service at no extra cost and being extremely successful at doing just that. The ultimate measure of success is having a family and reputation that I'm proud of, which is most important. It's not important about the numbers. I don't feel comfortable discussing it. I don't need that. What makes me successful is that I care about each person. I own it like it's my own. Ultimately, my motivation, first and foremost, is my wife and my family.

JILL RUDLER

HER REAL LIVING
Columbus, Ohio

#1 Gross Commission Income—Real Living Inc.

- Sales Volume: $52 M
- # of Units Sold: 258
- Gross Commission Income: $1.45 M
- # of Employees: 3
- www.AllAboutColumbusOhio.com
- Years in the business: 26

What is HER in the company name?

HER is an organization that was started in the mid-'50s by Harley E. Rooda, who was president until the early '90s. He started the independent real estate company, and it's grown into the largest in Central Ohio over the last 15-20 years.

How did you get involved in real estate?

My parents were in the real estate business in the late '60s. My mom owned her own real estate company. Although I never thought I would be in real estate, because I'm a little on the shy side in any kind of group, one-to-one, I do pretty well. I didn't think I was much of the salesperson type, so when I got out of school, I didn't know what I wanted to do; I thought, "I could try this for a while." Here I am, 26 years later.

I took some classes in college. I never finished with a degree. I finally decided to take some real estate classes. I didn't know what I wanted to do, and at the time, at least this was an opportunity for me to try my hand in it and see how it would go. I never dreamed I would stay in this long.

How did you get past the shyness?

It's knowledge. The more knowledge you have about what you're doing, the easier it is, especially on a one-to-one basis. I'm still very shy in a group, but when it comes to one-on-one, I can sit there and talk all day to clients. I can even get up in front of organizations and speak now because I'm speaking about something I'm comfortable with.

How did you realize you had a passion for real estate?

The passion came from working with Bob, my husband. The two of us got in to real estate at the time we met, and we were married shortly after that. We've worked together with our own clients for several years. We relocated to Columbus from northeastern Ohio in 1987, so we had been in real estate nine years. We moved to Columbus because it was a great market.

When we came here, we thought we had a lot to learn. At first, we worked independently, and then we decided this was a business. We need to run this like a business, so he took over the management of the office and the marketing, and I concentrated on the clients. That's when we started to grow.

How long did it take to figure that out?

We didn't have children at home, so it made us able to go out and spend a lot more time with clients. We started in December of '87. By 1989, we hired our first assistant. We decided to split this job in 1993. It's overwhelming for both of us if we're trying to split our time between clients and the office. By then, I think I had three assistants who worked for us. They weren't buyer's assistants. At that time, I was hiring support staff to handle the paperwork and the communication. I was also focusing on, at that point, trying to hire real estate agents instead of a secretary or people to just answer the phone.

Did you have your own office then?

We worked at an office of 90 agents, but I have 11 assistants who work for me, ten of whom are licensed. I have an office within an office.

You came to the conclusion that you and your husband needed each other.

He was a very important part of growing the business. You had to grow it like any other business, with the support staff and everything in your office you needed. We didn't take advantage of what the office had to provide us with its equipment. We went out and did it ourselves. We felt like this was our business, and our job was to go out and provide all the services we could. From years ago, we had our own fax machine, copier, all of that, so we could manage our office a little better.

What made you decide to hire agents?

At first it was great having a pleasant voice answering the phone instead of leaving messages with some secretary at the front desk. We found what was and wasn't helpful, coming home from appointments at 10:00 P.M. and still having a stack of messages to take care of. They couldn't answer calls in a way that could solve the problems. It would delay the answer. By hiring a real estate agent, we were able to take the pressure off us of spending those evenings returning the calls once we did get back to the office or home. I spend most of my day out of the office right now. I'm in the office maybe five percent of the time.

How did you get started?

Early on, in the late '70s, early '80s, it was about doing open houses and talking to people and getting your name out there. We did things like making little caricatures of ourselves and an ad in the paper. We tried to do some branding, at that point, with why people should call us.

Everything changed when we moved to Columbus. We started over in real estate. We didn't know anyone when we moved here. We had to decide how you get your name out there in the late '80s. Why do people call you? At that time, open houses were a way in which we could meet people personally, understanding that we had a lot to offer them individually. They would call us after the open house, and say, "We want you to work with us." That was, I think, the way I got my name out there initially. I've never done a lot of phone solicitation, and I've never done door-to-door. Since 1995, I haven't done any open houses. Once I got my name out there, it was word-of-mouth.

Through doing open houses?

Yes. Originally, it was holding open houses in areas that are for first-time buyers. Those people don't always know a realtor. They want to work with someone who they are confident will help them and do a good job.

Did you do a lot of advertising?

From day one, we felt that advertising was very important. We did a lot of full-page ads. Anytime we had anything to brag about, we would advertise it, whether it was a listing, even in the beginning, when we didn't list many homes, or advertisements, putting our name and faces out there, so people would start recognizing we were in the area. We would support different organizations, such as the Chamber of Commerce. We would buy the back page of its publication for several years. We try to make ourselves look like a dominant force in the community.

We didn't have a lot of overhead, so, when we made money, we put it right back in the business.

Did you take salaries then?

No. As a matter of fact, I still don't take a salary. My husband does, but I don't.

I am still self-employed. I haven't incorporated or anything like that. I felt like there was no advantage for me, with all the license laws in Ohio, to do that. The reason we decided to give Bob a salary was strictly so he could pay in to his retirement.

Have you had mentors or coaches along your way?

I haven't had any coaches or mentors. I moved to one of the top offices during the early '90s because I wanted to be around the people who are very successful. I learned from them a lot of things to do and not to do. I tried to be aware of what was going on around me. By 1993, I had accomplished something about which everyone had said, "You'll never be successful because you don't know anyone. You don't have children in school." I felt like it was not who you know; it's what people are saying about you. My reputation in the community is that I'm highly ethical. I get many referrals now, with people saying, "Jill's a great agent; you should call her."

How did you build that reputation?

By working honestly with the other agents and never playing games with them, and being very honest and up-front. The other thing I think they appreciate about how I work is that I have a staff of people when they call in, to negotiate a contract, get information, or schedule an appointment. They're able to talk to someone, and it's handled immediately. They don't have to leave a message for us to get back to them. Having that clear communication is important. People want it immediately. Moving to Columbus, I found that right away.

In 1988, I got my first cell phone. I thought this would help me. Then I found there is no way you could do those things out of the office, whether you're showing houses, meeting with sellers, at closings, or at meetings networking with realtors, and be available seven days a week to handle the things that have to happen.

I looked at realtors and said, "Okay, whom do I pick who would stay with me long term and be very successful?" I looked for the younger agents who had been in the business two or three years and were very successful, but hitting that wall with time management because they had children. That's where I was able to hire people, my salaried employees, who would stay with me long term. I have people who have been with me between four and thirteen years. It's critical that you hire people and keep them. It has to be a good job for them and they have to like it, or they won't be very successful with your clients.

And they're on salary. I do some benefits like profit sharing and vacations. We go on some company trips and things like that.

Since you're almost running a company within a company, what made you decide to stay with Real Living, instead of becoming independent?

I found there were some advantages: being stable and staying with a company that's known as the top company in your city, for relocation, if nothing else. A lot of people relocate in to Columbus, and want to deal with the top company. It costs me money to do that, but it has never been about every last dollar, or I wouldn't have spent money on the advertising as it was.

You added people as the amount of business increased.

Right. We tried to figure out how to delegate more of what we did, so we could be out with the client more. By 1994, I realized that I was not returning the buyer calls on the ads quickly enough, and I was starting to lose opportunities because I was playing phone tag. At that point, I hired my first buyer's agent. At that point, I had four assistants in the office doing the daily communications and all the paperwork, and then I hired my first buyer's agent. Two years later, by 1996, I had to hire two more. Now, I'm up to six in the office who do the daily communications. They work seven days a week, so I have a rotation on the weekend. I have five buyer's agents who work for me.

Did it make a big difference having your husband's constant support?

It was extremely important. The only reason I'm successful is because I didn't have the pressure at home of why aren't you home, why are you working so much? If I had children, I could tell you it would have been impossible to build it the way I did, because I did it with a lot of my time. I used to work 90 hours a week. I don't anymore. I work maybe 50-60 hours a week. That means a little bit more in the spring and a little bit less in the winter.

How did you end up working for the biggest or the best office?

I selected the company I wanted to work for. It had 23 offices. It's like the joke of the company; the first two offices I interviewed at wouldn't hire me. Of the two managers, one said they wouldn't consider me because they wanted to work as a team, and at the time they didn't hire husband-and-wife teams. If they had problems with one, they'd have to let the other one go, and they didn't want to deal with that. The second one I interviewed at said they would consider hiring me, but they weren't sure if they would. The third one said they would love to have me.

The fear was that we didn't know anyone, had no centers of influence, had no children in school to meet other families, and that, maybe, we wouldn't be successful. But, we always thought we would be successful, not based on whom we know, but how we build a business. Thinking of this as a business and not "I'm going to sell a home" helped build us in a way other companies are successful. Personal marketing, the opportunity to spend a lot of time to do it the right way, and our ethical background made it come true.

Mothers have a much bigger challenge in this business.

If they're as dedicated to being a parent as they are to their business, they won't stay in real estate full-time, or they'll work for someone else. That's the dedication it takes when you have nothing in your way. The minute you have to make a decision between going to the soccer game or going to show a house, you've lost, because those time management things are difficult to solve. That's why I've looked at people like that and said, "I can give them an opportunity to work either 40 hours a week, or if they're a buyer's agent, one or two days on call. The rest of the days, they can balance their life a little bit more. They can be as successful, if not more successful, as they would be if they were working hard, trying to do a few transactions a year.

The agents who used to be realtors and selling on their own are now real estate assistants to me, doing either the follow-up on listings or contracts, or whatever in the office. They're able to work a 40-hour work, get a salary, stay in real estate, and talk to buyers and sellers about real estate, but they don't need to go out and physically be gone nights and weekends.

There's such an immense turnover in this business.

Right. More than anything, it's about time management. It's out of your control. People get in to the business because they think it's flexible. They don't realize that they need to be flexible seven days a week, 24 hours a day, or they're not going to be successful.

Where do you focus your time and energies?

I work on appointments. My office gets the phone calls and schedules me for meeting sellers to list properties, listing presentations, and going to closings. Mostly, it's a scheduled day where I'm out of the office meeting people. Of course, when you close 250 to 300 homes a year, you tend to spend a lot of time at closings.

We still have round-table closings in Columbus. But since I represent mostly the sellers, I have buyer's agents who go to the buyer's closings. When I'm representing the seller, we coordinate it so that the buyer goes to the closing. Fifteen to twenty minutes is all we have to spend. They sign their papers, and then we're ready to go. We try to manage the time in a way where I'm not sitting an hour in a closing, when my sellers need to be there for only 20 minutes.

Do you work with buyers?

I do a little, but very, very few, only when necessary. When I have a buyer, a listing that I'm taking, or a referral from a past client, I usually give it to the buyer's agents and let them handle it. That way, they can focus on searching for buyers every day. When the calls come in on the listings, they can take those that day, and they're fresh and ready to go. People say there are certain things you can't delegate. So far I haven't found one thing I can't delegate, because everything can be delegated.

At some point, I will delegate my listing appointments. The last couple of years, my business has been a little flat, because I haven't been willing to take the steps to grow it again. I think that will change. That's another thing to delegate. I haven't negotiated a contract since the mid-'90s. People say, "If you get an offer on your listing, they want you to talk to them." Very rarely do they care. As long as someone competent is talking to them, giving them good advice, being supportive to them and helping them through that process, they don't care whether it's me or not.

A call comes in and they say, "We want to talk to Jill about selling our home." They'll get the information for the listing appointment, prepare the market analysis, put all of the information together, and put it in my schedule, and I walk out the door with the packet they give me. I sit down and present the listing to the seller, and present my information, as well as the market analysis. They may, at that time, go ahead and list with me or call me back to list it in the future. I do the listing paperwork with the seller and take it back in to the office. The office processes everything, advertises it, and follows up on it. If the house sells quickly, I don't even meet the seller again until closing. If it doesn't, many times, 45 days later, I'll sit down with the seller, and we'll review what's happened so far and decide if there are any changes necessary in the next 30-45 days. There's little involvement on my part on a personal basis with that seller if it goes smoothly.

I've been able to take vacations up to 12 weeks a year, and you can't have your business stop when you're gone. I've been gone as much as six weeks at one time. They've gone out, listed homes, put them in contracts, and closed, all before I ever got back in town. It can happen. It's all about how you tell them the benefit of working with a team. There's so much benefit. I can't be answering all those things happening right now in my office, but they're happening—negotiation, preparation of presentation listing, sellers calling to get information on something—or we're calling sellers for feedback, or calling the Realtors. Lots of things have to happen simultaneously.

What percentage of your listing appointments do you get?

If they list their homes, probably 70-80 percent.

What enables you to get that percentage?

I believe it's that people meet me, and I present a case where there isn't much more that can be done besides listing with me. They're in a position where they can't give any better service than someone answering the phone and someone handling their situation. If they do need to talk to me, it's easy. I'm paged, and between appointments, I'll return their calls.

It's explaining the benefits, the job as a Realtor, about how you're out of the office a lot and how there are a lot of people, all those things that have to happen in a transaction, all the communication.

It's not missing opportunities by having the right people in place, everyplace they need to be.

How long do your listing appointments normally last?

Usually an hour and a half.

Is there a specific process you follow?

Oh yes. When I go in, I usually view the house first, and then I sit down and present my staff and how I work. I try to set expectations. After that, I do the market analysis and show them the different homes that are available and what's sold. We talk about price range, and then I do a net sheet for them. If they're ready to go forward, we list it. If not, they call me back. A lot of times, I'm barely getting in the car, and they're running out the door, and asking me to come back and list the house. They'll call after interviewing other Realtors, deciding it was a very good presentation, and they feel like they could work with me.

Sometimes I'm not their first agent, but many times, I'm the last agent. I'm often the second agent, and sometimes, after interviewing me, they know it was such a different experience from their first experience that they feel like this might be something that works.

You don't do a hard close. In fact, it sounds like, if you want to list with me, okay, and if not that's okay, too.

That's how I've always done it. My staff tells me, "You never close a sale." I do in my own way, but many times people don't need to be hammered at this point. They want to be an educated decision-maker. I educate them on the process, and that's why I always thought I wasn't a very good salesperson, because I'm not good for the hard close. I don't like to go in and make people feel like I'm the only one who can sell their house, because I'm certainly not. A lot of very good salespeople are out there, and we could all do the job, but we do it in different ways. My way has been very successful for me. What I work harder at is not getting the listing. It's selling the house. People appreciate that. There is a lot of uniqueness in sellers. I don't want some listings I go on. It's not because they're not great houses. It's because I don't want to work with the sellers. You can't turn them down. Many times I still get them, and we've worked out our differences. They want you to create miracles or predict the future, which is impossible, obviously.

You have to put yourself in a position of the buyers, and sometimes that means you have to put the seller in that position, to understand that there's lots of competition, and if you're not competitive in the market, depending on what type of market you're in, your home will not sell. It might be runner-up several times, but you have to follow the market as it's changing.

How do you deal with the market changes?

The thing is to stay in contact with the sellers, to keep them up-to-date with the changes as they're happening, suggestions that will sell the house quicker for top dollar. Certain homes you put on the market will always sell fast, but, on the whole, it's definitely a buyer's market, where there are so many more sellers than buyers. At the same time, there are many resale homes. There's continual new construction going on, which, of course, affects our inventory.

Are you niched into a particular market?

I'm a little varied in that I sell everything. Last year, I sold a $50,000 house, which there are not many of here. The average sales price now is about $220 for me. But I've sold several $700,000, $800,000, or $900,000 homes as well. Right now, I have three or four salable homes on the market. They're very tough. I still do a lot of first-, second-, and third-time homebuyers. A lot of people are downsizing right now from the bigger to the smaller home.

I think the baby boomers are getting to that point where they want a second home, or they want to start saving more for retirement. They want to retire earlier, and be active retirees. They don't want the big yard, and they want to be on the golf course or in a patio home. I see it in my own neighborhood, where a lot of people are doing that right now. It's the beginning of it.

Since others are doing your negotiations, do you discuss the deals with them and how they're going to be negotiated?

No. I have one assistant who prepares the CMAs, who also negotiates most of the contracts when he's there. He's been with me 13 years, and he will review the net sheet I provided to that seller, any price reductions I've done, and any changes I've made in the marketing. Then he'll call them and not only review the contract but talk to them about what they're trying to accomplish, what they're feeling, and what changes they've made since starting to market their home. There may be some differences in their motivation, or anything like that. He tries to get a feeling for what they're trying to accomplish, and based on this offer, how they would put together a counter-offer that would try to attain their goals.

Even though I talked to them about their motivation, a lot of times, it has changed. If it's 60 or 90 days later, they may have a totally different feeling. Sellers negotiate with you as well. They're trying to tell you, "We won't come down; we won't do this; we won't do that." Once they experience what's going on in the market, they may have a change of feelings, so we want to find out at that moment what their feelings are.

It's waiting it out, if you can. Obviously, some people's motivation for selling is that they want to make as much money as possible out of it, and they don't have to go anywhere. If you have to go somewhere, you have to sell for whatever the market will bear at the time. That's why you can sit there and say, "I have to get this much out of my house." But when it comes down to it, you know the market is going to decide where your home will sell—not your Realtor and not you. You don't want to miss an opportunity, and that's where getting a good Realtor who has a team and a good organizational ability to not miss an opportunity is the best thing you can do for yourself.

I usually keep the client up on what is happening in the market. "I know we thought we knew what would happen, based on history, but this is current history. This is based on your house and other homes on the market. These are other homes that have come on the market. These are homes that have sold. This is our feedback. This is where we've advertised it." It comes down to you changing something about the house, the marketing, or the price. You lay out a reason for any necessary changes. Sometimes you have to be patient. Sometimes it's not going to sell as quickly as you'd like it to.

If that's the case, you keep lowering the price?

No. I think that that's only one thing. Many times it's not about price. It's about simple things that could be changed. People come in and say the house is too small. You know what? Maybe you have to remove some furniture. Maybe you have to lighten it up a little bit. Maybe you have to get more light in there. You might have to do some changes to make it appear different. You can't make the rooms bigger, but you can certainly make them appear bigger by taking things out and lightening it up.

When I list the home, I will recommend staging tips for them. If there's specific staging, I recommend that up front when I'm listing it. I'm educated enough to walk through a house and tell them what I think a problem is with selling it.

If I walk in to a house and there's a dog or a cat odor, I tell them, "A lot of people don't want to buy a house that has dogs or cats, so you have to make it appear that there isn't one here." A lot of time that means you have to get special filtering systems in your house so that it doesn't have an odor when you walk in the door. Sometimes it's major, like tearing the carpeting out, having it professionally taken care of. If it's as bad as that, they're going to know that either they're going to sell it under market value, considerably, or they're going to do the things necessary to get market value. Not many owners don't know their house stinks. They don't want to admit it, but they know.

What other things about the house?

Decorating and things like that.

If you've ever been to a wallpaper store and seen how many books are available, that's how many different opinions there are. The odds of somebody walking in to your house and liking every room being wallpapered differently are slim. You may have to take every other room down. If you don't mind getting below market, leave it the way it is. If you want to get market, you have to update it. If you want to get above market, sometimes you have to do special things, real surprises that people don't expect in a house. It's all about the price they want to get.

What did you learn from those highly successful agents?

I learned you have to be confident in yourself and your ability, and you have to go out there and guide people through the transaction. But I also learned that sometimes when people were very successful, they became...how do I say this nicely?...egotistical, that it's all about me. The clients don't like that. It's not all about you. It's about them. Don't forget that the reason you're there is to provide a service to that client, and without you providing the services the best you can, you're going to lose that opportunity. I learned a lot by listening to other agents. Some believe they're invincible. I always felt that this was an opportunity. I want the opportunity to continue to provide service. We are only there at will. When our clients decide that we're not a value to them, we're out of here.

A lot of opportunity is out there that's not being met. Once you think you've arrived, you've arrived. I don't think I've arrived yet.

The biggest thing is continuing to market yourself. I saw people being very successful, and then they tended to stop doing the things that made them successful. They kind of rested on their laurels and said, "I can do this, I can do that," not putting themselves in a position where people would want to continue to recommend them to their friends.

What do you do to continue getting people to recommend you?

The things that you started doing. Providing the service that you tell them you will. Being very honest and telling them the things you can't do. You can't change the market. You can keep in touch with them. If somebody has bad credit, you can't change that. But you can certainly say immediately when something happens that affects them. It's all about the communications.

What additional things did you learn about what to do or not to do?

It's more in theory, not specifics. There's more theory to it about running a business, having support staff. I saw a lot of them hitting that wall where they couldn't be everywhere, and they had upset clients because they didn't get back to them quicker. I thought providing a staff, more of a staff, would help me to be in more places. Again, that's where I learned having a licensed Realtor worked for you, as opposed to a secretary. It made a huge difference.

You mentioned that your business has reached somewhat of a plateau.

I had some personal things in my life, in the last two years, that have caused me not to put my heart in to continuing to grow my business—my dad's death two years ago and a friend of ours last year who was in a tragic accident. Those things affected me personally. And they affected me in such a long-term way. I had to reevaluate my life and my time. I've gotten past that now. I've gotten to the point where I can take it to the next level. You can't be continuing to build your business if you're not thinking positively about the future. I'm 47—at that point in my life, a lot of people hit, when they wonder what life's about. What should I be trying to get out of it? How much time do I have left?

And then reevaluating your priorities.

That's probably the thing. That's kind of got me to a point where I question a lot of things. I know the way to get to that next level. I have to start thinking about how to implement it.

What would those things be?

You have to keep putting yourself in a position where you can be in more places. I think I've handled the buying side of it, and I've handled the support side. Now, I need to ratchet that up and maybe have an assistant who helps me with listings, maybe who does some of them for me. I have help when I'm gone. My office manager, who used to be my first buyer's agent, has been with me ten years, and she will go out on listing presentations when I'm gone or out-of-town or whatever. If I had someone who did that full-time for me, and we could do more of them quicker, then I could obviously keep going to the next level.

Are you turning away business at this time, or not responding fast enough?

No, you delay long enough to fit it in your schedule that it becomes a problem, because you know you lose opportunities. Catching that opportunity quickly sometimes makes all the difference in the world. Certain times, at the end of the month, it's hectic, and you have to put it off a few days, and by then, you might have lost that opportunity. Not to mention, if I could hire somebody who's a good agent, eventually I could wean myself out of this business.

Are you looking for an exit strategy?

Yes. I have a few that I've been working on. There will be an exit strategy sometime in the next five to 10 years. It's very workable. I'll be able to sell the business the way we've arranged it, in a way that should be very smooth for the customer, and probably almost not noticeable.

There's always the next thing you're going to do in life. I never planned on doing this for 26 years, and obviously, I'll be doing it for another five to 10. I think I will do something else afterwards, but it probably won't require as much of my daily time.

What have you done to become that knowledgeable agent?

Realtors continue to think about this more as a business instead of as real estate. Look at other businesses and decide how to improve it, even your listings, how to sell them for more money. I think you have to be open; it's not about what used to work. I still see people in seminars talking about how you have to make this many calls a day. You have to knock on doors. You have to do open houses. I don't do any of those things, but business still comes to me. I focus on how I provide a level of service they don't expect.

An unexpected level of service. But you still have to get that phone to ring.

It's word of mouth and referral and continuing to market the homes as well as yourself. That hasn't stopped. I've continued to do all those things.

What type of marketing are you doing?

We do a lot of direct marketing. We go in to neighborhoods we want to work in or that we have listings in. We do a lot of the new listings. We sold a home in your neighborhood. We also do what we call a quarterly report, a report of the homes that sold in their neighborhood over the last quarter. It's for information, but it also gets our name and faces out there. It continues to make you look like you're the professional in the area who has the most knowledge.

We do a lot of specific areas. I think we probably do six to eight thousand a month, as far as the area with anything from first-time buyer price ranges all the way up to the $800,000 to $900,000 house to million-dollar homes.

We still do a lot of, what I've considered, corporate advertising, where you're on the back of the Westerville magazine. Every month I have the back page. It's not about houses. It's about me, keeping my face in front of them as the expert in the community.

Sometimes we'll send out a calendar at the end of the year. Or we'll send out an Ohio State Buckeye schedule of the football games. That's a big deal here in Columbus.

We do some radio advertising. It's not to sell a house again, not to try to promote yourself as an ethical Realtor, and not to make every deal that comes along. We're not going to use all the gimmicks, but we are going to sell their home for top dollar and give them the service they deserve. People are tired of these gimmicks. They're tired of going in and feeling like they're being sold. They would like to work with someone in a professional manner, like the radio advertisement for me that was to remind even my past clients that I'm still there, to call me, and to tell their friends about me. Word of mouth is so valuable.

How do you keep in contact with your past clients?

We do mailings to them. We do birthday cards, quarterly mailings, and stuff like that. Anything we're doing, we try to keep them involved in it. Extra things, grocery lists, or whatever, when we do that, we always include our past clients.

Is there a percentage of your budget that you use for advertising?

My husband, since he does all the marketing, uses an advertising budget every year. I think somewhere in the $150,000-$200,000 range, I'm guessing, that's print advertising. To be honest, I stay so far out of that, I have no idea how it's changing.

What makes you decide when, and if, to use radio?

He decided that. We've done television and radio. It's something to keep changing things and make yourself visible. When you hear other agents on there, it sounds like a gimmick. Let's do an ad that says we're not going to give you any gimmicks, and it's all quality service. Bob called me and said, "Meet me at the radio station." I'm like, oh, no, I'm not saying anything. They said, "Let me ask you a few questions." They get me in a sound room, they ask me questions, and a week later, I come back and they have it all pieced together. It sounds great. But, I'm not the type to go out there and say a lot of things about myself. They were able to put it together in a very, very pleasant way that didn't make me feel like I was bragging.

How do you differentiate yourself from the market?

In my advertising, I say, "There are a lot of things that I've picked up through the years. One of them is that not every home sells." Then it goes on and talks about how you have to review what's going on, and Jill's an expert at sitting down with you and, if your house hasn't sold, reviewing with you what it would take to sell it. Because of that, I get a lot of expired listings. I don't ever call expired listings, but they call me.

A lot of times, if someone has a house for sale, they're looking in the paper for their home, and their realtor is not advertising. They see my ads. They say, "We're going to call her if it doesn't sell."

Bob is a genius at marketing. He's great at putting a staff together and running it as a business. My success lies in him being able to get the phone to ring, and I go out and do what I love doing every day. He gives me the opportunity to do it, because he makes the phone ring, and he puts me in a position where I have lots of opportunity. My part of it is to be knowledgeable, to be a good agent, and to make them trust me to a point where I will not let them down.

When you work with the general public, there are always different levels of expectation. Even when you try to set them, they all want different things. That's sometimes difficult, to be everything to everybody. I do the best I can. If I can't accomplish the goal, which isn't very often, but when I can't, we leave on good terms and I wish them luck. If I can sell their homes, I still do.

How do you invest in yourself?

A lot of what I do is vacations, getting away, doing things that I enjoy. A lot of that, for me, means I have to get out of town. We have a boat on a lake about an hour from Columbus, so we'll get away there once in a while, for short little jaunts. We try to go away for a week every opportunity we get. Like I said, from the middle of December, to the middle of January, we usually go somewhere on a long-term vacation. The last several years it's been New Zealand, but prior to that, we explored all of the Caribbean. My husband and I, a captain, and a cook even took sailboats for two or three weeks out there in the middle of nowhere. That was fun, too. We've done things that maybe the average person doesn't do. We do something like that every year.

Is it being the best you can be that drives you?

Anything I do, I'm that way. I want to put my whole self in to it. I grew up with a very strong, ethical background, as far as making sure I follow the Golden Rule, doing the things I can do, and being honest with people about things I can't do.

What mistakes have you made along the way?

I've learned this business is not as easy as it appears on the outside. It's not necessarily about sales. There are different types of people out there, and trying to serve them all is impossible. It's not about getting the listings; it's about selling the homes once you get them. Don't over-promise things. The first time you feel you're not going to be successful with this client, based on his or her needs, work hard to confront the person and be honest. People appreciate honesty. Wishful thinking can only get you so far.

As you go down the path, their expectations change?

Yes, or their thought process. I try to be clear and pull out of them what their expectations are. But they don't always know what they are until they start getting some experience in it, and then they realize it's not what they were looking for.

I find that, unless they've gone through the experience of selling a home, in a market like we have their expectations can be bad as far as the match to what our market is. A lot of times they'll tell me, "I've sold every house in the first week." That's not always the kind of market that we're in here. It might take months to sell your home, and you might sell it for less than you think you should get out of it. It comes down to it being worth only what the market will bear.

We're experiencing that now. Anyone who listed a house 60 days ago probably had no idea what to tell clients could happen, and here it's happened. Now the agent is having to go back and say, "Oh my gosh, it's changed." As it's changing, it's a little difficult always to know why, but you have to tell them why. You don't always know yourself exactly why.

If you have to sell, you have to follow the market. If everyone's lowering their prices, and they're selling for a lot less, you better lower your price quickly, and not wait to follow everybody else. At that point, you may have waited so long that you get even less because you've been on the market too long. If you have to sell this home, you might lose money on it. If you do, you might have to accept that and move forward, because there'll be some other area someday in your life in which you'll make money. You can try to second-guess what tomorrow's going to bring, but you can only deal with now.

You can feel the market, but you always wonder whether it's a daily thing. Is it a weekly thing? Is this going to come back out of it in a week? Those things change that quickly. That's why you don't want to jump. If it's been a day or two, you have to drop your price. You have to justify to that client that they need to drop their price. You can't do it without justification. How do you do that if it's in the process of happening, and it's only been happening a week? You have no reason as a seller to think that the next week would be better.

Or, you might need to change whatever in the house will make it sell. You may be getting feedback that there's something you can change.

To get the price reductions, you have to provide evidence that you're doing what you should. If you're not doing what you should, they're going to blame you. But if you're doing everything in your power to sell that house, you're showing the house, and people aren't buying it, there has to be a reason. It's location, the floor plan, or the price. You can't fix locations or floor plans, so you have to change the price.

How often do you advertise a home?

It will be out there in print four to six times a month, probably. Sometimes it takes that in certain markets. In ours, it does. It's exposure, getting it exposed to a lot of different places.

By the time it comes out in print, the house is already sold.

That can happen, but I'm always listing another one. It doesn't matter. When they call, I'll tell them about that newest thing that came out last week that hasn't even shown up in the advertising.

What types of things do you do to stay motivated?

I'm the type of person who's fairly motivated to begin with. I'm not motivated by money. When I moved to Columbus, I had to start over. It took me about a year to be in a position where I could pay my bills. I had to start back at square one. At the point where I could pay my bills, and I wasn't borrowing money for my taxes, things like that, it was, like, okay, now the rest of it is easy.

I was always willing to spend the money on ads, staff, and bonuses, different trips, and stuff for my staff, things to keep them motivated. It hasn't been hard for me to be motivated to go out and work every day. I have appointments. It doesn't matter what day it is. I go and do them.

There seems to be reluctance to invest, especially when starting out.

I know. That's the biggest thing, because they don't have the money. But you shouldn't get in the business without a good amount of money behind you and the support of someone who isn't going to cause you to be pressured to try to be home, because you can't. You have to have support from anyone you have any priorities with because, if you don't, certainly you can't be successful. It would be impossible.

You were sharing with me that you went to see Tommy Hopkins.

When I went to a Tommy Hopkins seminar. I was going to school, and I was between two jobs. For the only time in my life since I was 16, I took a hiatus. That was for about three months. I said, "What do I want to do with my life?" At that point, I still didn't get into real estate. He gave you the confidence to know you could go out there and do anything, but you had to put your mind to it. If you didn't have experience in some job, you would go out there and say you could do that, and you learned how to do it.

The following week, I sent applications in to a company. I wanted to be a secretary. I thought I was going to be the best secretary. I didn't know how to type very well, but I thought I could learn. Of course, I sold myself. I got the job. I kind of glued myself to the typewriter the first week. I got very good at that job. I stayed there about two years. I thought, "I'm not the secretary type, but I can do the job." Then I got in to real estate.

There are few things I would say I couldn't do. I have to figure out how you do it. If they said to me, "We want you to do this or that," I'll learn how to do that.

Was it what he said, or how he said it, that it happened to hit you?

I've listened to a lot of speakers since. It's so much common sense on his part. He started in the real estate business the same time I did, around the age of 21. He was out there in a band uniform, because he didn't have the money to go out and buy nice things. He went out and bought a Cadillac, because that gave him motivation. He better start working to pay the bills. I thought that made a lot of sense. To motivate yourself, you put yourself in a position where you have to work.

When you're young, you're trying to get by. Always have big aspirations about what you would like in life. I would buy things, and I learned to live with a real feeling of being on the line with credit. I did a great job of keeping A-1 credit all those years because I felt motivated to work to pay off the bills. In the beginning, I had to borrow money for my taxes. I didn't mind doing that. It wasn't until I had the money in the bank, and had to take it out of my account and pay the IRS, that I got ticked off. So I didn't have the money. No problem, I'd make it.

As an independent contractor, one of the biggest follies is forgetting that the number-one thing you have to do is pay your taxes.

Absolutely. That's part of the business. I paid, even when I didn't have the money, because I was always leveraging. You pay this advertising, do this, do that. You get a line of credit on your house; you can have that fluctuation, so you can stay in the market and pay your taxes on time, and pay every bill on time. That's obviously critical.

Being willing to take the risks, even if you have to go in to debt. Doing what's necessary to get what you want out of life.

If you're not willing to risk anything, you shouldn't be running a business. Selling real estate is running a business.

When Bob and I split our duties, and he took over the management and marketing, I could focus on the client issues. It gave me clarity to concentrate on creating marketing plans and following up on them. He could run the business and deal with the things that had to be done on a daily basis to grow the business. There are two parts of this business: sales and marketing. You have to think about them independently. Other businesses do so. I'm not sure why Realtors think they can do it all.

With any successful business, the person who runs the business puts a lot of his or her time in to it. You're not going to run a successful restaurant by going in at 9:00 and leaving at 5:00. That's the same with real estate or any other business. You have to be involved in it, and you have to be involved during the hours of operation. It's seven days a week with real estate.

For the last five years, Bob has been able to delegate 90 percent of his job. There's not a lot of management involved. There's some constant tweaking, but that doesn't require a lot of time.

Several times during the year, he concentrates on marketing for a week or two. Then he can spend more time being semi-retired. He's very flexible with his job. Mine's based on the hours I have appointments.

When I'm off, I'm off. We truly love what we do. He loves growing the business. I love spending time with the client. When we have free time, we spend time with each other, and we do things we enjoy. Sometimes it's taking a glass of wine, sitting out in our backyard and relaxing. It all should be looked at as making the best quality time that you have. Some nights in the spring when I get home at eleven o'clock at night, it's sitting down and having a cup of coffee together and saying, "It was a very productive day."

It is finding that quality time, the two of you alone, when you don't have to be discussing business all the time.

What most people have problems with are children and finances. We have Cavalier King Charles Spaniels. We haven't had those concerns. That's probably made it a little easier for me. I have to remember that we're at different points in our business and different points in our life as well, because he's about 14 years older than me. He should be semi-retired. He's worked hard enough for a long time. He could be retired if he wanted to be. He probably will before long. I'll still do this for a while. At some point, we'll both be sailing around the world.

What's it like to work with your husband?

From time to time, we question each other. But we look at that as a challenge that will help us to improve what we do, instead of taking it as criticism.

What one piece of advice would you give to real estate people?

Focus on a business plan that will put you in a successful position, based on your customer service skills and what you provide a client, not on how many deals you can close. How fast can I close them? How much money can I make? The rest of it follows. The money will follow if you are out there, trying to represent the clients the best you can—not yourself, but your entire staff. You have to continue to let them know that this is not a paperwork business. This is a people-work business. When people focus on paperwork, they lose. You have to get the paperwork done, but you have to be there for the clients and act like, every time they answer the phone, they're the only ones who matter.

If you were to do it all over again, would you do anything differently?

Yes, I probably wouldn't do it at all.

I didn't know I was going to get in to this when I started. I would have been someone else's assistant, if I could have at that time, and been very happy doing that. But, you create this giant that you can't stop. You have to continue because you want to give them something they can't get somewhere else, and that's a good experience in their transaction.

Do you truly believe you would have been happy and content being an assistant?

I think I would have. It's funny, because as long as I'm put out in front of that client, I'm happy. I have a lot of benefits from running the business, but I put a lot of my life in to it. Would I have done it differently? I don't know. I've made a lot of mistakes throughout my life, but I've benefited from knowing that, boy, I don't want to do that again, and then figuring a way not to do that again. Mostly, you can't keep doing the same things and expecting different results.

You have to do something different.

When someone tells you it's not going to work, it does not mean it won't. I'm good evidence of that.

That's why I don't think there's one way to sell a house. I think there are many ways to sell houses, depending on what circumstances exist with that client and that location, and it's ever changing.

COUNSELING THAT WILL LEAVE YOUR CLIENTS LOVING YOU

Counseling is not an option, but an ethical requirement. As Gregg Neuman says, when you go to a lawyer for his or her expert advice, you wouldn't expect them to say, "It's up to you." You would expect to get great advice. That's what you're paying for, just like with your clients.

To be able to counsel someone, you have to have their trust and respect. They have to know you have their best interests at heart, knowing that it's about them, not you. Sometimes you have to counsel your client that maybe this isn't the best time to sell their house. Maybe they should continue to rent. If you're not going to be honest with them, who is? The trust that is established is part of the relationship. You can tell from the interviews that all these superstars let their clients know they would take care of them, be honest, and deal with integrity. They displayed the confidence, the "you can trust me," when they walked their clients through the sales process. In turn, the clients had the confidence about what they were doing, and could make better and quicker decisions.

Mentoring advice from the best:

❖ Pre-condition and educate your buyer/seller as to the steps, what they should be doing and valuing, realities, what's a good offer, what's a bad offer, what good terms are, what good conditions are, building inspection issues, and the process. Condition them with realistic expectations.

❖ Know the costs of construction and repairs. Then you will be able to give your clients informed options on what they should do. You can then advise them where they should be able to get one-to-one dollars, i.e., from painting and carpeting. Neutral, decent window covers are a good investment. You can then discuss the tradeoffs.

❖ If the client's house needs to be fixed or cleaned up, or if it has an odor, you have to be honest with them. You need to explain the implications of fixing or choosing not to fix. If they choose not to fix, then you know the house is going to be harder to sell, will take longer to sell, and will sell for less. If they say yes, then you need to be able to give them an estimate of those costs so they can make the right decision. When they see hard costs, you're not attacking the memory of their home.

❖ One idea is to counsel your buyer to tell the seller, "I want a physical inspection where I'll be looking only for safety and health hazards. I'm not going to be nit-picky about paint touchup, or leaky faucets, and I want to make the move as smooth as possible for you." You want your client to look reasonable, in the eyes of the buyer, and it makes the offer seem more real.

❖ A good idea for time management is to get your clients to take appointments during the day. Gregg Neuman says, "Let's see it in the light of the buyers." This is a great strategy and will lessen those night appointments.

❖ Know your clients' desires, the type of people they are, what they've lived through, what they bought before, their likes and dislikes, and their goals. Wow, if you knew your clients that well, you'd do an awesome job of finding them the right house.

❖ Staying with the "pulse" of the market requires you to be working with sellers. A couple of the interviewees still work with buyers. They say it helps them understand the market better by keeping a pulse on what the buyers are saying and wanting.

❖ Sometimes your clients don't have the reality of the market. Sometimes they have to make a mistake, not take your advice, and send in the wrong offer for the market. Many times you will have to take them out to several houses to get a feeling for what is available. That just has to happen sometimes.

❖ Give your clients their options, tell them what to expect, what type of offers may come in, what comparables have been, and what the market trends are. You might have a discussion with them about how much less they can pay for a property, or how much closing costs the seller could pay. In recent years, it could be discussions on how to win with the next property coming on the market $10,000 more than the last one sold for. Share what the seller expects from the buyer, contingencies and what contingencies to do, the strength of the contract, and what effect financing can have on the offer accepted by the seller.

❖ Sometimes clients don't know what they want until they start getting some experience. Then they realize it's not what they are looking for. So, the clients' expectations can change. That's why you always have to keep up with the "pulse" of your clients.

❖ When you don't know the answer, don't say, "I don't know." Say, "I will get that answer for you." Those responses are perceived completely differently. One says you're a person of action, and that it's not important you don't know, but that you will find out.

❖ One idea that has produced incredible results is to bring in a decorator. As part of your team, have someone who can come in and do the staging. Recommend what the best things are that will make the house more salable. Maybe furnish it differently. We heard several stories where they made double what it cost them to redecorate.

❖ It may not be the case of needing paint or carpet. You may have to advise your clients that they need to declutter a room or closets, shampoo the carpets, trim the bushes, move furniture, lighten up the room, or just paint the trim. There are cosmetic things you can do that don't cost a lot but will make the home look cared for.

❖ Analyze the offer before you meet with your seller. Get the financials out of the way. Then outline to the seller the positives and any concerns. Help them decide which one maximizes the dollar, timing, and financial credibility that works best for them. Guide them, but the decision is ultimately theirs.

❖ The best negotiators feel both sides of the deal. Most important though is knowing what is going to satisfy your client at the end of the deal. Know what they are thinking. Know how far you can stretch them.

❖ It's not always about the money, the price. Sometimes it's about convenience, timing, emotions, or security.

❖ Sometimes all clients need is a sounding block. Listen and be empathetic.

Your advice, your counsel, is critical to the success and ease of a transaction. The customer relies on you and counts on your expertise. They pay you big bucks for your knowledge.

NEGOTIATE LIKE THE PROS

The key in negotiations is understanding the motivation of the other party, really knowing what's important to your clients. What are their priorities? Is it getting that *home*, getting the best/right price, getting the date to close they need, or selling the house to someone who cares about it? What are their goals? Your responsibility is to sell your clients the house they want, not the house you think they want, but you know what they want because you asked the right questions, and listened. And the faster you understand your client, the easier it will be to find them the right house. You can either ask better questions upfront, or spend more windshield time.

Also, the longer a house is listed, the priorities of the client can change, which also may change the motivation. Keep a pulse on where your client is along the process.

Many times, the contract that's accepted has a lot to do with the reputation of the agent and the lender who's coming with that contract. That's where the Realtor's expertise adds value to the deal.

The more knowledge you have, the more control you have.

Gregg Neuman says to remember that typically the buyers have to pay more for the house than they want, and the sellers get less than they want. You have to help them understand that. Even if they don't get what they want, it's really a good deal for both of them.

Powerful Negotiation Strategies:

- ❖ You never know what someone is going to take: no matter what the buyer says, no matter what the seller says, no matter what the other agent says. Put it in writing and give it to your client. Take the extra step.

- ❖ If you want to negotiate what's best for your clients, it behooves you to talk to the other agents. Quiz them on what's important to their clients. What is their motivation? When do their clients want to move? What are their plans? What are they willing to do and not do? Does the seller want to leave anything? How important is that wood-deck inspection? Of course you want to be nice and establish a relationship with these other agents if you expect them to be helpful. They are not the enemy. Do not be confrontational with them. When you compete with the other agent, the clients lose. Keep them calm. Many times they don't know what to do, and you can help guide them along, which will make the transaction go better for everyone. Share scripts to use with their clients on how to close the counterproposal.

❖ By presenting your buyers to the sellers on a more human basis, you can establish with the sellers that your clients love their house and want to make it their *home,* and they want to be flexible. You can accomplish this by getting the sellers to let you present your offer in person. This gives you the opportunity to sit face-to-face with the sellers and have a strategic advantage in that you will be able to watch them respond. This will let you know when they like or don't like something you're suggesting. It enables you to present your "case" as to why the sellers should take your offer, now, and before any other. Always present your client in the best light.

❖ Have your buyers write a letter outlining what they and their family feels about the house. Include as much detail and emotion as needed to touch the heart of the seller without being gushy, phony, or too long. Have the letter read at the beginning of the meeting with the seller, whether you are present or not.

❖ If you get a chance, introduce your buyer to the seller. This again makes them more human.

❖ Don't do a lot of negotiating back and forth. All of the negotiations are hard on clients. Sellers will think the buyers are real grinders, and then when the buyers want something repaired, you may run into resistance to make the changes. They may even say no.

❖ When writing your contract, think, "What do I need to tell this seller that will help them know this buyer better?" Find ways to make it personal.

❖ Casey Margenau says that negotiations is knowing what to do and how things can come apart, along with how much and when to grind, when not to grind, and when to make an offer. Sometimes higher offers are better. Give them a little bit lower than they're expecting. It makes it hard for them to turn down. You obviously don't want to lose the deal.

❖ Most of these superstars think that, once you have an offer, as long as it's reasonable, and that can be decided only by the buyer/seller response, you need to find a way to work it out for both parties, not letting egos or lack of experience get in your way. If you aren't sure about what to do, ask an expert.

❖ Mary Ann Bendinelli had an excellent idea. When you present the offer to the seller, make sure your buyer is very close by. That way, if any changes need to be made, you can get together with them immediately, but the seller has time to accept another offer or have a change of mind.

❖ Another of Mary Ann's ideas: If you know you're in a multiple offer situation, provide the other agent with a summary sheet. Mary Ann says she would have to prepare it anyway, and it gives you an "at-a-glance" view of the offers. Include the price, terms, settlement date, and contingencies. (Summary included in Appendix.)

❖ If it's not a seller's market, always ask for the washer, dryer, and refrigerator. Then you always have something to give back.

❖ Don't sell houses as-is. It creates doubt and fear in the buyer.

❖ Don't give a carpet allowance. The buyer and the seller may have different expectations as to what that replacement should be. Put in real estate beige, neutral carpet, with an upgraded pad.

❖ Objections are part of the sales process. You can address them before the client even brings them up. If they aren't talking, you don't know what they need information about.

❖ As Cheryl Davis says, "Don't let your greed exceed your need."

❖ Take into consideration that what's written on paper can seem cold and mean and can be misinterpreted. What did the person really have in mind or intend?

Each of us has a style, a way of dealing with people. Some styles work better than others. These experts have shared what they've found works best. And what they say is pretty universal. You don't have to "sell" your client. You have to listen, counsel, and have his or her best interests at heart, and you'll be successful.

MARKETING IDEAS THAT WORK

There is a big difference between marketing and advertising. Marketing is something you do to keep your name recognition (over time), and you're not expecting an immediate response. Advertising, which you normally pay for, is asking someone to take immediate action. It's either "Call me" or "Come to my open house."

Why is it that most agents don't think they need to spend money on advertising? I'm not talking about sending out their Just Listeds, Just Solds. I'm talking about spending money to show the houses in the newspapers and real estate magazines. All of these superstars do. They do it for continuous lead generation. They are never affected by market changes. Year after year, they grow their business, regardless of the market.

You have to advertise continuously, regardless of the market, if you want to be really successful. They all advertise, usually on a weekly basis, in whatever the major newspaper is, and in the local real estate books. There ads are full color, full page. Some, like Cheryl Davis, use national periodicals. Creig Northrop does television ads. Several of them do radio advertising. One important element is to be able to track where you are getting the results. When you start out and don't feel like you have anything to advertise, hold an open house or advertise on the back of the Chamber of Commerce directory. Sue Frye runs ads in the movie theaters. Find out what works best for you, and do it consistently.

Here are additional ideas from the best in the business:

- ❖ Put your plaques and awards up on the wall. It establishes credibility.

- ❖ Web sites are a must. It is highly recommended that you have your own. Your name works really well.

- ❖ There are many layers of direct marketing. You have to be careful to spend your money wisely. Mailings alone, once or twice, are not going to get results. Name recognition takes time.

- ❖ Most send out the Just Listeds, Just Solds postcards. Some do quarterly mailing, Christmas cards, 4th of July cards, and open house announcements.

❖ Make your advertising about the property, not about you. You're wasting your money sending out a postcard about you. It just goes in the trash.

❖ When Gregg Neuman starts to mail out to someone, he'll mail once a week for the first three months, then three times a month for three months and then get to two times a month. People feel like they've been getting things from him for years.

❖ Creig Northrop provides moving trucks for his clients with his face and name on the side.

❖ He also follows the philosophy of Wayne Gretsky, "Skate to where the puck is going, not where it's been." Keep your mind open to new opportunities and where the market is going.

❖ Mary Ann Bendinelli sends out flyers for her Just Listeds, Just Solds instead of postcards. She has a tear-off at the bottom for a free market report. If she hasn't sold anything in a particular subdivision for a couple of months, she'll send out quarterly sales postcards.

❖ John Beutler writes Christmas cards to all of his past clients. Using a Century 21 system enables him to keep in contact with his clients in different programs throughout the year.

❖ Jill Rudler does what she calls "corporate" advertising by placing an ad about herself on the back cover of a major local magazine.

❖ Part of their advertising efforts includes letting other agents know about their listings. Some hold lunches and send flyers, emails, snail mail, and weekly sheets.

❖ When advertising your properties, don't give all the details. Give them just enough information to pique their interest to call. You use the ad for a lead. Chances are, the house will be gone, but now you have a potential buyer.

❖ One of the best ways to get your name out there is to volunteer. Find something you really love and commit time to help. The results will not be immediate. You never know when they will produce results.

Lead-Producing Open Houses

Open houses are part of your marketing plan. Many of these top producers still hold open houses.

- ❖ John Beutler says the secret to holding a great open house is to advertise it well and make sure the directions are correct.
- ❖ Invite the neighbors; they are going to come anyway.
- ❖ You can read in more detail the comments from:

Whatever your marketing plan, the important thing is to implement it consistently. If you try something for the first time, give it a chance to work. Find a way to track your marketing results. If you don't spend the advertising dollars, you will not have potential clients calling you on a regular, consistent basis. These experts say that, if you want to grow your business year over year, you must advertise.

THE 27 BIGGEST MISTAKES TO AVOID
They cost you time and money and affect your reputation.

These are the ones shared by Gregg Neuman, #1 agent for Prudential. They are not in any particular order

> - Putting yourself ahead of your client.
> - Trying to be competitive with cooperating agents rather than trying to work together.
> - Failing to continue to obtain education on changes and trends.
> - Not spending enough on marketing youself and relying on your broker to build your image.
> - Reacting to, rather than anticipating, changes in the marketplace.
> - Failure to embrace technology.
> - Putting too much information in your ads, removing the need for the clients to contact you for information.
> - Not learning and practicing scripts.
> - Not following up with past clients.
> - Not continually building new spheres of business.
> - Limiting yourself to geographical farms.
> - Not cultivating your points of difference (i.e., days on market, list price to sale price, and so on).

After listening to these pros, I would add:

> - Not taking consistent actions.
> - Not having good business habits.
> - Spending time on non-revenue producing activities.
> - Not spending the time upfront to get to know the seller before doing the listing presentation or the buyer before taking him or her out to look at homes.
> - Not following up on leads.
> - Not keeping the clients informed.
> - Working on one deal, getting it closed, and then looking for another, instead of having multiple deals going on at one time.

- ➤ Not really listening to your clients.
- ➤ Not dressing professionally.
- ➤ Spending time on lukewarm leads.
- ➤ Not having clearly defined priorities.
- ➤ Prejudging your clients.
- ➤ Not realizing that people are always watching and judging you.
- ➤ Not being available to your clients when they clients want you.
- ➤ Not knowing what is and is not a good value for your client.

ACTIONS THEY TAKE EVERY DAY

The one thing that separates top performers from everyone else is that they take consistent action every day.

I've attempted to capture as much as possible of what these people do. In the "What 240 Years Taught Me" chapter, you will learn how they think. No one is going to give you a blow-by-blow description of what to do because each of us is different, with a different personality, geographical location, and market. The most important thing is taking consistent action every day.

These superstars tell you stories about people who get in to this business, do well for six months, and end up failing. The reason was they got comfortable with their success, and didn't realize that you can't build a reputation overnight, and you have to have continual listings.

I find action to be interesting because we can convince ourselves that we're doing something, when in actuality we're doing something, but not the right thing. A real estate friend of mine said he met another agent who commented, "I've been in the business for 26 years," with somewhat of an arrogant tone. My friend's reply was, "You've probably been in the business one year, 26 times." All top performers know there is always more to learn out there. Take a look at this list and be honest with yourself about how much and what you do.

Another interesting thing about action is we all know what it means. It's not a mystery. If someone asked you, "What does it take to lose weight?" your answer would be to exercise and change your diet. So we know, but we don't necessarily do what we think about. Knowledge without action is useless.

I just learned something in my own business. Several years back, I met someone who marketed seminars in the real estate market. After meeting, we decided this would be a good partnership. Now he's going a different direction, so my company will be doing the marketing. I sat with him to learn exactly what he did. Then I went to replicate what he did. Instead of replicating what he did, I asked a lot of questions about how the process was working. I found there was a more efficient, and I believe successful, way to market.

How many of you have followed others around you, doing what they're doing, instead of learning it "right" from the start? It's like golfing. You have a habit of playing one way that may not be effective, but it's really hard to change it. However, by going to a pro, they can point out, and usually pretty quickly identify, what you're doing wrong. Learn from these pros.

Consistent actions they take:

❖ Mary Ann: allows one hour a day for lead generation.

❖ Allan, Gregg, and Creig focus on listings. They are always out on listing appointments. They spend the least amount of time at a closing that they have to.

❖ They all have an assistant who helps with the paperwork.

❖ They are constantly talking with people they meet about real estate. Now, because of their status, people know who they are, so real estate naturally comes up in the conversation.

❖ They constantly follow the market trends. They read real estate articles, keeping up on finances, legal issues, environmental issues, and construction and repair costs.

❖ They have advertising in their local publications and newspapers on a consistent basis.

❖ They are constantly looking for ways to build their market and grow their business.

❖ They get listings to get inventory to generate new business.

❖ They check the hot sheets each day to see what properties have settled.

❖ They pre-condition and educate their clients as to the steps, realities, and process of buying or selling.

❖ They consistently exceed their client's expectations by providing outstanding customer service.

❖ They keep their clients informed of changes in the market.

❖ They counsel their clients on what to do to make their house more salable.

❖ They return calls promptly.

❖ They set realistic expectations.

- ❖ They do the right thing, not the easy thing.

- ❖ They never leave their clients dissatisfied. If it needs fixing, fix it.

- ❖ Gregg Neuman marks some listing presentation documents "confidential" to get the seller's attention.

- ❖ Cheryl Davis says to wear your badge everywhere. That will help with name and face recognition. It can help generate conversations at the grocery store, the cleaners, or soccer games that may not otherwise arise.

- ❖ She also suggests that we all need a road map. Most of us need to write down our marketing plan, our goals. This reminds us and helps keep us focused. Otherwise you will hit and miss and not be consistent.

- ❖ Allan Domb makes 100 telephone calls a day. This includes calls to his past clients to say happy anniversary for each year they're celebrating their new home. He tries to call where it is most likely he can leave a voicemail and not disturb his clients, but let them know he's thinking of them.

- ❖ Allan will also buy his seller out of the deal if it goes bad. That's taking customer service to a new level.

- ❖ John Beutler tries to return every call the day he gets it. He keeps track of everything on a yellow legal pad. At the end of each day, he goes over it to make sure he has followed through on all his commitments and priorities. He also focuses his time on only the top 10 revenue-producing transactions.

- ❖ They gather as much information as possible about the client upfront so they can provide the best service in the least amount of time. Many use a questionnaire to interview the client.

- ❖ They have their materials prepared before the appointment. Mary Ann Bendinelli says you should be ready to leave your office within an hour for an appointment request.

- ❖ Duties they have delegated: interior home features; interior digital photography; virtual tours, daily updating of Web site; writing and negotiating contracts; attending home inspections; neighborhood market reports; ordering signs up and down; answering the phone; reviewing emails; dealing with termite inspections; holding open houses; removing lock boxes; delivering brochures; processing the contracts and the listings; making brochures; preparing and mailing Just Listeds, Just Solds, and Open Houses; calendar mail outs; meeting ad deadlines; meeting the appraiser; showing properties; bookkeeping; and marketing. Wow, think of how many more listings you could get if someone else were doing all of this.

❖ Set aside an hour a day to do nothing but call past clients, or for lead generation.

❖ When someone calls you about a house, don't say, "Let me know if you're interested." Get his or her number and follow up within a half day or the next day.

You have been presented with a smorgasbord full of ideas you can take action on right now. Pick one thing that you commit to doing and are willing to put some energy in to each day to move the idea forward. You will be astounded by the effect on your business.

WHAT 240 YEARS IN REAL ESTATE TAUGHT US
The #1 Producers Share What They've Learned

As you read these statements below, take a moment to ponder what and how they do things, what they've learned. Do you do them? If so, is it 90 percent, 70 percent, 50 percent, or 10 percent of the time? Sometimes we'll see something and say sure I do that, but do it how? The most interesting part of these lessons is that almost all of them reflect on your reputation. This is how these superstars live their lives. How many of these things would people say about you?

- ❖ Anticipate the market, rather than react to it. This means you have a gut feeling on where it's most likely to go, and could articulate that to the client.

- ❖ Do the paperwork right. Whether you're doing it or someone else is doing it, it has to be done right, and why not the first time. You're responsible for it, one way or another.

- ❖ Do the right things because they're the right things to do.

- ❖ You have a responsibility and obligation to counsel your clients in making the right decisions.

- ❖ Following through and paying attention to the details are important. Make sure your contracts are complete, follow through with what the contract says, and remove loopholes.

- ❖ Sellers typically get less than what they think they should get, and buyers pay more than they think they should pay. Counsel so they understand, and get the best deal for both of them.

- ❖ Be honest with the client about what they need to do to make the house more salable. Teach them why it's important.

- ❖ When you have multiple offers, make sure a lender with a pre-approval letter approves the buyer.

- ❖ Unless it's full price, the last thing you talk about is price.

- ❖ Present in person when you can.

- ❖ Call the other agent before you write the contract to find out the details and what's important to the buyer or seller that could affect your contract and enable you to negotiate better.

❖ Use transaction specialists, or hire someone else to do all the paperwork. Do what you're best at doing, which is being with the clients.

❖ Gregg Neuman looks at things as challenges, not problems. Therefore, there is less finger pointing and more challenge solving.

❖ You have to continue to invest in yourself, looking for new ways to make yourself more efficient and retain more profits.

❖ It's the agent, not the company they work for, who makes the difference.

❖ You have to build your own branding. Your company brands the company, and you brand you.

❖ Focus your time on buying and selling.

❖ The listings keep the motor running smoothly, so you're not chasing the buyers and your phone is ringing.

❖ Listings work for you 24 hours a day, and you have an army of agents selling for you.

❖ If you have properties to sell, the buyers come to you.

❖ They learned a lot from listening to what other agents were doing. Then they knew more about what to do and what definitely not to do.

❖ You don't get instant gratification in this business.

❖ It takes at least a year before you really have a feeling for it. Be patient.

❖ Get your face consistently in front of people.

❖ In advertising, you have to determine how you will get the best bang for your buck.

❖ Be sure to test your marketing. Pick a niche market or neighborhood, put different wording on the brochure, or insert a number for identification.

❖ Don't ever negotiate your commission upfront. You may have to do it on the back end, or pay for something out of your pocket.

❖ Great agents work hard and are ethical and honest.

- ❖ Allan Domb says to know your hourly rate so you know how the market values your worth.
- ❖ Try to do better than what you tell people you will do.
- ❖ It's easier if you find a niche or become a specialist in your market.
- ❖ Understand and get to know your clients. You have to adapt your style to them; you can't expect them to adapt to you.
- ❖ You make good money selling real estate. You make real money buying it.
- ❖ Take responsibility for your mistakes.
- ❖ You need to be in the market on a day-to-day basis. That is the only way to keep your pulse on the market. Otherwise, you can't effectively give good advice to sellers. If you want to work at this business part-time, you might want to consider becoming a buyer's agent. Buyers lead to sellers, and you can grow your business that way.
- ❖ Sue Frye says you have to be happy in order for the people around you to be happy.
- ❖ Sue also says that, if you help other people, you will get it back tenfold.
- ❖ Mike McCann says that, if you have the properties for sale, you control the market.
- ❖ You have to spend money to grow your market.
- ❖ Their market knowledge and customer service are the two things that differentiate them in the market.
- ❖ Your market knowledge enables you to price the seller's house at the best level.
- ❖ You have to put things in perspective and not take them personally. Learn to distance yourself enough so you can be objective.
- ❖ Their reputation is their best form of branding.
- ❖ Knowledge = Confidence, Confidence = Trust, Trust = Sale.
- ❖ People are always watching you, so present yourself professionally.

❖ You have to be passionate about this business or you won't stay in it.

❖ The markets change, you adapt, and you continue to grow your business.

❖ Other agents are your customers as well.

❖ These top performers don't compete with others; they compete with themselves.

❖ This is not a paperwork business; this is a people-work business.

❖ If you want to be successful, it requires the support of your family. Almost all had their spouses working in their business.

❖ Just one new idea can take your business to a new level.

❖ They do what they do because they love it!

❖ They love the challenge of the deal, and the fact that every day is a new day. They get to work with different people and circumstances all the time.

❖ Having systems in place provides you more efficiency, flexibility with your time, and better customer service.

❖ I love what Gregg Neuman says, that contacts are like strawberries; they have a very, very short shelf life, and if you don't work them quickly, they're gone. Those who are persistent will get them.

❖ Creig Northrop says the customer service part of any business is taken for granted. It gets harder to keep that as you build your business.

❖ Sometimes, to motivate yourself you have to put yourself in the position where you have to work.

❖ They modify their style to match their clients. They don't change who they are but how they present themselves.

❖ Keep an eye on every transaction.

❖ Always take care of any mistake you or your team makes. These top producers said to do this regardless of the cost.

Wow, now that's a lot of knowledge. That's a lot of lessons learned the hard way. Incorporate what they've learned into your daily life. You're now smarter and know better. Do it, don't just think it.

SUMMARY—THE RESULTS

How these superstars help the most clients in the least amount of time, with the most efficiency, and make them the happiest.

My favorite part of the book is looking at the big picture. What did we learn from these superstars? What did they have in common? What does it tell us about the best way to conduct our real estate business? Who can succeed and what does it take? I've summarized in each of the previous three chapters how they counsel, how they negotiate for and with their clients, and their marketing plans. The statistics and stories tell us:

- ❖ You can be married and be very successful in this business.

- ❖ You can have children and be very successful in this business.

- ❖ It doesn't make any difference what area of the country you are in. Karen Hoberg lives in a community of 1,800 homes and sells 236 units a year. John Beutler lives in a town with 115,000 people and 900 Realtors, and sells 281 units.

- ❖ The more expensive the homes you sell, the fewer units you have to sell to make comparable money.

- ❖ There is no doubt that knowledge is power and confidence. Allan Domb is the epitome of a knowledge expert. He has niched himself in a geographical area, with high-end customers, and specializes in condominiums. This enables him to have incredible focus and expertise. He knows all the buildings he sells inside and out. He has 75 percent of his market, and he's the highest-paid and probably the most profitable Realtor in the country. Obviously, if you want to make the most money, this is the best model.

- ❖ Your background has nothing to do with your success.

- ❖ Working for a major real estate firm gives you credibility and relocation business.

- ❖ To be successful, you really need to work 50-70 hours a week, but that includes fitting in those family commitments. You have to be willing to give it your all.

- ❖ Focus on what you're best at.

- ❖ When you're new, contacts are not required to be successful.

❖ Even superstars don't get every listing they go after. They average 70-80 percent.

❖ Top producers lose clients like anyone else. People change their minds.

❖ Foreclosures enable you turn over a lot of units, but not make the most dollars based on effort.

❖ Listings work for you 24 hours a day, and you have a slew of agents to help you sell.

❖ Be ethical and honest, and counsel your clients to make the best decision for themselves. You are the expert, and clients expect you to give them direction, not make their decisions for them.

❖ What motivates these top producers to work so hard and stay in the business is getting people the homes of their dreams, and facing the challenges. Every day there's something new.

It's in the details. Everyone has to do the same thing, but what can differentiate you is how you do it. Pay attention to the details.

How do they run their business?

❖ John Beutler is able to generate the most sales volume and units sold, with one assistant. He owns the office, and his wife runs it, which probably gives him an advantage.

❖ Allan Domb, the #1 agent in the country, has his own title and mortgage company, and he is a "listing machine." Because he sells at the top end of the market, and specializes in condominiums, he is able to sell the most units at the highest sales volume.

❖ Allan Domb has figured out a formula that enables him to do what he likes to do best, make the most money, and build his wealth. I'd dub him "The Wealth Machine."

❖ Creig Northrup is the youngest of these Superstars, has the most employees, is the third highest in number of units, and is a close runner-up for #1 in the nation.

❖ On the other end is Cheryl Davis who handles the top end of the market. She sold 55 units that took others over 200 units to make the same amount of commission.

- ❖ You have to have at least one employee who is handling most of the paperwork.
- ❖ The focus needs to be on profitability, not on sales.
- ❖ You must take your clients through the process A-Z. You can't cut corners, or the deal will not go smoothly.
- ❖ Always call the other agent and discuss the offer before putting it in writing.
- ❖ Show clients homes in the price range they say they can afford. Once they have seen what's available in the market, they may decide to adjust the price range they are looking at.
- ❖ If you have the properties to sell, the buyers will come to you. Otherwise you're out there looking for them one-by-one.
- ❖ Provide outstanding customer service.

What these superstars do:

- ❖ Focus on the tasks that generate the most revenue.
- ❖ Know the costs to bring a house up to salable condition.
- ❖ Know the costs of remodeling so they can present options on a property for which the clients may not see that will make it their dream home.
- ❖ Know the market better than anyone, and keep ahead of the trends.
- ❖ Keeps clients informed of market changes, what to expect, and what they're doing.
- ❖ Let things go when they don't work out. All of us have to learn from our lessons, and not beat ourselves up. They evaluate what they did wrong, and what they can do to correct it. It's the only way to have peace of mind, stay motivated, and be able to focus your energy on the future, instead of the past.
- ❖ Do what is right for the client.
- ❖ Treat their staff and vendors like team members.
- ❖ Adapt to their client's style.
- ❖ Take the time up front to ask the right questions, and get to know the client. Be a great listener.
- ❖ If they have a reasonable offer, they make it work.

❖ Advertise consistently, regardless of market, to keep that phone ringing.

❖ Most have licensed assistants who can take the calls and answer the questions while they are out of the office so they don't lose clients.

❖ Are available when their clients need them.

❖ Know the best values in the market.

❖ Never prejudge their clients.

❖ Take care of their mistakes—always leaving the client happy.

❖ Spend the time upfront with the buyer and seller to understand their wants/needs.

❖ Stay in contact with their clients on a consistent basis.

❖ Prepare for each day, even if part of it will be rearranged.

❖ Make time for family.

Hiring staff: The #1 preference is to bring family in to the business first.

❖ The size of your staff is based on the decision of how you choose to run your business, not necessarily how many sales you make, or how much money you keep.

❖ The reluctance to hire buyer's agents was that they didn't want to manage employees.

❖ In hiring another agent, be sure they will fit this role and not compete with you and where you're trying to go.

A suggestion as to when to hire:

❖ You have five transactions going on at one time.

❖ You're grossing $50-60,000 a year.

❖ You're spending way too much time doing things other than listing and selling.

❖ You're losing opportunities because of playing phone tag.

There was a difference of opinion about whether you need to have buyer's agents. Half of these superstars say yes and half say no. Now, they all have an occasional buyer, always a referral. Half still hold open houses. We know that the two top-volume producers don't deal with buyers and are making the most money. They have found a way to build a team of fully accountable, high-performing, customer-driven people. You can't do this business alone and expect to be highly successful.

Most of these experts say the market is changing. We're seeing baby boomers making new choices in their lives. They are downsizing, moving to where they want to retire, buying patio homes, buying a second home, locating on a golf course, or locating closer to their children/grandchildren. As people live longer, their homes are not coming available as quickly. Also, more and more people don't want to go to assisted living and want to stay in their home. What effect will this have on you? Are you prepared?

Key lessons I learned from these superstars, my ah-ha's:

What an agent wants:	What I want in an agent:
To help the most clients in the least amount of time, with the most efficiency, with the least amount of hassle, and make the client happy.	Know how to price and market my house so it sells quickly, at the best market price, with the least hassle, keeps me informed and fits into my schedule. That would make me happy.

Notice anything similar here? Mostly, clients and agents want the same things. The better the agent is the more everyone gets what they want.

❖ When the agent is knowledgeable, they will know how to price the house correctly for the market. That means that you can explain and justify your market price and therefore, should get a sales price close to the listing price. Based on this, when you do get an offer, make it work.

❖ Regular prospecting. If you're not getting the amount of business you want then what are going to do to drive more business? More marketing, more advertising or more calls. If you make a habit of making so many calls a day, then you will have more consistent results.

❖ One overriding comment made by all of these experts is that you can make good money selling real estate, but you make great money by owning it. Take advantage of your knowledge to build your wealth. I wish I had understood this earlier in my life.

❖ Always be looking for ways to increase your productivity and retain more profits. Depending on where you are in the business, that focus may be internal or external. You can either make more business from the money you have, or create more business to make more money.

❖ You can make as much money and help as many people as you choose. For all these superstars, it wasn't about the money but providing the best service they could provide, in the most ethical manner, and being the best they can be. These top producers helped other agents with the deal. They did not compete with them. Their only competition was themselves. By being an ally with other agents, they will help sell your listings.

❖ Reputation is everything. As Jill Rudler says, "It's not who you know, but what people are saying about you." Protect and grow your reputation. Providing outstanding customer service is what established these top producer's reputation. Making sure, at the end of the deal, that the client is happy affects people's opinions, referrals, and reflects on your reputation.

❖ Focusing your time on things you do best and letting someone else do the other things. After these interviews, I reformatted my business. I sought out people who could help me grow my business and had expertise where I didn't. I looked at each of the things I do, what I did and didn't like to do, and what is the most productive use of my time. For a little investment, you can achieve significant income.

❖ Allan Domb has three time management philosophies that if you follow them, you can't help but grow your business:

1. Spend 80% of your time doing the 20% that produces the greatest results.

2. Spend your day doing the 10 top dollar producing activities. This requires you to analyze your day. What was productive, what wasn't, and delegating those things that aren't productive. Of course, that assumes you have someone to delegate to.

3. What is your hourly rate? Now that can be a scary calculation. If you look at your typical day, take the actual numbers of hours you work, times the number of days a year you work, take out vacation days, divide those hours by the amount of your income you make, you may be surprised to find out your only making minimum wage.

❖ It's not in the money you make, it's in the money you keep. When you look at that figure, you can then be more effective at evaluating what and how you are doing things. Otherwise, you can have a false impression of how successful you really are. Focus on getting your asset value higher, debt lower, and increasing your cash flow.

❖ Have systems in place so you can be gone. In this business you can't be indispensable and expect to have a life. Systems allow you to be better prepared, saves you frustration, allows you to take care of your clients, and go on vacation.

❖ Keep in regular contact with your clients. Whether that's mailings or callings, if you don't keep in contact people will forget you. You need to keep top-of-mind presence.

Regardless of your job, if you were to focus on these key activities you can't help but be more successful. Listening to these superstars enabled me to refocus my time and energy to get more of what I want. I know it will do the same for you.

Each of these superstars found a formula that worked for them. Each of us has to find our own formula and decide how we define success. What are you're priorities? What is going to make you happy? Only you can make these decisions. These decisions will formulate what and how you run your business.

- If you don't want to or like to manage people, then that will determine the amount of money you will make. It will impact your responsive to your clients, customer service, and how much advertising you do.

- If you chose not to advertise and have a constant flow of clients, then you will limit your success in this business.

- If you decide that you can't be as available to your clients when they want you, then you will limit your success in this business.

- If you decide you want to do business by referral only, then that is the slice of the business you want. If that's enough to make you happy, great. If you want more, then you'll need to rethink your marketing strategies.

- If you decide that you don't want to implement any new changes then you are limiting the growth of your business.

- If you decide it's more important to be comfortable then taking risks, then you will also decide to limit your business.

Our choices, our behaviors will determine our future. We are the ones designing it and have to take responsibility for the choices and decisions we make. The most important thing is to enjoy what you're doing.

The real estate business is what you make it to be. Learn from the best in the business. Determine what you're going to do right now to take your business to the next level.

What is one thing you learned that you will implement consistently and immediately? Try it for the next 30 days. See what works for you.

Reach for your dreams. Design the life you want. It's possible if you are willing to work hard, follow what these experts do consistently, and give it your all. It's up to you.

APPENDICES

MARKETING PLAN[1]
MIKE McCANN, THE REAL ESTATE MAN

1. INFORMATION GATHERING
Collect all pertinent information about the property to assist in selling for the highest-possible price in the shortest amount of time.

2. MULTIPLE LISTING SERVICE
Input your home's description in the Internet-based Multiple Listing Service (**TReND**), a regional computerized information system that offers your home to real estate offices that are willing to give your property exposure to hundreds of real estate professionals with thousands of qualified and motivated buyers. **TReND** can instantly match new buyer prospects with available listings and make them aware of your listing immediately!

3. HOME BROCHURES
Create an informative brochure for your home, detailing its features and benefits. Home brochures are distributed to all Realtors in our company and to cooperating brokers who have clients interested in your area, and are also provided to prospective buyers.

4. IN-HOUSE AGENT TOUR
The listing of your home is announced at our weekly sales meeting. Our Realtors tour each listing obtained that week, enabling them to preview your home, which may be "perfect" for a buyer they may already be working with.

5. HANG "FOR SALE" SIGN
Our most valuable marketing tool! A sale sign draws attention to your home from buyers who may be shopping in your neighborhood without a REALTOR ®. (This accounts for about 20 percent of our sales!)

6. ADVERTISING
Your home will be advertised every week in your neighborhood paper. Special color ads are featured in Mike's personal display ad in the

---
[1] Complements of Mike McCann

Philadelphia Weekly, a free weekly publication and home of the city's premier real estate section! Ads are also placed in publications such as *The South Philadelphia Review, The Society Hill Reporter,* and *The Philadelphia Inquirer,* maximizing your home's exposure.

7.   OPEN HOUSE
An open house gives your home a tremendous amount of exposure to prospective buyers in a short period of time. After a quick preview, many return for a private showing.

8.   NETWORKING
Networking to the real estate community is key to success. Having a well-respected and very high profile listing agent ensures you the highest co-broker cooperation available. Mike keeps area Realtors up to date on his inventory with a newsletter sent to all area offices and direct voice messages detailing what's new on the market!

9.   DIRECT MAIL MARKETING
Announcements are mailed to residents in your vicinity, advertising your home for sale, creating a neighborhood "buzz" about your home, and encouraging people to tell their friends and family, who may want to move to your area.

10. www.McCannTeam.com
Today's buyers are computer-savvy. They want instant information. Mike's personal Web page links new buyers to Mike's team, enabling them to obtain information and photos of your home and communicate with a buyer's specialist to make arrangements to see your property. Your home is also placed on Realtor.com and Prufoxroach.com so that it is easily accessible to buyers searching the Internet.

11. VIRTUAL TOUR
Your home will be videotaped inside and out, with the footage posted on the Internet, with links to my personal Web page as well as Prufoxroach.com, Realtor.com, and Homestore.com. Potential buyers can go on a "virtual walk-through" of your property online!

12. BROKERS LUNCHEON
Much like the in-house tour, I invite all the area Realtors to preview your home and give them a bite to eat. This helps to obtain a lot of exposure within the Real Estate community as soon as possible. Nationally, 80 percent of all listings sell through broker cooperation.

13. CONSISTENCY
Not one of these items is the do all and end all to selling your property. However, done consistently and thoroughly, this marketing plan is proven to get your property SOLD!

14. ADDITIONAL SERVICE AND COMMITMENTS

- buyer's qualifications: determining the financial ability of the buyer to qualify for a mortgage

- financial information: preparation of the closing costs to the potential buyer and financing options.

- repairs: advising, assisting, helping, and overseeing any repairs needed to qualify your property for mortgaging or improving the sale of your property

- availability: committing to be available to potential buyers and YOU at your convenience.

- referrals: proudly offering and providing referrals upon request

- policy: returning every phone call every day, and always being accountable for every detail

HIRING A NEW BUYER'S AGENT[1]

I have been very fortunate and haven't had to actively recruit agents. I am often approached by an agent who wants to be a part of my team, whether he or she is a newer agent who needs help, or an established agent who wants the team identity.

I usually sit down to lunch with the prospective agent, and give that precious commodity—TIME! We discuss the agent's goals, strengths, successes, and problems, and talk about my team and what is expected. Through this, I get a really good idea of whether the agent will fit with my team.

- Buyer's Agent Contract—attached

- Buyer's Agents get:
  - Leads
  - Office support
  - Guidance and coaching, especially with closing offers and negotiating with other agents
  - A team identity that opens doors
  - Conveyance assistance
  - A stronger presence in the market, both with clients and other agents.
  - The ability to concentrate only on money-making activities. I don't ask agents to run errands and so on for me.
  - Coaching on closing techniques and the benefit of my years of experience.
  - Ability to take a listing. If the listing results from my lead, I usually go with the agent on the appointment. Every transaction goes under my name.

- My goals are:
  1. To treat my agents well, so that I keep them for life! I expect them to be with me long term.
  2. To spend my time listing properties, and coaching agents and staff.

---

[1] Complements of Mike McCann

HIRING OFFICE STAFF

- Ads in newspaper, using only a fax number to contact. No phone calls initially, just a faxed resume.

- Contact interesting applicants. Conduct phone interview, assessing phone manners.

- Meet applicant in person, in neutral location, to further assess.

- Remember to administer a typing/keyboarding test! These skills are still essential to a good assistant.

- Initially hire only as a "temporary" position, with a review at either 90 days or six months before making "permanent." When permanent, assistants are eligible for benefits.

- Encourage office staff to study for Real Estate License, picking up the cost. This makes them infinitely more valuable.

- Pay assistants $10-15 per hour, depending on experience. Supplement with bonuses occasionally, during that spring market, or after an insane week!

THE FIRST ASSISTANT

I often hear agents say that they need an assistant, but...

"I don't know how I could train an assistant!"

"I wouldn't feel comfortable letting someone else handle the important details!"

"My clients depend on me, need me, only me!"

What often holds them back is that they don't know how they could train an assistant, or let go enough to let an assistant handle those small details that are so important in our business.

I felt the same way! But I was lucky enough to have my wife as my first part-time assistant. One of the most valuable things she did was to set up checklists for each "job." There was a checklist for a new listing, a checklist for a pending sale, a checklist for a settled property, a checklist for the listing booklets she assembled for my appointments, and so on.

The amazing thing is that, 16 years later, these same checklists (modified and updated, of course!) are used by my staff every day. You can break your job as an agent into smaller, teachable jobs, and then set up a checklist for the smaller activities. This way, you can be more certain that all the little details are being handled.

As far as your assistant handling your clients on the phone, look for someone who has a great phone manner. That's why the second part of my hiring procedure is a telephone interview. Before I even meet the prospective assistant, I hear how they handle the phone. And once you find that person, you will be amazed at the positive response you get from clients who want to talk to a live person!

Yes, it's an adjustment. But hiring an assistant frees you up to do what you do best, sell real estate! And it is an investment that pays for itself almost immediately!

EXCLUSIVE ASSOCIATE AGENT AGREEMENT

Between Michael R. McCann, CRS, GRI, Associate Broker, and

_____

1. It is hereby understood that this agreement is for a term of 12 consecutive months, commencing on _____, with a temporary period of 60 days after which either party can terminate this agreement in writing. It is automatically renewable each and every period unless otherwise cancelled in writing by either party at any time with 14 days notice.

2. Michael R. McCann is the top-producing broker/agent for Prudential Fox & Roach Realtors, Philadelphia, PA, and is recognized as one of the nation's top Realtors. Because of this unique opportunity, _____ (hereby known as Agent) has joined Prudential Fox & Roach Realtors, Philadelphia, PA, with the intention of working and training under Michael R. McCann as an Associate Agent.

3. Michael R. McCann and Prudential Fox & Roach Realtors, Philadelphia, PA, will provide for the Agent the following:

   a. Limited use of Michael R. McCann, the McCann Team staff, and Prudential Fox & Roach Realtors, Philadelphia, PA, administrative staff to assist the Agent in clerical tasks, follow-up, and feedback functions and a variety of other tasks associated with the showing of, sale, and closing of each real estate transaction.

   b. Training through audiotapes, videotapes, and hands-on training with Michael R. McCann and other team members and staff. Training on networking, listing, selling, closing, negotiating, farming, etc. All forms, booklets, check lists, and other tools.

   c. Weekly sales meetings and as scheduled, Associate Agent meetings.

   d. Desk space, phone, voice mailbox, letterhead, envelopes, and basic office supplies, as provided by Prudential Fox & Roach Realtors.

   e. Use of all of Michael R. McCann's and Prudential Fox & Roach Realtors, Philadelphia, PA, equipment and facilities, such as computers, copiers, fax machines, etc.

4.   This renewing agreement shall be in effect for each 12 month period:

For a period of 12 consecutive months, the Agent shall be an Associate Agent for Michael R. McCann of Prudential Fox & Roach Realtors, located at 210 W. Washington Square, 2nd Floor, Philadelphia, PA, 19106. During this time and during subsequent renewals of his agreement, the Agent shall work exclusively with Michael R. McCann; and real estate transactions conducted during this agreement shall fall under the following terms and conditions:

   a.   The Agent will work exclusively with buyers. All listings or potential sellers generated by telemarketing, cold calling, and canvassing the market will be referred back to Michael R. McCann, and a 50% referral * will be paid to the Agent for the referring lead. (*When discussing referrals, percentages are of Michael R. McCann's gross commissions earned after closing, after the Prudential Fox & Roach Realtors splits have been taken.)

   b.   The Agent will receive a referral fee for each and every successfully closed buyer transaction that the Agent brings to fruition, based on the following scale:

Buyer Agent Net Commission   **% of McCann's**
Gross

Current listings that are McCann's are not part of this agreement. Nor are new ones coming in unless as a direct result of Agent. Agent shall be paid on properties that Agent sells, and listings that he/she refers to Michael R. McCann.

   c.   It is understood that all real estate contracts presented by the Agent will list Michael R. McCann, Prudential Fox & Roach Realtors, Philadelphia, PA, as the selling agent representing the transaction.

   d.   The Agent will make clear to all clients that he/she is working with Michael R. McCann as an Associate Agent and that McCann will be included in the final negotiating process.

    e.   Sales Associate Commission Schedule in Prudential Fox & Roach Independent Contractor Agreement paragraph 11 shall be replaced as outlined in section 4.

5.   Additional Guidelines

    a.   The Agent will always present and conduct him/herself in a neat and professional manner.

    b.   The Agent will provide Michael R. McCann with a weekly update of all activity, phone calls, prospecting, and all basic activities related to the sale of real estate.

    c.   Attend weekly office sales meetings and tour each Tuesday morning, and attend Buyer's Agent meetings as scheduled by Michael R. McCann.

    d.   Coordinate efforts and provide updates to all sales regarding lending pre-qualifications and approvals, inspections, and any information pertinent to closing with McCann and conveyancer.

    e.   From time to time, the Agent may be asked to help Michael R. McCann in the negotiating process or in listing a home, or perform some other related real estate function. As a courtesy, the Agent would be expected to comply.

    f.   It is the responsibility of the Agent to comply with the laws, rules, regulations, and conditions governing Real Estate Agents in the State of Pennsylvania, the Greater Philadelphia Association of Realtors, the Pennsylvania Association of Realtors and the National Association of Realtors.

    g.   Agent shall attend educational courses to enhance educations. Some are offered free through Prudential Fox & Roach Realtors, others to be paid for by Agent.

    h.   Agent will be available to work days, evenings, weekends, and Sunday Open Houses. Time off shall be scheduled with Michael R. McCann in order to provide full coverage by our Team.

    i.   Agent will work floor time and answer phones as needed to obtain new leads and exposure for the McCann Team.

    j.   Agent will assist marketing, networking, performing tasks to help sell listings and work with buyers.

    k.   Agent will be encouraged to think creatively and bring his/her ideas to the Team.

6. Listing Referrals

    a. In the case that the Agent receives a buyer lead either directly from Michael R. McCann, or through Michael R. McCann's advertising programs or lead generation programs, and the buyer eventually lists with Michael R. McCann, Michael R. McCann would pay a 50% referral of his gross.
    b. If the Agent should refer a past client or a relative to Michael R. McCann for the purpose of listing their home, Michael R. McCann would pay the Agent a 50% referral fee, provided the Agent could produce documentations showing that the client in question actually conducted a closed real estate transaction with the Agent in the past.

7. Competitive Clause

If, for any reason, the Agent or Michael R. McCann should decide to terminate this agreement, the following provisions shall prevail:

    a. It is understood that all clients referred to the Agent are, and always will be, Michael R. McCann's clients. The Agent promises not to solicit these clients after the Agent terminates this agreement for a period of 24 months. If for any reason the Agent solicits any of Michael R. McCann's clients, a 50% referred fee will be paid to Prudential Fox & Roach Realtors, Philadelphia, PA, and Michael R. McCann upon the close of any of these transactions.
    b. It is further understood that any and all databases developed by Prudential Fox & Roach Realtors, Philadelphia, PA, Michael R. McCann, or any of their subsidiaries are the sole property of same, and any attempt to use these databases after termination would be considered a violation of copyright infringements under Federal Law.

All terms and conditions set forth in this agreement are hereby agreed to on this _____day of _____, 20____.

_____

Michael R. McCann[1]

_____

[1] Complements of Mike McCann

NEW LISTING CHECKLIST FOR: _____

1. Add New Client Info To Top Producer   _____

2. Send "THANX" Letter To Seller   _____

3. Create Fact sheet – Distribute To MCCANN TEAM   _____

4. Place Fact sheet In Floor book @ Front Desk   _____

5. Copy Fact sheets/Seller's Disc For Office/McCann Files _____

6. Add To Board In Office   _____

7. Enter New Listing Into MLS   _____

8. Add New Listing to Realtor.com   _____

9. Call for violations   _____

10. Look up 2004 Taxes   _____

11. Add To "Office Tour List"   YES   NO   _____

12. Order Virtual Tour   YES   NO   _____

13. Track Referral   _____

14. Add New Client/Showing Info To MCSELLER   _____

15. Add New Listing Info To INVENTORY   _____

16. Order Sign   YES   NO   _____

17. Mail Tenant Letters   YES   NO   _____

18. Turn File In To OA   _____

19. Lockbox   YES   NO   _____

20. Add To Office Ads (Wkly/Review)   _____

21. Add To Open Houses/Weekly Ads   _____

22. Add To MCNEWS/Mass Fax Update Website   _____

23. Add To "JUST LISTED" Postcard List   _____

Confirm Installation Of Lockbox/Note On Lockbox Inv   _____

UNDER AGREEMENT CHECKLIST FOR: _____

1. Complete TRANSMITTAL and TURN   ____

2. Track 2nd Deposit + Mortgage Commitment   ____

3. Track Condo Docs   ____

4. Add To Board In Office   ____

5. Update Status In MLS   ____

6. Look Up Real Estate Taxes   ____

7. Call L & I for Violations on multi-units/rehabs 686-2445____

8. Fax TRANSMITTAL to Kolleen if settling w/i 30 days   ____

9. Add to conveyance chart   ____

10. Track Referral   ____

11. Pull Fact sheets/Disclosures   ____

12. File in pending drawer   ____

13. Cancel all showings   ____

14. Update Status On MCSELLER   ____

15. Remove From INVENTORY   ____

16. Transfer Keys To Pending Drawer   ____

17. Remove From Office Ads (Wkly/Review)   ____

18. Remove From Open Houses/Weekly Ads   ____

19. Add To PRODUCTION List   ____

20. Update Fact sheet In Floor book @ Front Desk   ____

21. Update Website   ____

AFTER SETTLEMENT CHECKLIST FOR: _____

1. Update Status In MLS   ____

2. Add to PRODUCTION LOG   ____

3. Confirm Referral Payment + Record In Top Producer   ____

4. Update/Input Buyer + Seller Info In Top Producer   ____

5. Delete Fact sheet/Listing From Top Producer   ____

6. Prepare NEW YEAR/THANK YOU Letters + HUD-1   ____
   (Store For Mailing In January 2004)

7. Send Philadelphia magazine subscription / Thank you   ____
   Letter To Buyer (only if it's our client)

8. File In Settled Cabinet   ____

9. Remove Client Info From MCSELLER   ____

10. Order Sign Down   ____

11. Remove Fact sheet From Floor book @ Front Desk   ____

12. Remove fact sheets   ____

13. Confirm Removal Of Lockbox/Note On LB Inv   ____

14. Add to "JUST SOLD" Postcard List   ____

15. Update PRODUCTION List   ____

BACK ON MARKET CHECKLIST FOR[1]: _____

1. Update Status In MLS   _____

2. Halt Conveyance   _____

3. Remove From Conveyance Chart   _____

4. Remove File From Pending Drawer   _____

5. Add To Board In Office   _____

6. Update Client Status On MCSELLER   _____

7. Return Listing Info To INVENTORY   _____

8. Update Fact sheet In Floor book @ Front Desk   _____

9. Redistribute Fact sheets To Mailboxes   _____

10. Add To Open Houses/Weekly Ads   _____

11. Confirm Reinstallation Of Lockbox/Note On LB Inv   _____

12. Add To Office Ads (Wkly/Review)   _____

13. Remove From PRODUCTION List   _____

14. Add To MCNEWS/Mass Fax   _____

15. Update Website   _____

---

[1] Complements of Mike McCann

ARE YOU AN A, B, OR C BUYER?[1]

When touring (Group/Team/Office), you quickly notice how busy the Buyer department is. For you—the Buyer—that's a good thing. You want a Buyer Specialist who is active and really knows the marketplace. During your tour you probably also noticed our Buyer Activity Boards. These boards serve a couple of purposes. One is to enable us to match properties with specific Buyer needs. The second and most important purpose is to classify all of our Buyers by urgency. In order for our team to focus on your real estate needs, we must first determine your readiness to buy. Since not all Buyers have the same needs, we categorize our Buyers by urgency as follows:

"A" Buyers   Are the highest priority Buyers. These are people who have to buy a home now. They have sold their home, they've transferred into town, or their lease has expired. In many cases, they could potentially be homeless.

"B" Buyers   Are the second highest priority Buyers. They are ready to buy, except that they have a home to sell first, have a lease to fulfill, or are in the stages of getting pre-approved.

"C" Buyers   Are the people who may buy a property when the right one comes along.

As you can see, being a "B" or "C" Buyer doesn't mean you are less important to us. Your needs are paramount. It only means that we want to identify customers with the most urgent needs and find homes for them first. Remember, you could quickly become an "A" Buyer and become top priority! We will always try our best to accommodate you. If you are not an "A" Buyer, though, please be patient as we work you into our schedules.

I/We have read the above and feel that I am/We are (an) _____Buyer(s).

_____   _____

Buyer   Date   Buyer   Date

_____

[1] Compliments of Howard Brinton of StarPower® Systems, Inc.

MULTIPLE OFFER SUMMARY[1]

Company: Agent: Purchaser:	Company: Agent: Purchaser:	Company: Agent: Purchaser:
Offer Price:	Offer Price:	Offer Price:
Escalation Cap:	Escalation Cap:	Escalation Cap:
Increments:	Increments:	Increments:
Contingency? Financing: Home Insp: Radon: Other: Good Faith:	Contingency? Financing: Home Insp: Radon: Other: Good Faith:	Contingency? Financing: Home Insp: Radon: Other: Good Faith:
Down payment:	Down payment:	Down payment:
Loan Type:	Loan Type:	Loan Type:
Additional Terms:	Additional Terms:	Additional Terms:
Settle Date: Settlement Co:	Settle Date: Settlement Co:	Settle Date: Settlement Co:

---

[1] Compliments of the Bendinelli Team, Weichert Realtors

List Prospect
Buyer Only   **Agent**_____
D . I . S . C
Type: A   B   C   **Date**_____

Buyer Information

1.So you're thinking of purchasing of a home? _____

Buyer_____ Home #_____

2.Are you currently working an agent?_____ 3.Have you spoken to a Lender, Who? _____

4.How long have you been looking? _____

5Do you own/rent? _____ 6.How soon do you need to move? _____

7.If we find the right property are you ready to buy_____8.Anyone else who will be helping you buy? _____

9.Tell me what you are looking for?_____10.When's the best time to get together_____

Address_____ Office #_____

City/ST/ZP _____ Cell #_____

Referred By:_____Pgr #_____

Email:_____

Company_____Fax #_____ Other #'s_____

Present Home	**WHAT DO YOU MEAN BY THAT??**	**Future Home**

Est. Value $_____   Price Range: $_____

Price Range: $_____   SqFt_____

Monthly Payment_____   House Townhome Condo Lot Income

#Bdrms_____ #Bths_____   #Bdrms_____ #Bths_____

House Townhome Condo Lot Income | Down Pymt |

SqFt_____   Pool: Yes   No   Parking:_____

Special Features_____ | MthPayment | Lot size:_____Backyard_____

_____   Special Features_____

AREAS,ZIPS

Comments _____
_____
_____
_____

1

---

[1] Compliments of Gregg Neuman

Contract Processing

Dates	Address	Purchaser	Seller
Contract		Name	Name
Appraisal			
Inspections:	Legal Description	Address	Address
Home			
Pest	List Price	Phone	Phone
Pre-Settlement	Sales Price	(O)	(O)
Settlement	MLS#	(H)	(H)
Occupancy			

Agent	Lender	Loan Information	Settlement Agency
Name	Firm	Type	Name
		Rate	
Firm	Loan Officer	Points	Address
	Processor	Loan Amount	
Phone	Phone	Down Payment	Phone
(O)	(O)	Application	(O)
(H)	(Pager)	Approval	(FAX)
(FAX)	(FAX)		
Notes			

	Date Due	Date Completed	Date Due	Date Completed	Date Due	Date Completed
☐ Change Status						
☐ Turn in sale to PRU						
☐ Contract—All parties, Atty & Lender						
☐ Just "Sold" to neighbors						
☐ Sold sign						
☐ Talk to mortgage company						
☐ Order well & septic						
☐ Order termite						
☐ Remove lockbox						
☐ Order sign down						
☐ Settlement gift						
☐ Thank you to selling agent						

MABCPCL

[1] Compliments of Mary Ann Bendinelli -- Bendinelli Team, Weichert Realty

Howard Brinton Script

Script:

On a scale of 1 to 10, with 1 being you are in no hurry to find a house and 10 being you're ready to buy a house today, where would you rate yourself? (Client responds)

And what would it take to make you a ten?

Script:

Mr./Mrs. Buyer, I am very excited about helping you find a home, and if you're serious about doing that, then we can accomplish that in just a couple of days. Now if you're not serious about buying a home, then let's not waste my time and your time and we can part friends right now. But that choice is yours. What do you want to do?

Phyllis Wolborsky Conclusions
#2 Gross Commission Income Producer: Coldwell Banker

Phyllis was gracious enough to share some of her key ideas:

"I still take buyers out. Many of the agents you have spoken to have buyer's agents or they are the owners of the company. Last year my sons and I sold $91 million of residential property (300+ homes): half listings and half sales. I still take buyers to be able to know what people do not want, instead of just listening to what they want as that may be only a dream."

I shared with Phyllis that I had looked at over 30 homes when I bought my dream home in Carlsbad, California. "I do not feel an agent needs to show anyone 30+ homes. If they know their product, have knowledge of the market, and make people feel comfortable, they will be able to find out what people do not want and eliminate many properties up front, and find a home in a realistic amount of time.

On listings, pricing is the key. I not only include closed sales, but also expired's and withdrawn's so my customer will see what happened to the properties that were overpriced. Also, you should make it clear that if the property does not move within 30 days it will need to be repositioned with a price adjustment. I tell my sellers that if the home is not positioned and conditioned properly it will sit, and sitting is not good for either of our wallets as, the longer it goes, the less you will get. Realistic pricing is a must.

When people have spent a lot of money doing normal maintenance projects, it does not up the price—new roof, painting, carpeting—yet it will make the home sell faster. And the faster it sells, the more you get, but it should not count as added value. The home simply becomes more show-able, and more salable, but not more valuable. Otherwise, it would not sell at all.

In one of my best lines to people who want to reduce my commission, I ask them how they could trust me in negotiating their equity if I cannot even handle sticking to my fee. It often soothes sellers when I have to present a low offer, and if they get upset, I simply remind them that this is better than the one we had yesterday. They say, "Did we have one yesterday?" That is my point. They should not be upset with this person making what they see as a low offer, but should be mad at the other 20 people who have visited their property and made no offer. Let's at least thank these people with a realistic response."

STAR POWER® Systems Presents:

Empowering Language

Empowering language is used to support transformation in reality through the power of language.
Words combined with sound (voice) are energy vibrations that affect the body's energy centers and have
the inherent capacity to give (energy) or to take it away. Words convey underlying messages to our
energy centers, creating physical, emotional, mental & spiritual responses in others and ourselves.

1. *Language originates from thoughts and feelings.*
2. *Empowering language is responsible, powerful and healthy.*
3. *"Dis-empowering language keeps us sick & weak." (Carolyn Myss)*

Replace:	With:
Should	Choose, desire, want
Need to	It's important to me to
Have to	Want or desire to
Can't	Not willing, choose not to
Always, never	Sometimes, often, seldom
Must	Choose, desire, want
But	And
Try	Intend, aim, will
Yeah, uh huh	Yes
Nah, unh unh	Not willing, choose not to
Maybe	Statement of worth, "I am"
Kind of, sort of	Eliminate these
I think	Clear statement of belief or fact

The power of "I" language:
1. *Take responsibility for your world, your situation, and your choices.*
2. *YOU are in the drivers' seat, not someone or something outside of yourself.*

"…We have no integrity when we attribute… our feelings and emotions to someone else, or the weather,
or to anything which we can't control… [and] deny our own ability to choose alternate behaviors."
--Julia Penelope

Victim Language:	Empowering Language:
You or they make me	I feel / felt---when
When you	When I
It's not my fault	I am responsible for
It's a problem	It's an opportunity
I'm never satisfied	**I want to learn & grow**
Life's a struggle	Life's an adventure
I hope	I know
If only	Next time
What will I do	I can handle it
It's terrible	It's an opportunity

Reframe negative statements into positive, as the brain doesn't hear don't, won't, never type statements.

Complements of Howard Brinton

ABOUT THE AUTHOR

DEBRA PESTRAK

Debra's life didn't start out remarkable. In fact, she understood at an early age that if she wanted anything in life she was going to have to work hard for it and that it was up to her to get it.

Debra progressed from telephone operator to a leading salesperson and manager for top telecommunication companies. In her mid 30s, she realized she wasn't using her full potential—but how do you?

She started researching top performers to find out what they did so she could learn to do it, too. In two years, she went from broke (actually $20,000 in debt), to the top one percent of the nation's income bracket. Her energy and tenacious style helped her build and lead new sales groups, manage a $20 million budget, and win every multimillion dollar contract she negotiated.

Debra's spell-binding seminars teach you what she did to reach her full potential, become a millionaire, and have the man of her dreams. Her confidence and power enabled her to get interviews with the best of the best. Debra unraveled the incredible secrets of the top business and salespeople, and she presents it so you know you can do it, too. Her passion to help you get *more* out of life enables her to use real-life examples that you can identify with and that will inspire you to action. She is also author of *Playing with the Big Boys: Success Secrets of the Most Powerful Women in Business* and past president of the National Speakers Association—San Diego. Debra has a degree in Business Administration and Management, and extensive experience in Neuro Linguistic Programming (NLP).

Want to empower your people for greater success? Call Debra Pestrak, the performance expert, at (888) 786-3777 today. Visit her Web sites at:

www.DebraPestrak.com
www.PlayingwiththeBigBoysandGirls.com
www.MostPowerfulWomen.com

If listening to CDs is the way you prefer to learn, then you'll want to get the 24-CD series from these interviews. At the end of each of the interviews, Debra recaps some of the important and unique strategies discussed. Every time others have listened to theses CDs, they have picked up at least one new idea that has made them more effective. Order on-line at the above Web sites or call 888.SUN.3777.

If you find yourself not satisfied to be where you are, but wanting to go farther, you've reached a point where you decided it would be a good idea to get some help, then call Debra because she can help you get to where you want to go.

My passion in life is to make a difference in others' lives. I would love to hear your story about how this book has changed your life. Please email me at Debra@DebraPestrak.com.

Client's Comments About Debra's Programs

"This was the missing link in my business. This information will help me turn leads into clients."
— Lori Zaw-Minway, Coldwell Banker

"Common sense methods that will produce uncommon results."
— Cynthia Allison, PMI Mortgage Insurance

"Debra's program brings out everyone's unlimited potential."
— John Dorilag, Families at Home Realty

Partial Client List

- Verizon
- Downey Savings
- Countrywide Home Loans
- Bank of America
- American Red Cross
- Captiva Software
- Marriott Hotels
- Sharp HealthCare
- SBC
- Bailey Properties

VISIT US AT

www.PlayingwiththeBigBoysandGirls.com

www.DebraPestrak.com

www.MostPowerfulWomen.com

Gifts for your friends

Order this book from your local bookstore or from Sun Publications at 619-884-7505. Orders may also be placed with Success Unleashed, Inc. at:

   Telephone orders: Call 888.786.3777 toll free or 760.434.3343. Have your credit card ready. **Fax orders:** This form to 760.434.7076.

   Web site orders: Go to www.DebraPestrak.com.

   Postal orders: Success Unleashed, 300 Carlsbad Village Drive, Suite 108A-#78, Carlsbad, CA 92008. USA.

Quantity discounts available.

The interviews are also available in a 24 CD package series.

Please send a copy of this book to me or my friend/s.

Name: _____

Company: _____

Address: _____

City: _____

State: _____ Zip: _____

Name: _____

Company: _____

Address: _____

City: _____

State: _____ Zip: _____

Number of books -- $19.95 each   _____

Shipping: 1st book $5, each additional $2.50   _____

For products shipped to California, add 7.75% tax   _____

Total order $_____

Name:_____

Address:_____

City:_____ State: _____ Zip:_____ Country: _____

Tel. No.: _____

Credit Card: Visa MC AMX No.:_____

Exp. Date: _____ Signature: _____

Please sign me up for Debra's *Success View* free e-newsletter: Legible email

address:_____